Speaking of Ethics

—m—

Living A Humanist Life

Joseph Chuman

ISBN: 1492804460
ISBN 13: 9781492804468
Library of Congress Control Number: 2013917572
CreateSpace Independent Publishing Platform
North Charleston, South Carolina

Acknowledgements

One of the joys of completing a project such as writing a book is the opportunity to thank those people who have been part of making it happen. In accordance with my philosophy of human nature that the self to a great degree is social, this volume in many ways is a composite of the thoughts, influences and good will of many people.

First, I want to extend my sincere gratitude to Dr. Marc Bernstein, the former archivist of Ethical Culture's national movement. Marc saw the potential for broader interest in these talks and strongly encouraged me to make them accessible to a larger audience. Beyond his emotional support, Marc applied his pen and formidable skill to editing the major share of these essays.

I also want to thank my writing group for helping to reinforce the idea that writing is a craft; a pursuit greatly enriched through the insight of others. Marc, together with Doris Friedensohn, Theresa Forsman, Patricia Lefevere, – all skilled and accomplished writers – have come together almost monthly for the past twenty years to share good food and warm camaraderie. In the spirit of friendship and mutual support we have critiqued our work, both before and after publication, and thereby have added value and confidence to my development as a writer.

All the essays in this book where given as public addresses at the Ethical Culture Society of Bergen County in Teaneck, New Jersey, a community I have served as a professional leader for the past forty years, and more recently at the Ethical Society in New York. I want to thank all those members and friends of

Ethical Culture who have opened their hearts and minds to my thoughts and deepest convictions on ethics, social justice, humanism and living the good life. Without them, this book literally would not be.

And finally, I want to express my loving gratitude to Linda, my wife and life partner. Many of the themes I present in this book have been developed and refined through conversations and shared exploration with Linda over many years. Her support, creative insight, critical acumen and belief in me have inspired me to a standard of excellence.

Contents

Preface

Marc A. Bernstein, PhD, Former Archivist, Ethical Culture Movement

Ethical questions can be framed broadly or narrowly. In a narrow framing, a concrete situation that poses an ethical dilemma is raised; an answer is then invited or proposed. Examples of this method abound in advice columns, whether commonplace or sophisticated. Here is a hypothetical situation:

"I was riding on the train the other day when I heard a young man seated next to me discussing the intimate details of his sex life in a cell-phone conversation. I was appalled. I wanted to tell him that it was inappropriate to be having such a conversation in public, but it seemed to me that my comment would infringe on his free speech as an American. I buried my head in my newspaper and said nothing. Was this the right thing to do?"

This is situational ethics. It has the virtue of clarifying principles involved in making moral decisions, but it has serious limitations as a way of thinking about ethics. Because it frames all ethical dilemmas as questions of individual choice, situational ethics does not, cannot, examine the conditions that create the dilemma. In this instance, the behavior of the young man is a given; how we might react to it is the ethical problem. But there is another way to view this issue. In one of the essays in *Speaking of Ethics*, Dr. Joseph Chuman asks, "What are the moral consequences that follow when a society blurs the distinction between public and private? Such broad questions cannot be answered—or even raised—if we think solely in terms of situational ethics.

In *Speaking of Ethics*, Dr. Chuman asks big questions: Can multiculturalism be dangerous? Should religion be immune from criticism? How are we to address Holocaust denial? He looks not only at societal questions, however. He is concerned with individual issues as well, just not those that lend themselves to the narrow framework of situational ethics. So, he asks: Is the pursuit of happiness a worthy goal? What are the personal virtues we need to inculcate to help others around us? Is there a value to merely being a witness to suffering that we cannot ameliorate? Ethical questions all.

Dr. Chuman comes to his task with two kinds of qualifications. As an Ethical Culture leader for more than forty-five years, he plays a ministerial role to his congregants. He helps people deal with illnesses and end-of-life issues; he counsels individuals as they consider divorce or other life-changing decisions. In a phrase, he deals with the flinty problems of living. But he brings another kind of training and experience to his task. Dr. Chuman is a trained academic. He holds a Ph.D. in religion from Columbia University and teaches in its highly regarded Human Rights Program. This academic experience has exposed him to currents of thought that originate in universities—postmodernism is a good example—before they filter down to a wider American audience. His familiarity with these trends allows him to critique various arguments about ethics and human rights that would be beyond the ken of all but a few religious leaders.

Although Dr. Chuman's considerable learning suffuses *Speaking of Ethics*, readers will find the book intellectually accessible. Composed of talks given to various Ethical Culture audiences, *Speaking of Ethics* has a conversational, not a professorial, tone.

Before readers begin these pages, however, they should know a little about Ethical Culture, and Dr. Chuman's philosophical stance with respect to ethics. Ethical Culture is a 137-year-old movement that has had at least two distinct goals: to raise ethical awareness and to make religion consonant with the findings of modern science. Although its founder, Dr. Felix Adler, was neither agnostic nor atheist—he had an unusual understanding of the meaning of God—the Ethical Culture movement is part of the humanist family and excludes prayer to a divine being in its Sunday morning meetings. For Dr. Chuman, as for many of his Ethical Culture colleagues, ethics derives from mankind's long effort at cooperative living, not from God's word.

This philosophical take on ethics helps explain the contents of part 3 of this book. After he deals with ethics in private and public life in parts 1 and 2, respectively, Dr. Chuman focuses on a number of humanist heroes. Some of the figures he discusses helped carve out a domain for ethics that was independent of religion (Giordano Bruno, Spinoza, Emerson, and John Dewey); others expanded the rights and liberties of the human family, widening the circle that could enjoy an enriched concept of human dignity (the Founding Fathers, early feminists).

The last section of the book offers some insights into Ethical Culture— what it stands for, why it is so small a movement, and why it offers, after all, a religious view of life.

Composed of talks given over a thirty-five-year period, *Speaking of Ethics* can be dipped into like a smorgasbord or read through like a four-course dinner. Whatever your preference, you will not regret having dined with Dr. Chuman.

Introduction: What Is Ethics? Why Does It Matter?

Let me begin by explaining what I mean by morality or ethics. Though there is a technical difference that is sometimes made between the terms, I will use them interchangeably. There are, in fact, several different ways of defining morality, but the one I will use is what I believe the average, reasonable person of normal intelligence conventionally means by the term. By morality I mean primarily the exemplification of such behavior as being truthful and fair, keeping one's promises, and repaying one's debts. Feminists have correctly reminded us that caring is an important moral value, and I would certainly agree. In addition to the harder, more objective values of being truthful and fair, there is a cluster of other not-so-quantifiable values, such as caring, compassion, and benevolence expressed toward others, which are essential aspects of moral behavior as well. So is loyalty. These are the kinds of values that reflective parents should teach to their children and want them to live by.

By stressing behavior, I don't mean to suggest that intentions and dispositions have nothing to do with morality. They certainly do. But sometimes the linkage between our intentions and our behaviors is hard to see. And this is one of the problems I want to get to. It is possible that we may intend to act in a way which is truthful, fair, caring, or loyal, only to find that we do not, for reasons that are, or seem to us, beyond our control. In my effort to express my caring about you, I may extend a compliment that ends up making you feel miserable. On the other hand, I may act in ways that in their consequences appear moral, but that are done out of motives or intentions that we might find hard to justify as moral ones. I might feel inclined to cheat on my income tax, for example, but do otherwise out of fear of being caught. Can my manifest honesty in filing my tax returns truly be said to be moral when my primary motive was externally coerced by fear of punishment rather than the claim of honesty itself? Perhaps not. If I refrain from stealing simply out of fear of punishment, or perhaps give a lot of money to charity not out of compassion for the needy, but because if I do my friends will think I'm really a marvelously generous benefactor, we can rightfully be skeptical about the moral quality of my behavior.

Without getting more complicated at this point, I think we generally consider morality as partaking, in some loose sense, of both motives and behaviors. Though, as noted, the two don't always fit together neatly.

So the moral person is the person who recognizes the importance of moral values and intends to act on them. In addition, because he or she cherishes such values, he or she will try to ensure that such intentions are expressed in behavior, even when it is difficult to do so. The moral person is one whom we recognize as a decent person, the person who manifests a high degree of integrity in both motive and behavior.

Often being moral in the way I am describing it—being truthful, fair, caring, loyal, and so forth—is not very difficult for us because there is not much at stake in behaving in these ways. But very often there is, and this is what makes the discussion interesting. Being moral becomes difficult, for example, when it comes up against what we perceive to be our immediate self-interest.

For the morally sensitive person these conflicts continually arise. Do I cheat on an exam in order to get the job or promotion I want? Or do I refrain from cheating and thereby decrease my chances? Do I deliberately misrepresent myself or mislead others in order to get ahead? When caught in compromising behavior, do I lie to my friend or my spouse in order to spare myself embarrassment, criticism, or rebuke? To ask a very comprehensive question, do I pursue a plan of life that is concerned overwhelmingly with maximizing wealth and pleasure, perhaps at the expense of others? Or do I factor into the way I live the concerns, interests, and needs of my fellow human beings? In this very large sense, too, I believe that we have at least some ability to direct our lives and our conduct.

How each person resolves these questions is determined within the inner recesses of his or her conscience, and different people will inevitably resolve them in different ways, some weighing the moral factors highly, others less so.

Each person must judge for himself where he comes out on such issues and other similar conflicts that we all confront every day.

But the first of two major points I want to make is that we must tread very lightly when making moral judgments about other people and how we think they ought to behave when they are confronted with such conflicts. I want to try to explain why I think we need to be cautious when assessing the moral behavior of people other than ourselves.

The older I get, the more I come to appreciate how complex and varied human beings are. It is perhaps part of the arrogance of youth to think that all people are essentially extensions of oneself; that the values that I hold are the values other people hold, or ought to hold. That all people think like me, or ought to think like me. That what I think best, all people, if they were in their right senses, would think best. In other words, it is part of the folly of youth to assume that others are more or less projections of myself, and that what I believe can serve as a type of universal standard for all others—one standard fits all. Yet the older I become, the more I marvel at the fact that people of goodwill can indeed see things very differently from the way I do, that they may look at the same data and see them through different eyes and from a different perspective and therefore interpret them very differently from the way I do. Thus they come to different conclusions as to what is right in a given instance. No doubt this results from the fact that all of us are socialized out of diverse experiences, some of which may be related to ethnic or class background, or gender, or a different stage of life. So before I render any assessment of the ethical merits of anyone's behavior but my own, I have to be a very good listener. I have got to make sure that I take on, as best as I am able, the standpoint of the other in order to see the facts as he or she sees them, and that my assessments are based on the most comprehensive view possible. Of course, I can never do this completely, but if I do not try to do it, my assessments about others, if judgments there be, run the risk of being gratuitously judgmental. Needless to say, some behaviors are, on their face, so volatile that it would be ridiculous and overly solicitous to take this stance. I am not particularly concerned with seeking out Adolf Hitler's viewpoint and moral perspective on genocide before assessing its immoral content. Nor do I have to go the full nine yards with rapists and murderers before coming to the conclusion that theirs is a morally reprobate behavior, though I must admit that in my role as leader of an Ethical Society, I do think that I need to extend myself further than if I were not in such a position. I am not referring to these extreme instances, however, but to those that we normally encounter in our interactions with others.

Second, I am reminded of the fact that doing the right thing is often difficult because people, ourselves included, are not always confronted with clear choices between what is good and bad, or right and wrong. Rather, more often than not, we are faced with having to make a choice between competing moral goods, and it is not always clear what we should do.

I may be strongly committed to being truthful, but sometimes my need to speak the truth runs interference with the loyalty that I feel toward a close friend. Do I lie to protect a friend or do I speak truthfully and incur his hurt? Here, two highly held values are in conflict, and how to resolve them is not always apparent. Sometimes there simply are no solutions that are morally satisfying. In a moral sense, sometimes we lose no matter what we do.

If it often difficult for us to know what is right for us because we are confronted with competing moral claims, how much more difficult it is to assess other people's behavior from afar.

And third, I've become appreciatively aware of how easy it is to set behavioral goals for ourselves, and how correspondingly hard it often is for us to meet those goals. Anyone who has been chronically overweight knows how extraordinarily difficult it is to alter one's behavior, even with the best of intentions. This is because we human beings are not simply rational minds, but rather a complex of drives, urges, impulses, and needs that we cannot totally control because we are unconscious or just minimally conscious of them. Again, I may want to do the right thing—I may want to respond to my friend's letter in a timely way when she writes to me, or extend kindness and support to my aging aunt—but find that my best efforts are thwarted and blocked by impulses, obsessions, or just bad habits that get in the way.

I have long ago given up a romantic image of the essential rationality of the human being. We are far more than transparent minds. All of us, I believe, experience a battle between reason and passion, and our ability to be moral is to a considerable extent based on our ability to master in life a relative integration between these dynamic forces, forces we internally confront all the time. One does not have to be a neurotic or an addict to appreciate the insight of the New Testament to the effect that "the good that I would do I do not; but the evil which I would not, that I do." Nor does one need to believe in sin, original or otherwise, or be chronically overweight to recognize that the spirit is often willing but the flesh weak. Such, I believe, is the universal human condition that often creates a gap between our moral intentions and our moral behaviors.

All these considerations—namely, that people may sincerely see the same facts differently and so come to different conclusions from themselves, the problems people confront when values are in conflict, and the fact the we all labor under the limitations of own humanity, so to speak—should lead us to more compassion than condemnation of others.

But having said all this, I want to turn my discussion around to make the declaration that, despite mitigating circumstances of which we need to be mindful, none of this is an argument against the supreme importance of moral values, ideals, and standards, and the need to strive continuously to make those values more keenly felt in our own lives and the lives of others. Though we often need to be circumspect, cautious, and compassionate in our ethical evaluations, none of these concerns should lead to the notion that we can abandon moral values, moral standards, and moral judgments about right and wrong.

I would like to end with one final question. And that is, why bother? Why should I strive to be moral? Unfortunately nowadays this is neither a question with a self-evident answer, nor a stupid one to ask. There are, in fact, many temptations not to be moral.

We might argue that by striving to be moral, one will not achieve more wealth, or power, or even admiration in the eyes of the mass of humanity. So why bother? I can think of at least four reasons.

One reason is that if I am moral, I will be rewarded with heaven, and if I am not, I will be punished in hell. For centuries, I suspect that this was the prevailing motivation for the majority of humankind to behave in conventionally moral ways. But of course it cannot be a motive for those who do not believe in heaven or hell or in a God who directs you to one place or the other. But even if you do believe in heaven and hell and a God who dispatches you there, I still don't think that fear of punishment or desire for reward is a very mature rationale for moral behavior.

A more compelling reason, I think, comes from the understanding that a society in which there were no moral values would not be a very pleasant society to inhabit. If we lived in a world in which people routinely lied, cheated, stole, murdered, and didn't care about each other very much, it is hard to imagine how we would find much peace or happiness there. It would be a condition that Thomas Hobbes described as "a war of each against all." It is a condition that wouldn't work to anyone's satisfaction, including our own.

But even this is not enough to compel me personally to be moral. One could argue that it would be nice to live in a society in which most people acted in a trusting, honest, compassionate way, but why should I? In fact, I might conclude that since most people are ethical, this provides a better opportunity for me not to be. After all, the society as a whole isn't going to be damaged noticeably if a few people are dishonest and totally self-interested, so why shouldn't I take advantage of the situation? And maybe I should.

But on the microcosmic level of interpersonal relations, this type of amoral reasoning breaks down. This is so because I believe that our most deeply held longings for love and for intimacy are based on our ability to live moral lives or sincerely strive to do so. I truly believe that without moral commitment, especially to truthfulness, there can be no trust, and without trust there can be no love. Truthfulness is the foundation for trust, and trust is the only ground out of which love can be nurtured and sustained.

But there is one more reason, even beyond this one, which partakes of a sublime intuition. And that is that in striving to be an honest, sincere, compassionate, and caring person, I am striving to realize and fulfill what it means to be a human being in the highest sense. That in my efforts to relate to others honestly, truthfully, and compassionately, without artifice or manipulation, I am somehow touching the wellspring of my being. It's an intuition, as Spinoza put it, that virtue does not bring us reward but is itself its own reward. It is the realization that in acting ethically toward others, I am fulfilling my humanity, my most distinctive nature as a truly human being.

Ethics in Private Life

Caring

One of the more unusual and unique aspects of my professional life, which is also very much my personal life, is entering into conversations with people who are actively dying. There is something very special about being with other human beings and talking with them when they and you know that the words, thoughts, and feelings they are expressing are among their last. It is not that what they say is inherently profound. It is rather that their words take on a deeper significance, at least in the mind of this listener, because they come at the end of life, and so implicitly have the feel of a type of summation of everything that has gone before.

So much of our talk is trivial when we think we have endless time to spend and endless hours to waste, but not at the end of life, when the press of time's winged chariot is at our backs. Whether it's talking with a young mother who is struggling to stay alive in order to raise her child, who will soon lose her protective care, or an elderly man who has lived a rich life he can review with a sense of fulfillment, or someone in midlife who relates to me her struggles on two fronts—against a ravaging disease *and* a medical establishment that depersonalizes her at a time when she is most frightened, and human kindness she most needs—these conversations, all of them, are thickened (I want to say "sanctified") by a sense that they somehow convey ultimate value. To enter into conversation with the dying is to enter into a very privileged conversation. But, I must admit, it is never easy. Nor do I ever want it to be.

I always enter these meetings with a sense of dread; like the trembling one would feel in walking to and peering over the ridge of a dark, endless abyss. I am not a romantic about death. Death is unwanted, death is final, death is unpleasant to think about, and death is incomprehensible. Perhaps it is unpleasant because it is incomprehensible. But having said that, the more important fact by far is that having engaged in these encounters with the dying, I always emerge from them in a way that leaves me feeling somehow more inspired. To talk to people in their last months, days, and, on some occasions, minutes is to cut through the quotidian bullshit of life, and to touch the deeper wellsprings of the human experience. Such conversations carry with them more genuineness, more authenticity, and more honesty than our normal talk, when we know that what we throw out, we can at some later time correct or take back. Communing with those near death is somehow to touch what seems more real, more significant, more gripping, in comparison to which other experiences come to seem more transitory and less important. I cherish such experiences, as painful as they are, because they give me a clue as to what matters most in my own journey through life.

This type of encounter in its uniqueness and specialness also serves as a paradigm for what I want to talk with you about.

In past addresses I have offered reasons why I think we should bother to strive to be ethical in this dog-eat-dog world. I suggested that beyond the notion that a moral society may simply work to the advantage of its citizens better than one that is not, on the personal level, an effort to live a moral life, to do the right thing by others, partakes of a sublime intuition. It is an intuition that this is ultimately what I live for.

Within this web of human relations, my highest purpose and my most sublime fulfillment do not come through wielding power and control over the largest number of fellows or beating out the next guy, however gratifying these may be. Rather, it comes through affirming the human bond, by my efforts to do the right thing by others, to meet their needs, and to enter into their lives with a sense of compassion and caring. And through the moral act, I reciprocally come into touch with the source, the wellspring, the essence of my deepest being as a *human* being. In this sense, we can understand the virtuous act and the life of virtue to be their own rewards.

Today I want to give attention to a particular ethical value, or, I might better say, ethical experience—that of caring.

We can think of ethical values as broadly falling into two different types, which we might in the first instance call "values of principle or judgment," and in the second, "values of intuition or feeling." Sometimes I have expressed these by referring to "hard values" and "soft values" with no hierarchy intended. In fact, it's my contention that an integration and balance of both types is necessary to begin a moral life.

What I mean by values of principle, or hard values, are those that are subject to rules and that are also relatively objective. They are public virtues. Among such hard values we may think of truthfulness, justice, fairness, and equality.

These vales have something in common: I can develop and articulate rules or principles as to when and how to apply them. Whether I have been truthful, or a particular social program has been executed fairly, is also readily observable to a broader public. Therefore, as I'm implying, I also need to bring my moral reasoning to bear so that applying such values in the right way engages my cognitive skills.

We are conventionally taught to think of morality in this way, that is, from the point of view of developing ethical principles and then applying them to particular cases. So if you open up an elementary text book on applied ethics or values clarification, you might find a problem such as the following:

Bob has promised his daughter Mary that he will take her to the amusement park to celebrate her twelfth birthday. The park is an hour from their home. They arrive at the ticket window to find that all people twelve years and over must pay five dollars to be admitted. Those under twelve pay only two dollars. By an oversight Bob left home with only eight dollars in his pocket. What should he do? If he tells the truth about Mary's age, they will be declined admission, and Mary will be very disappointed. Perhaps he should lie about his daughter's age. After all, what difference does a day make? What should he do?

What this problem brings to the fore is a conflict between a principle, "always tell the truth," and other important desiderata, such as maximizing your daughter's happiness and your own through a pleasurable day at the amusement park, or strengthening the father-daughter relationship, or enhancing the self-esteem of a child through celebrating her birthday. Some people looking at the problem might conclude that Bob should tell the truth and disappoint Mary; others that he should lie. More sophisticated moral reasoners might try to find some sort of creative or mediating third way out of this dilemma.

Whatever the case, my point is that we conventionally think of morality in this way; that is, the application of principles or moral rules to specific cases.

Needless to say, there is something abstract, cognitive, and remote in this way of thinking about ethics. You really don't have to know Bob or Mary personally, or know much about them, to come to a conclusion as to what is right in this situation. Although it's stretching a point, I suppose that you could develop a computer program that would give a credible response to problems such as these. To state that such an approach to moral problems is to do ethics at a distance, in the abstract, in no way is to denigrate such an approach. I believe that holding moral values and refining moral principles are essential to living a moral life.

But they are only one half of the picture. There is that other family of values that is not quantifiable, or easily objectified. Nor is it subject to rules or principles or judgments. What I have in mind are such values as kindness, love, compassion, and caring. What such values have in common is that they rely not primarily on reasoning, but on feelings and intuitions. They are matters of the heart more than the mind. They are not so readily articulated, nor are they very visible to a broader public. And most importantly, as I will try to show, such values are neither abstract nor applicable at a distance. In fact, values such as caring only come alive in concrete and specific circumstances, that is, in the very thick of our lived experience.

Both clusters of values are necessary. There's a beautiful passage from the book of Micah in the Bible in which the prophet asks, "What does the Lord require of you, but to do justly, and to love mercy, and to walk humbly with your God?" No doubt that very ancient wisdom recognizes that justice without mercy commits us to an abstract principle that in its rigor becomes ultimately devoid of humanity. Unmitigated justice can end up being nothing but cold and inhuman. But mercy without justice is ultimately rudderless, normless, and a formula for anarchy.

Perhaps the last clause of the quote, which bids us to walk humbly with our God, sticks in the craw of contemporary atheists and humanists. But if we metaphorically translate God as standing for that omniscient perspective from which all Truth is known, then we finite mortals better be humble, because we can never know how much justice and how much mercy we need to apply in a specific moral circumstance. We can always risk being too merciful or too overbearing in our application of principles.

Almost forty years ago, the Harvard psychologist Lawrence Kohlberg, following the work developed by Swiss educator Jean Piaget, embarked on a significant experiment that has become famous in the annals of moral education. He submitted dozens of young subjects to discussions of various moral dilemmas in order to discover how people think morally and develop their powers of moral reasoning. What Kohlberg found over many years of such research is that moral reasoning falls into six identifiable stages of sophistication. At the first, least sophisticated stage, people will conclude that what is right and good is that which enables them to be rewarded or avoid punishment at the hands of an authority. The sixth or highest stage is marked by an ability to embrace the principles of universal justice and human rights, which transcend not only self-interest, but also the norms and conventions of any particular culture, and even the law, when law itself violates a transcendent ideal of justice.

Kohlberg concluded that people could grow in their ethical sophistication by being exposed to other people whose moral reasoning was one, but no more than one, level higher than their own. Kohlberg's theory of moral development has had wide application and is used in prisons and in Ethical Culture Sunday schools.

But his theory possessed at least one major flaw. One of Kohlberg's students at Harvard, Carol Gilligan, observed that despite the fact that his research was extensive and truly cross-cultural, his subjects, whether they came from the United States, Mexico, or Turkey, were 100 percent male. In fact, if one submitted women to Kohlberg's methodology, they often came out on level three of his six-stage sequence. At level three, morality is conceived in interpersonal terms, and goodness is equated with helping and pleasing others.

Gilligan concluded that these findings did not mean that women were inferior in their moral development, or that if women were to move out into the world of work, they would in time rise to higher levels, as Kohlberg assumed. Rather, she concluded that the differences in these general responses of men and women had another explanation: women characteristically approach such problems and conflicts differently from men. Rather than look at moral dilemmas from the perspective of the detached individual who applies rules and principles to the issue at hand, women, she believed, characteristically look upon such problems from within a context of relationships and with a sense of personal responsibility foremost.

She wrote:

> When one begins with the study of women and derives developmental constructs from their lives, the outline of a moral conception different from that described by Freud, Piaget, or Kohlberg begins to emerge and informs a different description of development. In this conception, the moral problem arises from conflicting responsibilities rather than from competing rights and requires for its resolution a mode of thinking that is contextual and narrative rather than formal and abstract. This conception of morality as concerned with the activity of care centers moral development around the understanding of responsibility and relationships, just as the conception of morality as fairness ties moral development to the understanding of rights and rules.

> This different construction of the moral problem by women may be seen as the critical reason for their failure to develop within the constraints of Kohlberg's system. Regarding all constructions of responsibility as evidence of a conventional moral understanding, Kohlberg defines the highest stages of moral development as derivative from a reflective understanding of human rights. But the morality of rights differs from the morality of responsibility in its emphasis on separation rather than connection, in its consideration of the individual rather than the relationship as primary.

In short, it was Gilligan's conclusion that a woman's characteristic approach to morality partakes of appreciation of a human context, of relationship, and focuses on the values of responsibility and caring.

Following Carol Gilligan's seminal research, feminist moral theorists have worked to enlarge our understanding of ethical development and what constitutes moral commitment in the fullest sense. In this regard, it was not Gilligan's conclusion that women could not be principled or just, or that men could not be caring, but rather that by adding another voice, we all could gain a more inclusive understanding of the processes of moral development.

With that said, I want to spend the time remaining on the value of caring.

Caring results from a paradox of the human condition. On the one hand, as we move from being children to adults, we all strive, as we must, to stand on our own feet as individuals, as people who are powerful and free and who have broken loose from the psychological dependencies of our childhood. Much of the developmental psychological literature speaks of the importance of this dynamic of individuation. And this is true and good. But no matter how mature we may be, none of us is totally grown. We remain, to greater or lesser degrees, creatures of need, no matter how gloriously we may paint ourselves or others.

We need one another, and we need one another to grow. We need others to get by in times of doubt and weakness, in times when we fall or lose our way. Sometimes we may feel and act like Olympians, but most of the time, I suspect, most of us are simply human. The giving of myself in the effort to help another, not simply with transitory assistance, but in a way which leads toward his or her growth and greater actualization, is what I mean by *caring*.

Our expression of caring can either be superficial or far reaching. What I intend by *caring* here is not to be taken in its superficial sense. We can say that I will care for your cat while you are gone, or even your child, and mean it in a superficial way to signify a basic custodial responsibility. This is not what I mean.

What I have in mind, rather, is a profound relationship over time with a significant other person, perhaps one's spouse, one's child, or a dear friend for whom we have, for whatever reason, a special feeling of devotion. In this sense, caring is not something I can confer on everyone, or even a large number of people, but only a small, select few. I do not intend *caring* to mean a sentimental love of everyone, but a special and intense relationship with another person in such a way that our life becomes deeply interfused with the other's.

What are some of the factors that characterize the caring relationship?

In the first place, caring reflects the paradox I mentioned awhile ago. Namely, when I enter into a caring relationship, my life becomes attached to and invested in the life of the other, but in such a way that both he and I retain our separateness and independence. In this sense, the attachment is not parasitic, nor does it reflect a morbid dependence; nor an inequity of power or respect. There can be no place for condescension in a caring relationship. But rather, as the caring person, my interest in the other works in such a way as to help ensure his or her greater strength and his or her movement toward growth. It is not power or control that I seek, but rather the quiet satisfaction of feeling that the growth of the other is bound up with my own sense of well-being.

What caring also suggests is being fully involved with the other in *very concrete situations*. We have all heard of those people who love humanity but don't care much for human beings. Each of us probably knows someone who fights for abstract causes but in everyday relations to family and friends leaves much to be desired. The person who has the ability to care, as I am describing here, is not such a person, because caring as I mean it takes place in the lived concrete situation. It involves being able to sit opposite another human being and be present and receptive to the other. It means being keenly attuned to the other's feelings, facial expressions, and to his or her body language. To care means to be able to feel along with the other person, to feel as much as I can what he or she is feeling. It does not mean to reflectively say to myself, "What would it be like if I were in that person's shoes?" and then start to analyze her situation as if I were she. Rather, the caring posture suggest that as much as possible I receive the other into myself and see and feel what the other is feeling.

I suspect that mothers, when they hear their infants cry, don't say to themselves, "I wonder what it must feel like to wet my diaper. Let me put myself in my baby's position." Such thinking already suggests a stance of remoteness. Rather, the response to her child's need is much more intuitive than that. It's an *immediate* sharing of the feeling that something is wrong. The feeling, the identification, comes first and then the reflection.

My point is that the caring experience, in this profound sense, does not entail approaching the call for help with a principle or a judgment in hand. We do not begin by formulating or solving a problem, but by sharing a problem, or by sharing a feeling. It means being receptive and being able to listen very carefully and very attentively. The caring orientation draws its conclusions from the full range of feelings, words, and sensitivities that I apprehend in the other. It means experiencing the reality of the other as fully as I can. It is this interfusion and identification with the other that I mean by *concreteness*.

To care for another in this sense also means moving away from my own needs and toward the needs of the other. Not in a self-denying or self-sacrificial way, but in such a way that her joy becomes my joy and her pain my pain. The husband or father who leaves the house in the middle of the night to take his ill wife or child to the hospital doesn't feel this as a burden or a sacrifice. Rather, in being present for the other in the caring situation, there is a convergence between what I need to do and what I want to do, because I am fully devoted to the person who is the object of my caring.

If a result of the caring relationship is to help our friend or loved one to grow, then a further element of this relationship needs to be *trust* or *faith* in the other. Caring for another implies having the faith that he will grow in his own way and in his own time. In this sense there is always an element of risk and danger when we enter into a caring relationship. There are no guarantees. Our best efforts at extending ourselves, often in ways that leave us vulnerable, may turn out badly. But to care for another person means to take that risk. It means letting go of the temptation to control the other, or to impose solutions to his problems that may be ours, but not his.

To care for another also means to have faith in myself. It means having faith in my ability to be a caring person and to believe that my motives in wanting to help the other are genuine and sincere and not a covert mask to dominate or control. Since, as I am implying, the ability to care resides so much in feelings and intuitions, rather than in rational deliberations, I need to be able to have faith in my own instincts. I need to be able to trust my capacity as a feeling, intuitive person. And I need to trust my ability to learn from my mistakes. If I lack such faith and get too hung up on whether my actions, thoughts, and responses are correct or not, this self-doubt will surely get in the way of my being able to be a caring presence for my friend.

There is much more that characterizes the caring relationship, and much more that I could say. I have not spoken at all about the disposition of the one who is cared for. Without an openness to receive the caring of the other, there of course can be no such relationship. But as I draw to a close, there is one more question I would like to ask, and that is simply, why care? Why strive to be a caring person? To answer this question is to arrive at one more dimension of the caring experience: its reciprocity. For the truth is that through the process of giving myself to another in a caring way, in helping a dear friend or a family member whom I care about through a difficult trial or time of life, it is I, as the helping person, who receives back in an exquisite way as much as I have given.

If we are runners or cyclists, through practice we increase our speed or our distance so that one day we may run or ride faster or farther than we have ever gone before. We transcend our own limits and experience, thereby achieving the quiet and sublime joy of having done so. As it is with our physical self and its limits, so it is with our emotional self also. Through the act of caring, through giving of myself to another to whom I am devoted, I come to touch the farther reaches of my innermost capacities as a human being. Through the act of caring, I may even tap and liberate emotional resources that have remained latent or that I scarcely knew I had. In short, by helping others to grow through caring, I myself grow as a caring person. I develop that side of my humanity.

This reciprocal phenomenon is not simply a cliché of those who like to mouth vapid moral or human-relations platitudes. Anyone who has invested himself or herself sincerely in caring about and for another in the intense way I have been trying to describe knows that it is a very real part of the lived human experience. This sense of reciprocity is one of the sweetest rewards we as social beings can experience. In short, the act of caring for a selected other is not something for which we expect an extrinsic reward, but it is very much its own reward.

Let me close with this: for humanists, the value of caring and the experiences which it entails need to occupy a very special place. By caring, and by caring for others I think we help to build a sense of meaning into our lives.

When we leave the womb, we are all saddled with the burden of separating from our parents, growing to adulthood, achieving independence, and then reintegrating ourselves into the matrix of mature human relations. It's never a perfect fit. All of us remain, I believe, at least slightly alienated. All of us are, I believe, slightly bereft and slightly hungry for the attention and support of the fellow members of our species. All of us are, in this sense, wanderers through life who are searching for a home. But to be at home in the world, our world must truly be a human one. We must be able to recognize in the face and in the needs of the other not a stranger, but ourselves, and that we share a common humanity. It is through caring for another that I come to touch her humanity, and thereby my own.

Life is short, life is fragile. We all have needs. And among these needs is the need to be needed. Through reaching out in a caring way to touch the humanity of the other across the divides that separate us, we weave the threads that bind us together, and by so doing we build for ourselves, in this dangerous world, a home.

Through acts of caring we come to recognize that amid the trials and tribulations of life, and through its shared joys, what truly count most of all, beside which every other pursuit is of secondary importance, are love and friendship.

December 1992

The Pursuit Of Happiness

Search for it and you'll probably never find it. If there were a God, it would be hard for me to depict him, or her, as anything but a devious trickster. We all want to be happy, yet what we desire most, often persistently eludes us. After three thousand years of collective, civilized wisdom, there is little sturdy knowledge, and certainly no consensus, on this most far reaching of human issues—namely, how we can achieve happiness, if at all.

Most of us would agree that happiness is the primary end of a person's life: what he or she wants for himself or herself above all things. Ask your friend what he or she desires of life and you'll get myriad responses. Some will want economic security and more. Some envision a rich home and family life. Others aspire to some great, creative achievement: to be an actor, writer, athlete, or statesperson. Perhaps almost all would include good health and the respect and love of others as tops on their list. But ask them further why they want these things, and they will probably answer, "Because they will make me happy." A final question—why do you want to be happy—will probably bring only bafflement in response; bafflement because it is self-evident that to be happy is our ultimate desire, needing no further qualification or legitimization. I believe this, and so did Aristotle and endless proponents of happiness from Epicurus to Marianne Williamson.

But not everyone did. Among those who didn't was our founder, Felix Adler. In an address given in the early part of the century, Adler said, "The purpose of man's life is not happiness, but worthiness. Happiness may come as an accessory; we dare never make it an end." That's strong language. As a religious thinker, Adler inherited both the Hebrew conception of holiness and the central Kantian notion of obedience to the moral law as central to life. For many religious minds, *righteousness,* that is, how you morally comport your life in accordance with a higher standard, is far more important than winning personal satisfaction in life. Moreover, Adler was most concerned, as both a philosopher and an activist, with vouchsafing the unconditional worth of the person. He wanted to ensure that human beings are worthy regardless of their wealth, reputation, or happiness. If our worthiness as human beings depends on our happiness, Adler might argue, then we are all standing on very shaky ground. For so often in life, our happiness depends on things beyond our control—on devastating illness, the death of loved ones, or reversals of fortune. Adler would not say that because a horrendous disease has left a person miserable all his life, he is therefore unworthy as a human being. I don't think that we would say this either.

Though I admire Adler's moral tough mindedness when it comes to what we should value most, I simply cannot dislodge happiness from first place. Despite the sublime appeals of living a life in higher, more selfless dedications, it is ultimately too self-denying, except, perhaps, for a few extraordinary humans beings, none of whom I have ever met. As a creature of the flesh, I yearn for more. All of us, however we define it, or don't define it, desire to be happy.

This quest for happiness is an eternal quest. It is part of the existential reality of being human. But in our times the quest for happiness seems to be driven by powerful anxieties about a society in disarray. What to value and where to anchor one's life seem more tentative now than they have been in a long time. Consequently, the yearning for happiness is increasingly packaged and marketed as a technique. Go through the requisite number of steps, recite the proper mantras that touch upon deeper inward realities, and happiness can be yours. Much of the pop psychology we see today, though it has its place, mimics the very consumerist values that, in my view, offer a false solution to social discontents that are wide and deep. Like a new religion, pop psychology at times hopes to transcend the human condition.

In a more severe sense, our culture oscillates between the anxieties brought by diminishing expectations and hope on the one hand, and, on the other, the titillation of consumerism, celebrity, and commercialized sex as a means of escaping those anxieties. Wealth, status, and power are the symbols of happiness in our culture. Yet is the reality of happiness to be found behind those symbols? I don't think so. Much of what is held up as a happier life seems to appeal increasingly to the desire to escape. The mistake we are making on a grand scale is to equate happiness with pleasure; the ancients called such a philosophy hedonism.

Yet most of us would probably agree that, although much of happiness consists of pleasurable moments and experiences, happiness and pleasure are not the same thing. Even the depressed person can on occasion experience the pleasure of a laugh or a momentarily happy thought. But we would hardly describe such a person as happy, even if he or she had a succession of such laughs or thoughts. Pleasure by its nature is transitory and usually results from a release of tension, which itself is neutral or unpleasant. We tend to think of happiness, however, as something deeper. Perhaps we think of it as a state of well-being and contentment that endures beyond the flux of life's ups and downs, as something more rooted in our characters. Surely much of our happiness is affected by our outer circumstances and environment. But unless there is an inner sense of equilibrium and richness, the joys of external circumstances quickly disappear. The ancient story of King Midas, of course, teaches that.

What is it that makes for happiness? Is it something that can be cultivated by the way in which we live? Within degrees, I think the answer is yes.

At first glance, the questions may appear too broad to answer, for there appear to be as many roads to happiness as there are people on their own individual paths. Some people can't be happy unless they are fishing, others unless they play the corporate game, still others unless they commit themselves to the daily service of people in need. Despite an almost infinite number of pursuits directed at happiness, are there certain things that they hold in common? Somewhat tentatively, I would say yes.

I am a humanist. It is not an identity I was born with, but one I have chosen. I chose to become a humanist for a number of reasons; I made the choice not only because I thought that what humanism has to say about nature, God, and people is truer than what I was getting from elsewhere, but also because the values that humanism professes make for a more satisfying and, in some sense, happier life. So when answering the question "What makes for happiness?" I find it most accurate to respond from the cluster of values which comprise my humanist identity.

First, I need to say something about temperament. Temperament is something we all have, yet why and where temperament comes from is rather mysterious. Some people are prevailingly optimistic and buoyant by nature. Like Walt Whitman, they find it easy to sing of life and themselves. Others are more grim and somber. Some are weighed down by the heavy burden of negative emotions; others just slough it off. Insult some people and they'll brood for weeks; others will forget it in hours. Some are quick by temperament; others torpid.

In addition to innate temperament, each of us has our share of neurotic dispositions. By *neurotic* I mean those emotional responses that issue from and are fixated at an earlier time in our development. Feeling deeply threatened or enraged by the passing slight of another might be appropriate for a five-year-old who is relatively powerless and insecure. It is out of phase with reality, and therefore not conducive to happiness, if you are a fifty-eight-year-old. And on top of our temperaments and neurotic acquisitions, there are those mysterious daily vicissitudes we call moods. Sometimes we know why we are in a bad mood. Other times we simply wake up that way.

Perhaps there is not much we can do with our baseline temperaments, except to get to know them better and accept them, not as moral defects, but just the way we naturally are. As a recent article in the *New York Times* reported, new research points to the possibility that there may be a gene influencing anxiety—but this is very tentative. The fact that some people by birth seem to be more slated for happiness than others may be one of those cosmic points of unfairness meted out by the designs of an impersonal Nature. As the article mentions, the interest of Nature is not whether we in life have a good time or not, just whether we survive long enough to reproduce and launch our genes into another generation. The task of all of us is not to whine about our condition, but to deal as successfully as we can in life with the hand we have been dealt.

Despite the supports and obstacles of our native temperaments, I believe there are approaches we can take to build the possibilities of greater happiness. Again my view is shaped by my humanist commitments. There are four things I wish to focus on, though I could discuss many more.

First, I believe that happiness has something to do with living an active rather than passive life. In our overworked times, I know that many people hunger for more opportunities to simply do nothing, to be idle, and to waste time in the service of restoring their energies. This need for relaxation, for balance between work and leisure, is necessary and good. But I suspect a life of couch potatohood would bring happiness to few of us. What I mean by an active life is not an overheated, frenetic life. Rather I'm speaking of an orientation toward life that is zestful because one sees the world in novel, creative, and interesting ways, and acts accordingly. A person reading appears still, yet she may be mentally and emotionally fully engaged, alive, and active.

A multitude of philosophers from Aristotle to John Dewey, psychologists, and happiness gurus of all stripes have seen the human being as a dynamic, not static being, for whom happiness has a great deal to do with the expression and development of our powers and potentialities. Leave our potentials untapped and stillborn and we remain, to that extent, frustrated and unhappy. Allow our potentials to exercise themselves and develop, and in that process of unfolding, despite all the small temporary frustrations along the way, satisfaction that makes for happiness is to be found.

The example that most vividly comes to mind is the development of the powers of the artist or the creative person. But more to the point is the very development of our emotional potentials. I am speaking of the expansion of our capacities to love, to care, to laugh, to cry, to empathize, to feel compassion. We can do this at any stage of life. The person of deeper, richer, and wider feelings who senses the world in more engaging, sensuous, and emotional ways is someone to whom life will be less sterile, and to that extent more fulfilling.

Likewise in the areas of thought. Two people can look at the same object—let's say, a landscape or a piece of art. To one person it is full of interest and wonder. To the second it is a matter of total indifference. The object is, of course, the same. The difference lies in the minds of the observers. One mind is actively filled with associations and surrounds the object with a sense of play and wonder. The second brings nothing to it. His mind is passive. Again, I am not talking about a single pleasurable experience, rather an orientation by which we can approach life not as passive consumers of experience, but actors who bring our own imagination, interests, and energies to what we think, feel, and do.

This is something we can continually cultivate. Aristotle once tersely said, "If you wish to be courageous, you must do courageous things." It sounds trite, but it is true. By taking risky steps you can immerse yourself in new environments that will pull at your capacities to feel and to think in new and broader ways. It is that growth which is happiness inducing over the course of a lifetime.

Erich Fromm had a lovely phrase to the effect that when it comes to one's life, each person is "both an artist and the object of his art." In other words, at birth each one of us is confronted with a task, and that task is to create and mold a life. Happiness is not to be found in shirking or avoiding that task, but rather taking on the assignment.

This leads directly to the second closely related point. Each man and woman, I believe, is endowed with certain gifts. Where they come from, either by genes or by early processes of socialization, is hard to determine. Part of the journey toward a fulfilling life is to know oneself, as it were to sense one's inner contours as the wood carver might sense the pathways in the wood.

There are too many unhappy people in psychiatrists' offices who became doctors and lawyers because their parents pressured them to, when they would have preferred to do something else with their lives.

I am reminded of Stephen Jay Gould, the paleontologist whose father would take him, when he was a young boy, to see the dinosaurs at the Museum of Natural History. There he fell in love with those giant reptiles, and today he is still playing with them as one of the world's most eminent evolutionary scientists. In a marvelous way he was able to transform the passions of his youth into the career of a lifetime. Few people are lucky enough to have their work be a vocation that is an expression of themselves rather than primarily a way to make a living. For many, earning a living is a vehicle for buying the time to do what they really want to do most, be it pursuing a hobby, advancing a cause, becoming a fully invested family person, becoming an artist or a gardener, or whatever.

David Norton, a former leader in our movement and a professor of philosophy at the University of Delaware, has written a book entitled *Personal Destinies*. In the book, he lays out his theory of what the Greeks called *eudaimonia,* which we may translate roughly as "happiness." What it means literally is to be in touch with one's *daimon,* one's inner true being or self. When you are identified with your *daimon,* you are eudaimonious, "well daimoned," as it were, or happy. To be eudaimonious means to live in truth with oneself, to feel that one is where one wants to be, doing what one wants to do. One is reminded of the words to the Shaker hymn, "'Tis a gift to be simple, 'tis a gift to be free, 'tis a gift to come down where one ought to be." And it truly is. The person who loves his work does not feel it as labor or as a burden, because what he has to do, he wants to do. He is eudaimonious with his work, and thus it is a source of happiness.

The achievement of eudaimonia has much to do with reflective maturation—stripping away what is not essentially us in the process of refining our characters and interests. I long ago came to peace with the reality that I simply was not going to become a great ballet dancer, or a ballet dancer at all—it simply wasn't in me. Closer to home was the realization that I would not be an astronomer. My proficiency in math just wasn't strong enough. So I turned to ancient languages instead, where the complex but elegant grammars of Latin and Greek had a strong and aesthetic appeal to me. I love the interplay of words, their histories and nuances. The whole verbal enterprise is close to who I am. It is an expression of my *daimon*.

Happiness comes from growing older and wiser—from giving up without much remorse what one cannot have in favor of a truer, more authentic self. As we travel through life, we can steadily make those little adjustments that will move us closer to the center of where we ought to be, as it were.

Third, I am reminded of a Jewish maxim to the effect that "life is with people." Certainly this is something that humanists should value as well. While it is true that many people find happiness in isolated and solitary pursuits, humanism affirms that we are first and last social creatures. Other people can be the sources of our greatest torments and miseries, but in a social life can we also find the greatest joys, pleasures, and fulfillments.

We are more social than we know. Our lives are lived out within a human arena. Our possibilities for fulfillment, for a reputation, and for our sense of self-esteem depend on our interactions with others. We do not become ourselves except as we relate to others and they to us. This is true of our moral and emotional abilities most of all.

John Lovejoy Elliot, a leader in our movement, once observed that "the most important things in life are love and friendship." Though it is a simple observation, I believe there is much to be said for it. There is great happiness in cultivating the human bond through love, caring, mutual support, political solidarity, acts of charity and kindness, and the repartee that comes with easy socializing and friendship. Though this seems such a basic constituent of happiness, one fear is that these simpler humanistic pursuits are being lost in the midst of a frenetic, fast-paced society which is overly enchanted with pleasures to be derived through possession rather than from fellow human beings.

So far, all the aspects of happiness I have mentioned relate to what we might call a philosophy of self-realization or self-fulfillment. But I think that one more ingredient needs to be added, and here I return to appreciate Adler's respect for worthiness as an end of life.

We can experience happiness in either crass or sublime ways. If our happiness is to reach more deeply, I believe that we must understand our sense of fulfillment in more sublime ways.

It's a complexity of the human condition that we cannot really live fulfilled without a sense of meaning and purpose. And that sense of purpose usually suggests that we see our own individual lives and our fulfillment not as ends in themselves but in the light of larger dedications. We need to feel that we are part of a larger whole. We perhaps want to feel that the very process of our own individual self-realization serves a purpose greater than ourselves.

The sage Hillel has said, "If I am not for myself who will be for me?" then added, "If I am for myself only, what am I?" And Bertrand Russell has observed, "The value of a person's life is to be measured by his commitment to something that outlasts him." There is irony here. The flourishing of our individual selves that contributes to our happiness is made more meaningful when we subordinate those selves to something greater than we are.

How many creative artists need to feel that by their creation they are adding to a cumulative tradition? How many creative people feel the urge to teach so that they may give of themselves to future generations? How many people of achievement have the need to give back to society some of what they feel that society has given to them? There is much discussion today about the need for the fulfillments that come from spiritual experience. To my mind there is a spiritual realization that comports so well with our humanist values. It is a sublime sense that our deeper satisfactions are met when we appreciate our connection with the wider world; when we take what is best in ourselves and recognize that we can use it to enrich and expand the lives of others and thus humankind.

As I think I've implied, happiness is not something to be won as a prize in a game where one applies hard and fast rules and can expect to walk away with the prize. Nor does it result from applying easy formulas to the vagaries of life. Nor do I believe that there is a way to protect ourselves from the hardships, miseries, and tragedies of life that sooner or later visit almost all of us. I don't believe that there is nirvana for us, nor are there paths by which we can bootstrap ourselves out of the basic human condition.

Life confronts us with many challenges. Many things in life we cannot change, and it is itself a source of that happiness known as "peace of mind" to accept calmly and with resignation those things we are powerless to alter. Others we can slowly bend, mold, and create to our own satisfaction. The pursuit of happiness is a lifelong endeavor. But it is a strange and sly object indeed. It resists capture. For the ironic truth is that happiness will be ours not while we are pursuing it directly, but only when we are doing something else.

December 1996

Being A Witness For Others

I begin with a rendering of my favorite Shakespearean poem, sonnet 29. It goes as follows:

When in disgrace with fortune and men's eyes
I all alone beweep my outcast state,
And trouble deaf heaven with my bootless cries,
And look upon myself and curse my fate,
Wishing me like one more rich in hope,
Featured like him, like him with friends possessed,
Desiring this man's art and that man's scope,
With what I most enjoy, contented least,
Yet, in these thoughts myself almost despising,
Haply I think on *thee*—and then my state,
Like to the lark at break of day arising,
From sullen earth sings hymns at heaven's gate.
For thy sweet love remembered, such wealth brings,
That then I scorn to change my fate with kings.

The poet's sentiments are totally humanistic. It is part of the human experience that all of us, at times, experience hard luck and the criticism and scorn of our fellow human beings. We feel like outcasts. We all fall prey to feelings of isolation and despair, sometimes deep despair. Shakespeare tells us that God is indifferent, "deaf," to our self-pitying cries for help. Rather the only force that can lift us out of our sullenness, the only point of leverage, is the image, the recalled image, of another person who loves us and believes in us. It is the presence of another who pierces the darkness, and because of his or her love, we are able once again to find faith in ourselves. It is the human bond, the ability to weave the web of human contact and love on which our own happiness and well-being are emotionally dependent. Sometimes we fail to recognize this until we lose it, and we are once again "all alone to beweep our outcast state."

Today, inspired by Shakespeare, I want to reflect on a simple human experience that I believe goes underappreciated. It relates to the important, if not vital role we can play for other people in enabling them to believe in themselves and to rescue themselves from despair. I call this phenomenon "being a witness" for others.

What is a witness? For an answer to this question, I refer to a paper titled *The Healing Presence*, by Dr. Hank Seiden, published in the *Psychoanalytic Review* of October 1996. Dr. Seiden had presented earlier versions of this paper to a meeting of Ethical Culture's National Leaders' Council. He writes:

> It seems safe to say that coherent experience—to perceive what is and to think straight about it—requires, sometimes explicitly, sometimes implicitly, the confirming presence of other people. To believe in and trust what one sees requires a sense that another person in the same place and at the same time would see the same thing the same way. We need the sense that our experience is shared in order to feel that our experience is firm, that what we know to be true is true, that what we feel is valid. This is so, of course, even in terms of identity and self-definition—it is the confirming presence of others which allows us to go on believing that we are who we think we are. All of which is to say that a coherent self requires, explicitly or implicitly, its witnesses.

For Dr. Seiden, "the need for a witness is a vital human need." And I agree. Upon reflection, we realize how our own experiences need the validation of others. In a more extreme way, we may conclude that an experience is not real in a certain sense until it receives the confirmation of at least one other person, and preferably many people.

This is most dramatically true in a legal sense. When a person is a witness in a trial, he or she testifies as to what has happened and when. When on the stand, the role of the witness is far from a passive one. The witness is not a mere observer. The witness records what happens and, under oath and subject to penalties, takes responsibility for what he or she has recorded and verified. Legally, it would almost be correct to say that an event is not a real event until the witness takes responsibility for saying that it is real.

In the history of social action, especially religious social action, there is the honorable concept of "bearing witness." To bear witness means to testify to a truth, a religious or moral truth, by putting oneself on the line through public demonstration and willingness to accept the consequences. The person who bears witness says to himself, "This moral value is so crucially important that I cannot sit on the sidelines. I cannot be a secondhand player. If there is risk, then so be it. I am morally compelled to my actions, and I cannot conscientiously do otherwise."

In the early days of the Christian Church, to bear witness to one's faith, especially in times of persecution, meant to put oneself in danger, at times great danger. And so the word for *witness* in Greek became synonymous with the word *martyr*. In Greek, a martyr is a witness.

When I officiate at weddings, I welcome the guests and mention that despite the private feeling that couples have, weddings are actually public events. I suggest that those who are invited are not merely passive observers, but active witnesses, who, by their presence, are helping to legitimize the change in status of members of the community. Once again, the role of the witness is active and necessary, in this case, to complete the reality of the marriage union.

What pertains in law, in the realm of political action, and in marriage ceremonies is part and parcel of our normal everyday experience also. This is certainly true for our beliefs. In our egotism we tend to think that the ideas we believe spring fully formed from our own creative minds, like Athena from the head of Zeus. But this is assuredly false. In order for me to believe just about anything, I need the validation, the shoring up, the corroboration of others who are witnesses to my experience. If I have humanist beliefs, such as belief in the dignity of human beings, or if I believe it preferable to treat people with compassion rather than cruelty, I humbly admit that I did not create these beliefs, nor did I invent humanistic philosophy. These philosophies were present at my birth and in my environment for me to choose. More important, the fact that others continue to hold these beliefs works to sustain them for me. In fact if all the world's humanists were to disappear tomorrow, and humanist ideas along with them, it would become monumentally hard, if not impossible, for me to sustain my own beliefs and convictions. They would erode in time.

What is true with regard to belief systems and values pertains even to our most basic perceptions. I cannot doubt that there are chairs before me in this room. But if, through some diabolical force, everyone I ever met denied that such a thing as a chair exists and banished totally the word *chair* and everything related to it, including erasing every written reference to chairs, I suppose that over time I would come to doubt that there were chairs, and then come to doubt my sanity. Though it's a radical conclusion, our ideas, conceptions, and beliefs are themselves socially created and socially sustained—as is the very coherence of our own minds. We need confirmers, witnesses, in order to stay sane. And witnesses, again, are not merely passive. By confirming what we say, think, and feel, they actively help keep our minds as well as our world coherent for us.

This understanding is implicit in the use of solitary confinement as a most awful form of punishment. Without the confirming experiences of others, our minds become incoherent and disintegrate over time. It is for this reason that people held in solitary for long periods report that they will continually pace and measure the cell or engage in solving mathematical problems in their heads as a way of trying to maintain mental coherence in the absence of social confirmation. Anatoly Sharansky, the prisoner of conscience who was held in a Soviet prison for more than nine years, much of it in solitary, stated that he preserved his sanity by playing games of chess, of which he is a master, without a board, needless to say.

What goes for our thoughts, ideas, and beliefs pertains to our feelings also, especially our feelings about ourselves and our self-evaluation in the most intimate sense. It seems to be a fact, and in my view an absolutely horrific and terrorizing fact, that our own sense of self, our capacity to love ourselves and feel good about ourselves in our own eyes, needs the validation of other human beings. Whether we feel worthy is contingent in the greatest measure on whether other people esteem us to be worthy and express it in both confirmatory words and deeds.

Imagine, if you will, the following nightmare. Imagine that in a flash all people who loved you and confirmed you grew icy cold. Every man, woman, and child without exception either disparaged you or became totally indifferent to you. No reasoning, no efforts at persuasion, however powerful or persistent, made the slightest difference. You became utterly and totally alone. The question we ask is, given such utter isolation from the care, love, and affirmation of your fellow human beings, would you be able to sustain your own sense of esteem and self-love? I think the answer is: not for very long at all. We would soon lapse into a condition of depression, probably followed by madness and death. We are social creatures, and we are dependent on others more than we usually realize.

Our own Felix Adler was himself horrified by the idea that in the modern age a person's worth, including his or her sense of self-worth, depends on whether other people deemed him or her worthy or not. Remove God as the Watchful, All-Knowing Custodian and the Benign Sustainer, and we left with human beings doing that sustaining task. But, as we know, human beings can be fickle, and their validation of us can be withdrawn for reasons of their own. Adler did not like at all the conclusion that out worth rests on the flimsy fact of whether people think we are worthy. Many people deem Mary worthy; but no one deems Sally worthy. Should the ultimate worth of Sally or Mary be dependent on mere human sentiments, with all their prejudices and mutability? Adler thought not, and his entire philosophy is an elaborate effort to ground human worth in something more sturdy and secure. Adler wanted to ensure that, like the tree that falls in the forest and makes a sound even when no one is listening, each human being is worthy even if no other human being thinks so. While his efforts were notable, most people today would probably judge his technical philosophy in this regard an erudite failure.

Modern people in the late twentieth century would probably assume and accept the difficult thought that whether we esteem ourselves *does* depend on whether others affirm us or not. Such is a brute, existential fact of human experience. Most people are fortunate to have such an affirming presence in their lives. Many others tragically do not. It is ultimately, especially in the younger years, a matter of accident. If I am fortunate to have been nurtured by loving parents and have been able to bring around me people who affirm me, my chances for self-affirmation are good. If, on the other hand, by cruel luck, I am born into an unloving, brutal environment, then my life story will most likely be much harder.

A few exceptions, who constitute something close to a human miracle, qualify the somewhat fatalistic assertion. Developmental psychology tells us that for a person to develop a sound ego, with a sense of esteem and mature self-love, one needs to have had a good start in life—a family of origin in which one receives love, security, structure, and positive attention to one's needs. A lack of such a nurturing beginning, it is often said, sets the stage for severe psychopathology later in life. Yet I have long been powerfully moved by stories of people born into the most brutalizing of environments, homes in which there is not only poverty, but substance abuse, violence, and neglect; a home in which each child has to fend for himself, competing with five or six or a dozen siblings for a scrap of food, or a small corner of a bed; homes in which there is seemingly no nurturing foundation at all. Yet, out of almost total deprivation, sometimes there emerge people who grow up reasonably intact and go on to lead productive, successful lives. Ostensibly defying the canons of developmental psychology and bereft of nurturing childhood foundations, they are able, somehow, to construct out of their own experiences a foundation of their own as they travel through life.

But when we examine their backgrounds more minutely, we sometimes notice that out of the overwhelming emotional barrenness of their childhood, there was one person, and perhaps only one—a teacher, an aunt or uncle, a neighbor, a minister—who recognized something special in the child that no one else saw or cared to see, and by so doing gave the child a lifeline, a germ of affirmation around which he or she could construct a functional, self-affirming personality and go on to lead a normal life. This single instance of affirmation and belief in him or her made the difference between salvation and destruction. For most children caught in the grip of crushing adversity, there is only lifelong despair, but for a few, with the help of what I am calling a witness, there is a way out.

Several years ago, there appeared on the television show *20/20* a vignette on a Dr. Benjamin Carson. Dr. Carson, who practices at Johns Hopkins Medical Center, is one of only three African American neurosurgeons in the country. The program explored how Dr. Carson, who grew up in a Detroit ghetto with all the dislocations we associate with an impoverished childhood in an inner city, was able to pull himself up and achieve what he did. His lifeline was his mother. He explained how his mother, when he was in elementary school, insisted that he and his brother sit before her and read their written compositions assigned to them in school. What made this story so poignant, as he explained, was that his mother herself could not read.

This story leads to my central point. And that is that we can all be witnesses for other people. We can have an effect for good on others to an extent greater than we can predict in advance. For some who walk around feeling bereft of love and appreciation, we can play a role of far greater significance than we may know or imagine. As humanists we should expand and multiply our opportunities for doing so. We could be that aunt, uncle, teacher, or neighbor who plays that disproportionate, if not saving role for another, especially a child.

All of us live both public and private lives. The public sees only the surface we present to others. Others can do little better than guess at what lies beneath that surface. We all walk around among others as if playing a gigantic, continuous guessing game. We interact with other people daily, but we never really know what they are thinking within the privacy of their own selves. We get clues and hints from what they say and how they act. But these are merely clues and hints. The full story remains behind the curtain and is unknown to us—unless, of course, we live with them, or they are intimates who choose to fully and with nuance convey the contents and significance of their innermost thoughts and feelings. But one thing we ought not to be naive about: the inside story behind the curtain of privacy is always more complex than the public mask people always and indeed must wear. To wear a public mask is not hypocrisy, but a necessary demand of our social existence. We simply could not bear revealing our intimate lives to all.

An intriguing aspect of the human condition is that people tend to fill the gaps in their knowledge of others through imagination. We project onto others assumptions of how they are, and these projections are usually rooted in our own sense of inadequacy and insecurity. In some ways, we all feel insecure and inadequate. We look at the performer, the pianist whose talent and genius seems to ooze out of his fingers, or the ballet dancer who flies with the grace of an invisible hand that gently propels her through the air. We look at these performers, and we make the assumption that the outer competence and grace we see in the public self must be matched by an inner sense of competence and grace that they must subjectively feel in the intimacy of their private selves. We perhaps look upon these others with feelings of awe, with a belief that they are larger than life through and through. Perhaps in our unknowing imaginations we amplify their greatness and reinforce our own sense of inadequacy with comparisons that are foolish to make. Wouldn't we be surprised to learn, as we sometimes do, that those people who are most competent in their public personas, be they performers, teachers, politicians, bankers, or parents, are themselves wracked by gnawing sensations of their own inadequacy, and that sometimes people who are publicly the most competent privately experience themselves as incompetent and inadequate. Our lives are not coherent and in fact are, to varying degrees, divided, often uncomfortably so. The line between the objective and subjective selves, between the public and private selves, is more often than not neither smooth nor untrammeled.

My daughter, who is a social psychology researcher, tells me that some surveys report that upward of 40 percent of the American public suffer from what is called the "impostor syndrome," or at least from impostorlike feelings. Many people, by all objective measures very competent in their fields, feel nevertheless that they are undeserving of such estimations. Rather, they feel inauthentic. They feel like phonies and walk around saying to themselves, "If people really knew how incompetent I am, how it's all a contrived act, they would withdraw their positive acclaim." We can seldom know by looking at the outside what feelings, what pains, lurk within the subjective experience of the others we so admire. The person who looks great may not feel that way. The person who is competent may be disturbed, perhaps greatly, by emotions of inadequacy and inauthenticity. And more to the point, the child we see playing on the next street, who may greet us with a diffident smile, may in his little body be consumed with feelings of anguish. He may be forced because of his age to return home each evening to parents who treat him with brutality. Perhaps that child goes to bed each night with nothing but his own longings that someone, someday, will come into his life and say, "Johnny, you are not alone. I understand what you are going through, and it is not fair, it is not just." In other words, the child hopes that out of his desperation, impotence, and misery, a witness will appear, if not to rescue him, then to at least confirm that what he is experiencing is real and awful and in no way his fault. We can imagine how powerful, how crucially important, that act of witnessing would be to a suffering child who feels so neglected, unloved, and alone. Most important, can we imagine ourselves being a witness for such a child?

Though I am perhaps being a little melodramatic, we can wonder how many hurt, grieving children live on the peripheries of our lives, and how many adults we encounter who are lonely or feel their lives bereft of the confirmation they profoundly need. I suspect many.

I have a good and much-admired friend who in her adult life has made something of a career out of taking under her wing people young and old whom she senses have a need for more affirming human contact, whether it be a young woman with personality problems, a needy child, or adults who may come into her life whom she senses are lonely. She has an ability to sense their need and to respond with caring and friendship. What's needed is not technical skill, but a capacity for empathy, an ability to see in the person positive qualities that others may have overlooked, and a desire to believe in that person when others have not. The humanity and caring of my friend is indeed a gift to those who have been fortunate to have had her as their witness, so to speak.

All of us can do this, of course, by rearranging our priorities. Each of us can serve as a witness to another person, perhaps an acquaintance, or a child who is not our own. Each of us can extend a kind or supportive word in recognition of the skills we see others struggling to master. We can work harder to empathetically take the standpoint of the other, try to see the world as he or she sees it and express ourselves to the other through a confirmatory word or gesture. Sometimes witnessing people's inner lives by recognizing their struggle is all they really want from us, and sometimes that can be very much indeed. This goes beyond merely learning what troubles another or desiring to be helpful. Rather, to be a witness often means helping to bring clarity, order, and even reality to that person's experiences by helping to uncover, name, and validate them.

When we think of Ethical Culture and its mission, we often think of the big picture, of the struggle for justice in the wider society. Yet, the mandate to bring out the best in others applies in the smaller, more personal dimensions of life even more.

I would like to close with a passage from Felix Adler's *An Ethical Philosophy of Life* that expresses in his elegant words the phenomenon of witnessing that I am bringing to light. He says:

> No greater boon can anyone receive from another than to be helped to think well of himself. Flattery is the base counterpart of appreciation. Appreciation of the inner self despite the mask, is the greatest of gifts, to manifest it is the greatest of arts. In its supreme form it is the art of going down to the lowest of human beings—the man in the ditch, the woman on the street—and making them think well of themselves because of possibilities in their nature they themselves hardly surmise. It is also the art of making the most developed and advanced human beings realize in themselves something still higher and better than they have ever reached. It is this art by which the supreme human benefactors have worked their spiritual miracles, and it is the art to the extent of our ability we must each acquire and practice if human society is to be redeemed.

March 1997

Seven Values Worth Preserving

To say that we live in a time of change carries the deadly ring of cliché. Our society, our culture, and we ourselves are always changing. Time and life do not stand still but, like an ever-flowing stream, forever course forward. Yet events unfolding in American life and across the globe in just the past ten years do seem to bring us into a stage of political and economic development that looks and feels very different from the Cold War era we have left.

The rapid collapse of the Soviet Union, the current triumph of the free market, which has become a global market, and the rise of religious fundamentalism are all phenomena signaling a categorical change. It is as if massive earthquakes erupted all at once and rapidly realigned the landscape. Harvard political historian Samuel Huntington recently published a thesis proposing that with the end of the Cold War, nationalisms and ideologies won't matter so much anymore. Such allegiances will be powerfully replaced with a loyalty to "civilizations" fueled by a heavy religious component. In the future the globe will be realigned into Western, Islamic, and Chinese civilizations, and they will clash with one another. In his view, the West is in decline. Rather than attempt to assert our values into the other domains, the best we can do is hold on. These shifts, whatever they may be, although seemingly remote because they are global, in this world of instant communication, do have impact on our personal lives, our aspirations, and the kinds of values we individually nurture in our minds and hearts.

And so does the rule of the marketplace. The free market has been let loose in America and across the globe. With it has come a dismantling of government controls and protections; the consequences for our values have been tremendous. With fluctuating markets, we are open to greater vicissitudes and insecurities than before. Hard-won victories have been quickly swept away. Worker/management loyalties, a secure job with ample benefits, a good retirement to look forward to—these fixed points of American life have quickly become a thing of the past. Instead, more and more wealth increasingly moves upward to the richest Americans while the middle class gets smaller and works harder, struggling just to stay in place. The love affair with the open marketplace has helped to erode leisure and stress families, often beyond the breaking point, and has raised consumerism to frenetic levels. It has generated greater social isolation, and foments a war of each against all. It has banished from American life the idea that there can ever be enough. If it's profitable, do it—and the more profit, the better. Pull out all the stops. While you would expect this is in the commercial arena, the allure of the market has co-opted the nonprofit sector as well. Education, teaching, and the exploration of the free mind, which we would think would be the heart and soul of universities and colleges, are no longer. Today, the rewards go to those who produce objectified data and publish material that can attract large and remunerative research grants and contracts. And the tentacles of the octopus have even ensnared religion: religion, whose purpose, in my view, is to promote those values that money cannot buy—love, compassion, and service to others. Religion is being co-opted by the market as ministers become entrepreneurs and churches become more preoccupied with body counts and expanding budgets.

This is where I come in. In these changing times, I believe that we humanists must stand firm and continue to declare those bedrock values that we believe give deeper meaning to life and are necessary for the survival of the human race. In my opinion, some values are of eternal significance; they are fixed stars in the human experience. They belong to both liberals and conservatives. They are not transient, but permanent. They are values that must resist the vicissitudes of changing winds. They are human values.

There are seven values I believe need be preserved no matter how radically the social, cultural, and political landscape shifts under our feet. They are among the anchorages of life. This short list is by no means meant to be exhaustive.

1. *First, we need to preserve a love of knowledge and an appreciation of the importance of ideas.* I see these values fading on the American landscape. We live, in my view, in increasingly anti-intellectual times. On the most basic level, illiteracy is on the rise. The schools are not doing well. Among the more fortunate, many read less than they used to. There is less interest in, and greater impatience with, ideas. The public intellectual is all but gone from society. At one time, large segments of the public were interested in what great minds were thinking. But no more. Knowledge of the world, of history, of politics is increasingly gleaned from movies and television, not from books. The two approaches are not the same. Reading is a time-consuming process, involving rapport with a book. It generates reflection, depth, and what the critic Sven Birkerts refers to as "inwardness." The visual media, for the most part, don't, and can't.

In the last few decades, ideas have been flattened, at best into artifacts of culture or at worst into the fabric of entertainment. Look, for example, at journalism, which provides the lifeblood of democracy, and see where it has gone. Increasingly, journalism has become absorbed into an entertainment mind-set and its critical edge dulled.

For my immigrant grandparents, my parents, and for me, living in the afterglow of the immigrant experience, ideas were revered because they were valued as vehicles to achieve upward mobility, which also inspired social change. Ideas had power. Being knowledgeable and thinking clearly were respected and valued personal assets.

Indeed, ideas did have power. In the nineteenth century, unlike our own, it was passionately assumed that ideas were an engine that could, would, and did change the world. Marx, Darwin, Elizabeth Stanton, Freud, Einstein, and countless other political theorists, scientists, and men and women of letters molded a new world by unmasking and deploying ideas and inspiring others with their insight into the nature of things. Today we don't see ideas, except for technological ones, as having much power to transform society or ourselves. Their luster is gone, their potency drained. We have lost our faith in them. And we have also lost a sense of their beauty.

The pursuit of knowledge is not only of great practical purpose; it is also worthy of aesthetic contemplation. Exercising a curiosity to know the world, pushing aside the curtain of ignorance, feeling a sense of wonder before the mysteries we confront, and yet getting a handle on them, however small, by the power of our mind as it forges coherence out of it all—all these joys emerge from the interplay of life with ideas. But this repository of joy seems today not to be as much in evidence.

When I discussed the liberal intellectual tradition and the primary mission of college education to foster that tradition, to nurture the life of the mind, my students would honestly respond that they were not in college for that purpose. They were putting in their four years to get the "paper," the diploma, the credential. I don't blame them. They were merely absorbing and reflecting the predominant values of our times.

But as humanists, I believe that we must stand against these currents. We need to appreciate that a love of learning, of knowledge, of the life of the mind is a beautiful thing. It's an uplifting thing. It is a quality of character that deepens life. To be a reflective person, and not merely an entity driven by appetites, is an essential way to cultivate our humanity. We ought not to give it away.

2. While we need to cultivate our minds, we also need to strengthen and broaden our hearts. *My second value is compassion.* Of all the virtues, social as well as personal, compassion for me is the most cherished. Neither as intense nor as exclusive as love, not as condescending as is pity, compassion is the ability to feel along with another person. It's the ability to be moved by another's suffering and another's joy. It's to recognize that the feelings the other experiences are emotions that I experience in myself. It is this ability to sense a common experience that leads me to appreciate a common humanity. In my view, compassion is the ability to sense the humanity that lies behind another person's eyes and to be moved to care and to help. Compassion is the matrix from which ethics is born.

In times of stress and strain it becomes more difficult to feel compassionate or to want to care. I can give a dime to a homeless person, but when I am approached by twenty, I become overwhelmed. I begin to tune out as a matter of self-protection. I begin to care less. And so many of us feel overwhelmed these days, needing to protect the integrity of our marriages, our families, and our homes as our first and increasingly only object of compassion and caring.

And these are hard times; times of insecurity, of stress. The outside world has a raw and sometimes nasty edge. This too blankets our compassion. Our ability to care constricts until it envelops no one but ourselves.

I believe that we are at bottom social creatures. Our individual destinies are tied to the destinies of others, and ultimately to the fate of the human race and of the planet. So is our humanity. "If I am for myself only, what am I?" rhetorically asked the sage Hillel. There is great wisdom in that; wisdom that comes through compassion. Perhaps it will take greater powers of reflection as we look deeper into ourselves to find our strength. Perhaps we will have to carve out specific venues in which to cultivate compassion. But if we lose our ability to be compassionate, to care, our humanity also slips away. Above all things we cannot let this happen.

3. Compassion is a state that applies itself to the personal and interpersonal realms of life. Wordsworth speaks of "that portion of a good man's life, his little nameless, unremembered acts of kindness and of love." This is where compassion dwells also. As a humanist I think that we need to look beyond the interpersonal sphere to the well-being of the broader community. A third value we need to preserve is that of *activism*. Humanism is antiquietistic. This doesn't mean that there aren't times to sit idle and go with the flow. But to throw one's hands up and say "I am paralyzed, it is hopeless, and there is nothing that I can do" is not in our spirit.

As with compassion, the activist commitment arises from an understanding that the self is social. There is no human being who stands apart from the human family. We are all enmeshed in the web of humanity—present, past, and future. We are all the legatees of the labors of those who share our planet, our nation, and our neighborhood. We have what we could call an associative obligation to those who inhabit our community and make our lives possible.

Aristotle long ago said that to live a good life was to live the life of the *polis*, the community. For John Dewey, the wall between the citizen and the community is a fiction. We become ourselves through interacting with others toward common ends, toward what we might call "the common good."

People under the sway of economic forces, influenced by political leadership bordering on demagoguery, have directed their frustration toward the least of our brethren or have turned inward, forsaking broader social commitments.

We need to restore a devotion to the common good. We need to work for it, not only directly through neighborhood groups, environmental coalitions, civil liberties, rights, and women's organizations, PTAs, etc., but also through lobbying our government to move again in the direction of economic justice in the name of all of us. It is hard to find a way amid all the impediments and distractions of life. But democracy is more than an electoral form. It is a character trait; a character trait of a free and fulfilled people. Without it we lose robustness. We become parochial and small, almost trivial. On the national level, without a people filled with a democratic commitment and an activism directed toward solving common problems, we become a nation of sheep, and the door is opened for fascism.

4. Having raised the concern for fascism, it might sound odd that the fourth value I find worth preserving is *authority*. Authority is not authoritarianism. The latter is an arbitrary, coercive, and incontestable abuse of authority. It is authority's malignant expression.

Without respect and honor for authority, our lives are rendered shallow and superficial. *Authority* as I mean it is an appropriate, legitimate, and enhancing phenomenon. It is the power that a person has to legitimately command my appreciation and my attention. If I am in the presence of a person who has spent her life researching and reflecting on a certain area of thought, or is a masterful singer, or has commanded a skill or a talent by virtue of effort and native gifts, then it is due for me to appreciate what she has to present. She knows something or can do something that I cannot, and such is worthy of my respect. This does not imply that I abandon my power of dissent. It is the approach, the attitude, the valuing of the other that I'm speaking of. By so doing I bring honor to that person and I deepen my own spirit by attending to what the other has to give me, which, again, I lack. I fear that in our age, authority is being increasingly replaced by celebrity. Substance counts for less, and image is coming to mean everything. The consequence is that life loses depth. A sense of history disappears and thereby the claims of tradition upon us. What counts is momentary gratification, because there is little beyond us that we recognize as rightful authority to claim our attention and mold our thought and attitude. Too much, in my view, is determined by uninformed and immediate feelings and intuitions.

Without a sense of authority, there ultimately cannot be any ethics either. In order to say "this is good and that is not," "this is preferable to that," "this right, that wrong," one has to recognize the authority that certain claims and arguments have over us. Yet the fear of authority has led in some cases to what looks like a total moral relativism. College teachers have reported to me that in class discussion involving values, students often refrain from standing up and saying to other students, "I think your opinion is mistaken," or "I think you are wrong." The hidden assumption is that there cannot be any court of higher appeal; there can be no authoritative reasoning invoked by which to say, "I think you are wrong, and here's why." The only test of truth is whether the person is sincere in his or her opinion. There used to be an adage that went, "You have a right to your opinion, but not all opinions are right." This is slowly being replaced by a new rule of thought and conduct: "You have a right to your opinion, and if you are sincere in feeling that way, there is no authority, mine or anyone else's, to say you are mistaken."

Without a sense of worthy authority, we have no outlet for the expression of honor or respect. We trade in depth of spirit for the momentary and tawdry. We become superficial in our appreciations. Furthermore, we lose criteria by which we can assert what we believe to be true or right or good. We fall into a maelstrom of abject relativism. Let us not take that plunge.

5. Related to the demise of authority is a deep skepticism as to the value, or even possibility, of *objectivity*. Subjectivity is all the rage today. It is on the cutting edge in the academic world, in political theory, in literature, and in philosophy. Objective knowledge is not possible, it is said, because any assertion that a person or class of people makes must be an expression of their interests. In this regard, the objective claims of the dominant, that is, European class of men are nothing but an expression of their political dominance, and claims to objectivity are merely tools to maintain that dominance.

There is, of course, considerable insight to this claim. In a philosophical sense, there might be no great Truth out there. But, in my view, all of science, modern moral theory, and our judicial procedures issue from a commitment to objective values that strive to hold in abeyance our subjective feeling about the issue at hand—whether measuring the weight of gold or determining a person's guilt or innocence in a court of law. However imperfect the implementation of objective procedures might be, I simply cannot imagine an approach that would conceivably, or in practice, be better. Remove the consensual quest for objective values, however illusory, and you have opened the door to endless and brute power struggles with no way whatsoever to arbitrate between completing claims, except by force.

Jefferson's denial of basic rights to slaves, despite his authorship of the Declaration of Independence, is an often-invoked example of the false values of objective claims. Humanity is reserved only for those who have the power to define it. And so slaves, women, and nonlandowners were denied rights that on their face were declared objective, natural rights. Objectivity is assumed to be a sham, an illusory and genteel mask to hide the power interests of the dominant class. "The golden rule," as Marxists would say, is "He who has the gold makes the rule." The problem with this argument is that it doesn't recognize that the Declaration of Independence holds within it the very tools by which to remonstrate against its own abuse. It bears within it the seeds of its self-correction. The abolitionists and Martin Luther King used the words of the Declaration and its objective claims of human rights to show how the lofty ideals of the Declaration in principle were denied in fact. They didn't reject the objective claims of the Declaration. They strove to bring them to fulfillment.

In a similar vein, there are some in the developing countries who are arguing against the concept of universal human rights. They assert that the Universal Declaration of Human Rights is a Western, European document, and thereby reflects the interests of its originators. Developing nations have a different consciousness, are at a different stage of development, have their own traditions and histories, it's argued. Therefore we cannot accept that human rights have any objective claim. There are no human rights, and it is a form of Western tyranny to make them global and impose them on the rest of us.

Having worked with Amnesty International for twenty years, I can only shudder at this. First, if all principles reflect the power interests of those proclaiming them, why should I not be skeptical of the interests of those in developing countries who make such claims? And I am. Second, if I am tortured in Iran, it is as agonizing as if I am tortured in Canada or England. And last, I have never known an oppressed people anywhere who did not lay claim to their interests in universal and objective values such as freedom, equality, and justice.

Whether objective values truly exist in the clouds or not is an interesting philosophical speculation. But exist or not, they are tools for which we reach. They partake of a common language we must employ if there can be any hope of mediating conflicts among peoples in a civilized way. To erode our commitment to objectivity is to open the door to chaos. It is a door that, at the end of the twentieth century, has been opened. We should not walk through it.

6. Having reflected on some weightier issues, I propose my last two values as necessary tonics. My sixth value worth preserving is *humor*. Life, including my life, would not be possible unless it were suffused with large doses of humor.

Humor changes perspective and puts our lives, with all their worries, problems, and anxieties, into a proper and manageable space. Our day-to-day problems are either cosmic or not cosmic. And most that we confront are not cosmic, though often they may feel that way because we are so immersed in them and can't see beyond them. An ability to laugh, and to laugh at ourselves, to lighten up, is a crucial ingredient in our survival. It can evoke the comic elements in the tragic and nudge us to see that most of the problems that loom large are usually transitory. Our humor keeps us interesting and keeps the burdens we confront further away from us. We need to preserve it in the face of life's hardships, and we must retain our sense of joy.

When we confront the world around us, perhaps it's easy to lapse into the mind-set that nothing can ever be good. But if we look at the world with open eyes, there is much to celebrate. In our religion, we just go around one time. Let us not forsake the gifts that we can experience of life, of nature, of beauty, of friendship, and strive to renew them every day.

7. And last, we must recapture a sense of *grandeur in life*. Our horizons have constricted. We don't live in a time of grand vision, of elevating thoughts or expansive hopes. Our lives need more grandeur. When Darwin completed *On the Origin of Species*, he reflected upon the intricacy of nature, which he had so marvelously revealed to the minds of men and women. He concluded with the observation that there is "grandeur in this view of life." And there is—to see life, including our own, as part of an evolving flux of nature, to sense the powers of nature working through us. When the writer Anna Quindlen addressed a graduating class at Barnard College, she bade the students to reject the fashionable mode of pessimism. Rather, she said, "The only way you can save the world, or any small part of it, is to firmly, passionately believe that it is so grand that it is worth saving."

I believe there is a reality out there, beyond our own perceptions of it. Yet at the same time, our lives depend, in great measure on what we make of them and how we see ourselves. We can view our lives in small, petty, and futile terms. Or we can see ourselves as part of a larger tapestry. We can see ourselves as part of a grand unfolding drama with contributions for ill or for good in how we direct our lives and by the choices we make.

As we approach the end of the twentieth century, many sense that these are not the brightest of times. Let us attempt to illuminate the darkness by holding aloft those enduring values that enhance others and ourselves with intelligence, compassion, good deeds, honor, objectivity when needed, a sense of humor— and hope born out of the grandeur of life.

May 1997

The Perfect Is The Enemy
Of The Good

Temperament has a lot to do with the way in which we look at the world. Some of us are happy-go-lucky; others are serious and reflective. Some are gregarious and revive their energy from being with other people; others are more solitary and consult their own resources when in need of strength. Some people are dreamy and live to a greater extent in their imaginations and wishes, while others are more down to earth, practical, and sober.

These different temperamental styles, I believe, have much to do with the types of philosophies of life we find congenial. I want to look at two contrasting orientations to life, two philosophical styles that are fueled by two different kinds of temperaments.

Let me start this inquiry by looking back almost two-and-a-half millennia to ancient Greece and the golden age of Athens. There were great and original thinkers back then, and one of the greatest was the philosopher Plato. It is said that, like the philosopher Pythagoras, who preceded him, Plato had a particular love and aptitude for mathematics. He was impressed with numbers and the roles that they performed. For example, here in front of us were oranges and dates and pomegranates that we could touch, smell, and eat. But behind these substantial things, there were formal relations between them. So if we added two oranges and two oranges, we got four oranges. We could replace our oranges with dates, pomegranates, or whatever—soldiers, ships, or city-states—and when we added two of them to two others, we still got four.

The things themselves could change, but the formal relationship between the numbers that represented them always remained the same: $2 + 2 = 4$.

What also fascinated Plato was that each orange was different from every other orange; each had its own imperfections, and within a short period of time the orange would begin to rot, shrivel, and then disappear altogether. But this was not true of the numbers and the mathematical formulas that described the relationship between different oranges. Unlike the oranges—and, for that matter, anything else that we can see, touch, hear, or eat—mathematical equations such as $2 + 2 = 4$ never change. And unlike the orange, which has a short life span, mathematical equations are here forever; they are eternal, the same in Plato's day as they are in our own. But beyond being deathless and changeless, these mathematical concepts are unlike oranges, dates, or ourselves, for they are without any blemishes. In other words, they are perfect.

And then Plato did a strange thing, to our modern way of thinking. Plato concluded that these mathematical concepts, these ideas, are not mere figments of the human imagination. They are not imaginary. They are, in fact, real. They have all these marvelous attributes—they do not die, they do not change, and they are absolutely perfect. Plato concluded that these perfect ideas, which reveal themselves only to our thought—let's call them ideals—are more real than the world that we experience through our five senses.

So Plato taught that there are two worlds, not one. There is the world that we know through our senses, and there is a higher, more pristine, purer world of ideals that we can know only through organized, rigorous thinking and philosophical contemplation. Although this ideal world is more real, Plato taught, it is not so easily perceived. In fact, he believed it is sort of clouded over by the world we primarily live in, the world of sight, sound, smell, taste, and touch. It is as if we are walking around in a fog, and only at moments of special insight and illumination do we see this more glorious realm of perfection.

This kind of philosophy, because it posited two worlds, not one, is called dualism. And lest you think that it is merely esoteric and quaint, the historical fact is that because Plato thought the way he did, he set in motion one of the great strands of thinking that has served as a pillar of the Western world. Indeed, Christianity itself, which proclaims a dichotomy between spirit and body, Creator and the created, heaven and earth, takes the dualism of Plato's philosophy and brings it to the masses. The consequences for how we live and think have been unimaginably great. Saint Augustine, the great early doctor of the Christian Church, believed that of all the pagan philosophers, Plato came closest to the spirit of Christianity.

The premise is that this world and reality are not what they ostensibly seem to be; that behind this world is a truer, more solid, more perfect world, which we catch glimmers of only in rare moments.

But we don't have to go all the way back to Plato to encounter this kind of idealism and the attribute of perfection that it manifests. Our own Felix Adler, the founder of Ethical Culture, was very arguably a disciple of Plato. Adler believed, literally, not metaphorically and poetically, in another realm beyond this one; a sphere that is ideal and therefore perfect. In fact, Ethical Culture is based on the existence of these two realms and the tensions between them. It is the recognition of the distance between the ideal realm and what he called the actual realm, in which we live out most of our lives, that is the inspiration and the stimulus for ethical growth.

Here we are living out our lives, with all their imperfections, their pains, their sorrows, and their moral failures. But through the powers of our mind we recognize that there is an ideal realm, a perfect realm, a realm of perfect justice, perfect righteousness, and perfect peace. We recognize this perfect realm and we long to identify with it. It provides us with the vision, the lure, and the inspiration to want to close as much as we can the gap between the actual, imperfect realm we painfully inhabit and the ideal realm that beckons us. For Adler, it is our utmost purpose in life to strive by the light of the ideal to close that gap, recognizing, perhaps tragically (because we are inevitably finite and imperfect) that we may nudge ourselves closer, but never fully succeed.

Adler's flowery prose invokes this metaphysical dualism all the time. He never tires of telling us of the reality of the ideal and the perfection that we should incorporate as our standard for moral action. So it was typical of Adler to write:

> The perfect man has never yet appeared on earth. The perfect man is an apparition of light and beauty rising in the boundless infinite, an ideal to be more and more clothed in particularity. The purpose for which we exist is to help create the

perfect man, to incarnate him more and more in ourselves and in others.

Or,

The perfect society, which is our vision, is known now only in some of its pattern, in some of the conditions which it must fulfill: liberty, freedom, that is, inner freedom in the service of personality; widespread power, that is creative energy unbound in every human breast; life, that is mutual life enhancing other life. But from the development of this vision there can come to us the fullest and truest measure of undying inspiration.

In short, ideals inspire us—ideals of the perfect moral human being and the perfect society—to work to create such a society given the raw materials of our imperfect lives.

Ideals and the vision of a perfectly just society that they hold before us have, and have had, undeniably great power in transforming the world. Ideals, like brilliant guiding stars, are pristine. Ideals are glorious, beautiful, elegant, and pure. To be enchanted by the power of ideals is to be exalted, ennobled, and uplifted, and for many of us actively inspired. Although Karl Marx condemned idealism as the imaginary fantasy of bourgeois thinking and asserted that appropriate class consciousness emerges from the correct understanding of the ironclad laws of history, it seems to me that those in the working class who joined the cause of the Marxist revolution most likely did so primarily because of the inspirational moral power inherent in the vision of a classless, egalitarian society. In other words, despite Marx's pretensions to the "scientific" nature of his historical materialism, revolutionaries are primarily motivated by moral ideals, like everyone else.

This kind of idealism and its vision of a perfect society have great appeal. But they have their downside as well. Appeals to perfection may be ennobling and spiritually uplifting, but they can be psychologically paralyzing as well. If my standard is perfection, and I know that I can never reach it, I may very likely conclude that there is no point in trying. If I know I will never make music like Mozart, or shoot hoops like Michael Jordan, I may simply say to myself, "Why bother?" and whatever joy or accomplishment I may gain from what I might be able to do, though less than perfect, may be lost forever. In short, the perfect can be the enemy of the good.

But there is another danger in permitting perfection to be our standard. And that is the danger of moralism or excessive judgment directed at ourselves or at others. There is something unforgiving about the concept of perfection. If I strive seriously and hard toward a goal, employing perfection as my guide, and I fail to meet that standard, which I inevitably must, then, armed with an overheated superego, I might painfully conclude that if I am not perfect, I am therefore worthless. The paradigm in itself does not stake out any mitigating middle ground. It is all or nothing. If one uses the ideal as one's standard, the consequence may lead to excessive self-punishment.

Some perfectionists not only delude themselves into thinking that they have achieved the ideal, they begin to identify with the ideal itself. Everyone else can then be deemed as less than ideal, as inferior, worthy of derision and contempt. When this idealism becomes ingrained into the national character, it becomes especially dangerous. I would think that Nazism, for example, suffered from this self-deluding idealism in a catastrophic way—the Aryan type becoming the ideal and perfect form of humanity.

Short of that, there can be something brittle and perhaps self-absorbed in the person guided by perfectionist standards. There is little grace and little forgiveness in perfectionism. And certainly the unmitigated pursuit of perfection is humorless. This is one reason why religion generally has no sense of humor.

But there is another way of looking at the issue of improvement and self-improvement. This way does not jettison ideals altogether, but it places them gently in the background. Unlike the idealism of a Plato, or even of Felix Adler, this philosophy does not commit itself to dualism. It does not say that ideals are something "out there," untouched in their pristine remoteness from us, perfect crystalline models for us to admire and, if possible, emulate.

This approach does not look to perfection, but merely to improvement. It values ideals, but does not give them magisterial power. Rather, it sees ideals as mere tools that emerge from our problems and frustrations. Whereas ideals in the first sense are remote, in the second, they are used in immediate problem solving and overcoming the difficulties and frustrations that confront us. The term for this outlook is *meliorism*, which comes from the Latin word *melior*, which simply means "better." Hence, if your approach to life is meliorist, you don't seek perfection, but merely to make your condition or situation better than it is. You seek not perfection, but incremental improvement, and then you move on to the next problem. Your approach will be more engaged, more in the moment, more experimental; in a word, more pragmatic.

It is sometimes observed that this approach to handling life's problems is more typically feminine. There is something detached about ideals, making them more stereotypically male. The ethicist Nel Noddings, who wrote a marvelous and influential book on caring, a virtue that, unlike justice, she views as particularly feminine, was getting at these differences when she wrote:

> Women enter the domain of moral decision making through a different door. It is certainly not the case that women cannot arrange principles hierarchically and derive conclusions logically. Faced with a hypothetical moral dilemma, women often ask for more information…We need to talk to the participants, to see their eyes and facial expressions, to receive what they are feeling. Moral decisions are, after all, made in real situations; they are qualitatively different from the solution of geometry problems. Women can and do give reasons for their acts, but the reasons often point to feelings, needs, impressions, and a sense of a personal ideal rather than to universal principles and their application.

In other words, there is a dimension of concreteness and active engagement that seeks redress and improvement, rather than the imposition of an abstract ideal state on the conditions and problems at hand. Surmising that this approach is typically feminine does not mean to suggest, of course, that men don't have it or do not apply it.

So what practical implications does this meliorist approach have for the quests for improvement of oneself and of society? The answer is lots. Let me give some examples that I struggle with, and that you may wrestle with also.

For the past thirty-two years I have deliberately eaten meat or poultry on very few occasions. I have been a vegetarian for a slew of reasons, all of which together seem morally compelling to me. The most compelling is my desire not to have complicity in causing gratuitous pain to sentient creatures. And although I call myself a vegetarian, I am not really one, since I put no restrictions on eating fish—for reasons that are not morally compelling. In the final analysis, I have to confess that I am too lazy to go through the process of balancing the proteins I would need to sustain a healthy diet.

Now to declare oneself a vegetarian is risky business in several ways. When I declare it publicly, not infrequently I see people looking down at my shoes to see whether I am wearing leather. The unspoken—and sometimes spoken—response is to expose me, joyously, as a hypocrite. And if my standard and theirs is perfection—the ideal of pristine and pure vegetarianism—then they are right. I am undeniably a hypocrite.

But this isn't the only way to look at this moral commitment. One could argue, and I do argue, that if it were the ideal or nothing, the world would be making do with one more carnivore, because, given all the other demands of life, which are also very compelling, I would not be engaging vegetarianism at all. Is it not better, if one feels that it is morally wrong to consume meat, to eat less of it than more? And my own moral reckoning tells me that, yes, it is better. And furthermore, to carry my pragmatism one step further, by adopting the meliorist stance and by succeeding in achieving partway vegetarianism, I can feel the self-confidence of my success, and then incrementally move ahead to progressively consume fewer of my aquatic neighbors.

Let me invoke another example, which I suspect is a moral dilemma for all of us who are ethically and environmentally attuned. If you are like me, you will conclude that consumerism in American society is badly out of balance. Not only is it aesthetically excessive—a type of material gluttony—but it is ethically selfish in such a way that American excess deprives billions of our fellow human beings who are desperately poor, many too poor to even stay alive, of a dignified way of life, while it despoils the environment in ways that, if unchecked, will be irremediably catastrophic. The scientific consensus tell us that global warming caused by human agency is real, and in our excessive burning of fossil fuels we are perilously playing with the fate of the planet.

With that said, what am I as an individual going to do about it? There are several responses. One is to invoke an ideal of personal asceticism and whittle my possessions down to the minimum I need to sustain life and decent health.

I can abandon my middle-class lifestyle, give it all away, live in poverty, become a renunciant, and thereby consume little and do little damage to the earth. Some people do make this kind of choice.

There is a lot to be said about this response. In the first place, it does minimize environmental damage. Second, the person who proclaims concern about the environment and responds with this kind of saintly self-abnegation does live out his or her values to a very high degree, and thereby avoids the charge of hypocrisy. In the spirit of egalitarianism, he or she joins the ranks of the poor while trying to avoid being an exploiter. He or she also provides a living example of what, indeed, is possible for human beings.

But there is a downside to this kind of idealistic expression as well. In the first place, although such conduct is admirable and does demonstrate the limits of what is possible, the reality is that very few people are going to make this extreme choice. Hence, the actual practical value of this exemplary renunciation may be quite limited. Moreover, since other people know that they cannot match its heroic proportions, it may even generate a backlash of hostility born out of hidden and sublimated envy. There may be other, not-so-obvious problems with it as well. The person who is driven by conscience to be so pure in his commitments might overlook the fact that the exercise of conscience can sometimes be a form of selfishness that breeds self-righteousness. The zealous pursuit of conscience can at times be a very antisocial pursuit.

Other responses to consumerism and environmentalism can be less pure but ultimately more effective. In the meliorist spirit, one again can make a serious effort (if not go all the way toward environmental ideals) by at least consuming and polluting less. The meliorist position recognizes that the modern condition is a complex one, and that we are inevitably confronted in our lives with a multitude of competing demands and interests that make trade-offs necessary.

Consider the following example. What if, in the pursuit of an environmental lifestyle, I choose to forgo my car and use public transportation to get to work? I can drive to work in forty-five minutes, but it takes an hour and a half to commute by bus. What if I choose the latter, but it forces me to get home after my child is already in bed, and my child has been having problems that my active presence and parenting will help remediate? I am caught in a dilemma that pits my environmentalist commitments against my child's interests. What am I to do?

Here is a different example. Let's assume I am a surgeon who, in order to do my work in the best possible way, needs a solid night's sleep. If I don't get that solid night's sleep, my concentration suffers, and so do my patients on the operating table. It is summertime, and unless I use the air conditioner at night, my sleep is shot. But I also want to be loyal to my environmental values. What am I to do? Perhaps I need to consider a trade-off. I use the air conditioner, but purchase a car with far better gas mileage, or maybe my family realizes that it can live with only one car; or I drive less.

Dick Cheney famously observed that conservation is a matter of personal virtue. What he meant was that it is a matter of *merely* personal virtue and so practically a foolish indulgence. Cheney's was a snide, patronizing, contemptible remark, coming from someone who, unlike the rest of us, has been in a real position to affect the environment for the better, but chooses out of lavish self-interest not to.

But in a certain sense, there is some truth in Cheney's snide throwaway. It is environmentally a good idea that we recycle, for example, but in the big picture, individual recycling makes little difference compared to the damage caused by industrial pollution in the United States. If I am a middle-class environmental activist with some authority in the community, is it better for me to renounce my middle-class lifestyle in the pursuit of personal ideals? Or is it better to consume and pollute less, preserve whatever leverage my middle-class status brings, and then use my resources to organize the public to push for political change and new laws that will affect industrial pollution in broad sweeping ways? The answer depends on what I am trying to accomplish. If personal authenticity, virtue, and idealism are my goals, then I will choose the path of renunciation, and perhaps thereby forsake my political leverage. If I want to make a real, practical difference in the world, which is becoming dangerously polluted, then I will do something else that would require me to increase my resources, not give them away. What we are confronted with here, as we are in much of life, is a utilitarian calculus in which we weigh the benefits and harms of our choices in particular circumstances in order to educe what we believe is the right or better thing to do.

The real world forces compromises on us all the time. It demands action in areas where perfection is not in the cards. In the Bergen Society, four years ago, we started a project to assist political asylum seekers who are fleeing persecution and war in their own countries. We are playing a very modest part in helping to assist, through our sanctuary program, a small number of refugees, who are torture victims, from being returned to the site of their persecution, and in helping them begin new lives here in our country, where they are at least safe. When I think of the four million people who have died in the past five years from warfare in the Congo, or the two hundred thousand who continue to be slaughtered in the Sudan, our contribution is very modest indeed. It is easier to say, why bother? But it certainly makes a difference for those few people we help, and *that* is appreciably more than nothing. I am sustained by the wisdom of the Talmud, which states, "To save a single life, it is as if you have saved an entire world."

We, as actors in the world and as concerned citizens, are confronted with momentous ethical decisions at every turn. And I suspect that there is not one unified ideal response that fits all. Rather, we are more likely to engage in trade-offs that will be less than ideal, less than perfect. But it is certainly better than doing nothing. Life is like that. We need look to the stars, but we have to keep our feet on the ground.

I return often to a penetrating insight of the writer Albert Camus, who as a humanist was asked to speak about his beliefs to a group of Christians at a monastery in France after World War II. Camus said,

> We are faced with evil. And, as for me, I feel rather as Augustine did before becoming a Christian when he said, "I tried to find the source of evil and I got nowhere." But it is true that I, and a few others, know what must be done, if not to reduce evil, at least not add to it. Perhaps we cannot prevent this world from being a world in which children are tortured. But we can reduce the number of tortured children. And if you don't help us, who else in the world will?

June 2009

A Humanist Looks At Sin

At the center of humanist philosophy stands the inspiring belief that moral progress is possible. As humanists we hold very dearly to the conviction that through our efforts alone, as manifested in our intelligence, science, and good will, we can transform this world into a better place. We believe that individual people, and society as a whole, are not static entities, but grow in understanding, in goodness, and in kindness. Humanists affirm that the drudgery of the past can be reworked into a bountiful future. As we have progressed in our understanding of nature and have used that understanding to generate material progress, so the humanist believes that we can grow in our knowledge of human nature and employ those insights, likewise, in the service of social and moral progress. The humanist holds to the belief and is guided by the conviction that we might not achieve perfection, but that we can move ever closer to it.

If there were a humanist creed, it might be something like this:

As a matter of brute fact, we human beings are alone.

As a matter of faith, we can create a better world.

And as a matter of purpose, the act of so transforming the world into one of greater peace, justice, and happiness for all ought to frame for us our highest loyalties and dedications.

Such is the faith of the humanist. It is also the implicit faith of anyone who calls himself a liberal or a modern. Clearly, such a faith is high minded, ennobling, and optimistic. It is a faith that also makes, as all faiths do, certain claims about human capacities and limitations, and about the nature of the human heart.

The question I want to pose, in its awful nakedness, is whether this faith in human beings, this faith in humankind's ability to improve its own condition through human effort alone, is in any sense warranted. Or is this talk about improving the human condition, which sounds so pleasant to liberal ears, in the final analysis, nothing more than empty rhetoric, devoid of any real substance or credibility? Is it worthy of us, given what we know about human behavior? Or is it like Santa Claus, a happy illusion that makes us feel good and keeps us cheery but is ultimately made out of illusory material? Must the faith of the humanist end ultimately in despair because it never touches ground with the brute facts of human existence and experience? Or perhaps it sustains itself through a continual blindness. When we open our eyes wide and take a good hard look, can we really believe in human beings and the collective capacity of humankind to create a more humane world?

Indeed, these are not the easiest of times in which to sustain faith in human beings and in the capacities for human benevolence. All one needs to do to challenge this rosy assumption is to take a long, sober look at the world around us and the way human beings really treat one another. Take a look at all the stupid wars, the wanton cruelties, the starvation, the mass destruction of entire peoples, the heedless despoliation of the earth, our nurturing mother, and the ferocity of interpersonal and bizarre crimes performed in the absence of any conscientious restraints whatsoever. And yes, there is the persistence of institutionalized torture (the most immoral of acts)—the deliberate infliction of sustained physical agony. In the past, evils that would dare not speak their names are today perpetuated and promoted with blithe moral indifference.

Take a long, hard look at the masses of the chronically poor, the masses of hopelessly disenfranchised people who will be born to a life in which they will know little else but uninterrupted drudgery and will die a lonely death and fade instantaneously into anonymity. Look at how those who live in luxury want to keep what they have at the expense of those who have little. Look at how those who could help choose to turn away and encapsulate themselves in self-serving ignorance, or cynically construe clever ideologies to protect and perpetuate their own privilege and selfishness. Look at the abuses of power in high place—the manipulation of the public trust. Take a hard look at the frenzy, intensity, competitiveness, predatoriness, misery, and raw, wanton brutality of life on this planet, and then come back to preach the goodness and beneficence of humankind.

Our advances in science and technology don't seem to prefigure any moral progress at all. Rather, what seems more realistic is that such new knowledge simply enables us to pursue our own evil aggressions with ever more refinement and efficiency. In the remote past, no matter how brutal men were, there was a limit to the number of their fellow human beings they could destroy in warfare because of the limitations of technology. Today, through the wonders of science, we haven't grown any more peaceful, simply enormously more efficient, so that we can, and do, as we all know, live under the constant threat of the total annihilation of every man, woman and child on earth. One of the ancients had once said that "man is a wolf to man." Upon greater reflection, we might conclude that that formulation is really unfair to wolves. As I said, our powers of observation, our sense of honesty, and our gut feelings all conspire to make a sham of the notion that moral improvement of our species is at all a realistic possibility. A sober look at how people really do behave appears to mock our liberal hopes.

There is, of course, an older theory about human nature. It presents itself as an alternative to the liberal, modern progressivism to which we humanists subscribe. It is also making a comeback, in part because of the awful and seemingly incorrigible realities I've just superficially glossed over. It is the theory of human nature that proclaims that the persistence of evil that we see around us is not due to our ignorance, lack of education, repressive social institutions, or want of better social programs. Rather, the evil we see arises because there inheres in all human beings a quality of character called sin. Try as we might, we can never free ourselves of it, because sin is an intrinsic aspect of what we are. To deny it, as liberals and moderns have done, is an act of folly and arrogance, based on illusion, which can only bring us greater despair and tragedy.

What is the theory of sin? Is it more worthy of our belief than the liberal theory of moral progress?

Although the theory of sin takes many forms, some very literal, others very sophisticated, the concepts I'm using are those put forth by the so-called neoorthodox theologians, of whom the great Protestant theologian Reinhold Niebuhr is the most famous exponent. In fact, most of Niebuhr's thinking was shaped by the concept of sin, which colored his ideas about political and social theory. His religious philosophy, which he expounded for decades at Union Theological Seminary, put him in continuous battle with his academic colleagues in the Columbia University Philosophy Department, such as John Dewey. Dewey and many in that department were philosophical liberals and naturalists who based their philosophies on agnostic science.

What is this concept of sin, which is, of course, a theological concept? Its proponents claim that it is more hard headed, more truthful to the facts of human nature and experience, than the moral progressivism of liberals and moderns. While liberals will proclaim the theory of sin, which speaks of man's disobedience to God, the Fall from Eden, and the need for divine grace, as so much illusion, those who uphold the theory of man's sinful nature stand this liberal critique on its head. They proclaim that it is the liberal, the modern, and the humanist who are basing their beliefs on a fantasy, and they are therefore doomed to impotence, political and otherwise—and to failure.

According to Reinhold Niebuhr, human existence by necessity is involved in an eternal paradox it cannot escape. On one side, man is a finite, that is, limited creature; on the other side, he is infinite in his desires and in his visions. He knows he is mortal, but in imagination can look beyond his own death. He conceives of the ideal of altruism and perfect generosity, but in any act of altruism he is still bound to parochial and egoistic motives. When we claim to be objective and dispassionate, we still contain a kernel of subjectivity and personalism in our perspectives. We are limited, but we are always dimly aware of a perfection that is beyond our grasp. In short, man is a creature living tensely between two worlds: one is the actual and limited world in which he lives, but from which he cannot help feeling alienated; the other is an ideal world for which he longs, but from which he is permanently excluded. As Niebuhr puts it, "man's whole moral life requires him to seek after an impossible victory and to adjust himself to an inevitable defeat."

What is the result of being this creature existing in this middle state between finitude and perfection? Niebuhr says that it is *anxiety*. The fate of man is to be existentially, chronically anxious. And since anxiety is by its nature intolerable, man seeks to escape from this anxiety. It is the effort to escape that drives us to our greatest acts of creativity, intellectual productivity, and ennobling self-sacrifice. It propels us to produce whatever is good and marvelous in human life.

But this anxiety is also the source of something else. It is the source of man's sinfulness. The pain of anxiety drives us to mechanisms of escape. We may seek to escape through the excesses of sexual indulgence. We may attempt to obliterate our anxiety or desensitize it by losing ourselves in drink or drugs. Or, like Nazism, which is the most egregious example, we may try to escape it by identifying with total and absolute power here on earth. We may make the mistake of identifying our finite power and existence with infinite power and being. We may commit the act of ultimate idolatry. Any fanaticism commits this mistake. And we all in little ways identify our limited and relative powers with the Absolute; we all submit to this temptation. We all aspire to be self-sufficient, like God, and thus commit the sin of pride.

According to Niebuhr, there is in man an ineluctable perversity, which is original sin. It is a discordance in the human spirit that echoes a larger disharmony in the relation of man to the universe: The source of all man's highest achievements is also the source of his greatest wickedness and folly.

What Niebuhr is saying is that all our acts, however virtuous, are forever tainted because they are tied to the same origins. Our existential anxiety will always drive us to escape in the form of sin, and this is simply unavoidable. Man's wickedness is not a product of bad education, or repressive socialization, or the lack of more comprehensive scientific understanding. It has to do with man's fundamental nature. It manifests itself in history and dooms us to inevitable failure in our efforts to significantly transform the human condition for the better.

The antidote to this fact of human existence, from the Christian perspective, is to recognize that there is an Absolute that stands outside of history, beyond man's effort. Through faith man needs to open himself up to God's grace, which has broken into history in the form of Christ's love. In accepting this grace we can establish a type of reconciliation that in some respects leads us to transcend our own anxious state and find salvation. Humanists, moderns, and liberals, of course, have forgotten all this in their commitments to science, reason, and moral self-sufficiency, and by turning their backs on God's loving presence. They will continue to sin because they continue to mistake their finite powers for the Absolute, and because they feel that they can go it alone, without God's assistance.

The insights of the great American psychologist and student of religion William James are relevant here. James distinguished two personality types. The first he called "the once-born soul"; the other, the "twice-born soul." The once-born soul is the person who looks at life as a Promethean. Life is a progressive challenge, a medium for self-improvement and self-transcendence. The "twice-born" person experiences the pains, frustrations, travails, and tragedies of life, exhausts his energies in fighting to overcome life's hardships, soberly reflects deeply on life in all its aspects, and comes to the conclusion that he can't go it alone, that life is perforce a problem and that there has got to be something "more" to which he opens himself. In his examination of religious experience, James concluded that there indeed is something "more" in the universe.

In terms of scripture, we see that the Bible lays out the problem and provides the cure. Adam, the first man, disobeyed God and ate the fruit of the tree of knowledge of good and evil. In so doing, man turned away from God and established himself as the author of good and evil. No longer was God needed as a source of moral authority. Human beings could establish themselves as self-sufficient and autonomous. Adam's eating of the fruit was therefore the first act of secularization, of creating a world in which God was not necessary. In a sense, Adam was the first humanist.

Through the Fall, man became estranged from God, and in his separateness became lost with regard to the certainty of his own purposes. He was thrust into the condition of anxiety that we mentioned earlier. The path to redemption and reconciliation, through acceptance of the higher power, is revealed through scripture and by means of faith.

While I don't believe that Niebuhr would have accepted the story of Adam and Eve as literal history, I assume that he would have affirmed that the biblical account does portray in mythological terms a historical development of man's commitment to greater and greater self-sufficiency, culminating in the modern commitment to total self-sufficiency. I suspect that Niebuhr would have taken very seriously the need for access to God's saving power.

Well, what are we humanists to make of this theory of sin? Can we believe it? Should we? Does it more adequately explain the persistence of the antisocial and destructive behavior we see in our society and in the world? And is the theory of sin correct in its condemnation of liberal hopes and moral betterment as chimerical and therefore foolish and even harmful?

The answer I give to these questions may surprise you, and therefore I need to emphasize the qualification that I am speaking for myself alone.

In my reflections on this very complex topic, I come to the conclusion that there are aspects of the theory of sin that I accept, and other aspects that I deny. Let me try to explain what I mean.

First, as a theological statement, which it basically is, I disagree with it. I disagree with it because in my understanding of the way in which this universe is put together, I locate myself on the side of the moderns, liberals, and secularists. I affirm, for reasons that have little to do with the theory of sin, that the world of nature, including human thought and feelings, is all that there is, and there is outside of nature nothing *supranaturam*, that is, nothing supernatural. In this sense, I am a "once-born" person. I thoroughly accept the idea of human finitude, but I also accept the notion of existential anxiety and the feeling that human life is essentially problematic. In this regard, I can understand the feeling that gives rise to wanting something "more" to save us. Anyone who has been in the depths of despair and has exhausted his resources can identify with this feeling and with this need. But honesty compels me to believe that we can do no better than look for mundane, that is, this-worldly, solutions to these problems. Consequently, I do not believe, obviously, that there is divine grace. And so the highest level we can rise to when confronted by unresolved problems is what we might call "stoic resignation": acceptance of our fate, things that we can't change, and things that we can. That realization might not be pleasant, it might not fulfill our needs, but I do not believe that there is any cosmic guarantee that our lives must be so fulfilled. As Freud once said, "Experience teaches that life is no nursery."

I know that theistically committed people will say that with my stubbornness and unwillingness to open myself up to the saving power of grace through faith, my life is spiritually truncated. But in the absence of any other compelling evidence that outside the natural system there is a personal God who bestows grace, I always find such attacks to be suspiciously circular in their reasoning and unacceptably self-congratulatory in their purposes. "I'm more spiritually sensitive than you are," they seem to condescendingly imply. I don't buy it. For whatever someone might profess, we can never know what sensitivity lies privately in the inner recesses of one's heart, naturalist or supernaturalist. As should be clear, on the level of theology I dismiss the theory of sin, because I can't accept the whole theological enterprise.

But I don't think that the religious argument can be so easily dismissed. Here, I disagree with hard-core secular humanists. I am one of those people who believe that religion at times may be expressing truths about human nature, but doing so in the wrong way. In other words, religion can be metaphorically expressive of psychological and existential truths about human nature.

If we look at sin in this way, is it a valid theory of human nature? My answer here is yes and no.

If the person who upholds the theory of sin points to the liberal or secularist and says, "You are wrong to believe that humankind can achieve perfection through its own efforts," I would say that I agree, I don't think we can achieve perfection. But I don't think that this is what the liberal doctrine truly says. I don't believe that utopianism is possible, and furthermore I believe that it can be very dangerous. History is replete with the carnage of millions of people who have been slaughtered on the altar of one perfectionist program or the other because they did not fit.

If the man who upholds the doctrine of sin says to us, "You liberals have been too optimistic in the way you have depicted the goodness of human nature, and also naïve. You haven't entertained seriously enough man's great capacity for evil," I would respond, "Yes, at times, for many liberals that has been true. But don't overstate your case. Many liberals have also been wary of the evil capacities of human nature."

But if my interlocutor gets to the core of the matter and retorts, "The mistake you progressives make is that you don't recognize that the heart of man is perversely and forever evil, and that progress is therefore impossible and illusory"—at this point I begin to part company.

I do accept the fact that there seems to be a self-frustrating dimension in human behavior. Freud analyzed that self-frustrating element in secular and nonmysterious terms, elaborated in his brief masterpiece *Civilization and Its Discontents*. And I sadly concede that certain individuals may be incorrigible.

But the person who upholds the notion of human sinfulness and I differ in one crucial respect. It may at first glance seem like a minor difference, but it is one that entails a radically divergent perspective on human history and human nature.

What the concept of sin has done is to transform an observation about the human past into a doctrine about how human beings essentially are. It has dogmatized, and therefore conceptually foreclosed, the possibility of change and progress. Where my sin-minded friend sees damnation, I see the raw conditions with which we have to deal, just as death, human body size, and intelligence are conditions with which we have to deal. Such limitations do not foreclose opportunities. They set the conditions under which opportunities have to operate. In other words, human beings, with their drives, instincts, conflicts, and paradoxes, are the raw material with which teachers, parents, legislators, social reformers, and Ethical Culture leaders are compelled to work.

The crucial difference between the person who upholds the doctrine of sin and me is that he proclaims that there is a governor in human behavior that forecloses and limits moral progress. And my response is, *even if there are limits to human progress, we do not know where those limits are.* In other words, for me, the question of incremental human improvement remains an open question. I can never claim with absolute certainty that such progress by necessity is impossible. The person who proclaims the doctrine of sin does.

This apparently small difference has monumental consequences for the way in which we respectively approach the human condition. In the words of the philosopher Charles Frankel, the liberal or progressive hypothesis "is not a prediction about the future; it is a statement of policy for guiding human behavior, a policy which puts the status quo on the defensive, and of refusing to decide in advance that any given problem is beyond the power of human beings to solve." That is the essential difference. It is one of attitude and mood. One says we have a closed situation here; the liberal says we have an open problem that we need to dedicate our best efforts to try to solve.

The problem of the notion of sin is that it makes a fetish and a celebration out of a particular aspect of human experience. It seizes upon and dogmatizes pessimism. In this sense it partakes of its own romanticism. But it is a joyless celebration that we could well do without. I submit that life is hard enough without the additional burdens imposed by the concept of sin.

Yes, we are all partial creatures, in the sense that we are limited, and we all strive to be recognized, fulfilled, and loved. These limitations in the human condition should evoke in us compassion. They are at the same time the given conditions of the human experience that need to call forward from us our best efforts. Human limitations are the starting points from which we need to struggle to continuously build a humane and decent and civilized society. Friends, we need not, and should not, give the human limitations we see about us the last word. There is much in this world that needs our attention.

October 2008

Public Questions

Should Religion Be Immune
From Criticism?

I want to address the issue of manners and good taste. But the problems I will raise go far beyond manners alone or simple courtesies. They veer into territory that is deeply political and highly consequential. The issues I will discuss deal with our relationship to religious beliefs different from our own and the people who hold them. This question, though it has always been important, has become exceedingly relevant, even urgent, in our times.

The question has become urgent because of two major social forces that intersect at this historical moment. The first is the emergence of *tolerance* as a salient and highly touted virtue in our political discourse and in our social relations. In its traditional meaning, *tolerance* has always born a certain negative edge. On analysis, tolerance is a kind of grudging virtue in the sense that we tolerate what we otherwise cannot stand. Tolerance emerges from the realization that it is better for mutually contemptuous groups to tolerate one another than to annihilate one another. To *tolerate* is to declare a truce and to "live and let live," but tolerance acknowledges neither wholehearted acceptance nor appreciation nor love—just formal respect and the right for others and ourselves to be left alone.

But it is my observation that *tolerance* has changed its meaning under the pressures of multiculturalism and diversity. If you ask young people today, "What does tolerance mean?" often you will receive a response that suggests that to their minds tolerance means something like "the need to withhold judgment." The current assumption is that it is in bad taste to criticize the sincerely held views of other people, even if you think that they are wrong. For many young people, including my students, to criticize the views of other is simply impolite.

The emergence of this type of tolerance is, in many ways, a very good thing. I think we have made real headway in our society toward a condition of greater social inclusion because we have mitigated traditional hatreds and bigotries that were often laced with cruel judgments about the inferiority of people who were different from ourselves. The advances of American society in the past sixty years toward the inclusion of minorities, women, the disabled, and homosexuals would have been unthinkable to earlier generations. All this is not say that we don't have long way to go, but some remarkable progress has been achieved.

But there are also problems with an ethos of tolerance when it leads us to refrain from making judgments, in the sense that it can be taken too far. In the first place, I believe that judgments must inevitably be made. Without the capacity for judgment, there can be no ethics. Ethics is based on the necessary willingness to judge that this behavior is good and that one is bad; this idea is right and that idea is wrong. I often tell my students, both graduate and undergraduate, that it is a valuable skill to be able to criticize the ideas of their fellow classmates while, at the same time, protecting the egos of those with whom they disagree. It is a skill that I think is actually being lost.

This skill, or ability, I likewise believe is absolutely essential to maintaining an open, free, and progressive society. Democracy and freedom survive on the adversity of ideas, as John Stuart Mill noted long ago. Society also moves ahead through an active competition of ideas, a competition in which the most truthful and socially useful ideas generally, in time, percolate up to the top. Without the adversity of ideas, society stagnates and leaves itself vulnerable to the emergence of totalitarian forces. If we are lulled to give up our desire to critique ideas, actions, and policies under the mantra of tolerance, we undercut the vibrancy and adversarial energy necessary to sustain a dynamic and open society.

All this is another way of saying that as crucial and as necessary as an ethic of tolerance is, there is also a category of experience that we might call "false tolerance." In other words, there are behaviors, beliefs, and ideas that we should not tolerate, and, depending on the circumstances, there are ideas we should criticize, condemn, and actively oppose.

So the first emergent social dynamic that leads me to my subject is that of tolerance. The second is the resurgence of religion, and of religion as a powerful political actor on the American and global stage. The flexing of religious muscle, especially in its conservative political expressions, is something that we who are humanists find distressing, even dangerous; and it challenges the values we stand for and that we feel make for a desirable society.

But there is an added aspect to this resurgence of religion in American life over the last thirty years or so. Religion now enjoys a certain type of immunity from criticism that no other system of belief is able to claim for itself. A religious leader can mutter the most inane, insipid, and irrational utterances, which from the perspective of reason would embarrass even an elementary school child, and will win the accolades of multitudes of followers. If said by anyone who not did claim the authority of religion, such statements would be derided as the ramblings of an ignoramus. Indeed, religion stands almost alone as a domain of human authority, which, by its nature, is often counterfactual and irrational and stands against the test of evidence.

The same person who Monday through Friday works as an engineer, computer technician, or even a scientist, and bases his beliefs on rational consistency, banishes that reason when he professes his religious faith, a faith that might include a belief in miracles, whether it be the parting of the Red Sea, bringing dead people back to life, virgins giving birth, or God making the sun stand still. The need for logical coherence and consistency, which govern the lives of most of us most of the time, is thrown to the winds when the topic under discussion turns to religion. Indeed, from the standpoint of reason, much of religion is worthy of no more credibility than a belief in Santa Claus or the Tooth Fairy, no matter how it is gussied up and defended by the speculations of learned theologians. Yet religion not only persists—most of humanity exalts and honors it. Indeed, Americans seem to have a love affair with religion. More than 90 percent proclaim a belief in God, 70 percent believe in angels, and about 44 percent believe that God created man pretty much in his current form within the past ten thousand years. This contrasts with only 10 percent of Americans who believe that human beings evolved from other forms of life by a totally natural process.

Yet, oddly, religion gets a pass in the minds of most people, a type of exemption from criticism both intellectual and moral. If a person would say that he believes that the dead can be made to live again, or that he heard voices from on high espousing moral instructions, you would be right to doubt his sanity. But if another person says exactly the same things and cloaks them within the mantle of his religious faith, he walks among us as an upright man, in many cases worthy of honor and respect, and maybe even a seat in Congress or the White House, his religious faith being a testament to his appropriateness for high office. Criticism and the demand for logistical consistency seem to stop at the door of religion. Why should this be the case?

There are several reasons for the protected, indeed exalted status of religion. The first is the presumption (I believe false) that religion is the repository of many human goods that only religion can provide. Most important is the assumption that religion is the paramount, if not the exclusive source of morality, which almost all people cherish and which human society needs for survival. If we wish to know what is right and wrong, if we wish to know what are the highest goods in life, then religion provides the answer. As the origin and repository of morals, values, and the highest goods of life, religion claims an honored place. Those who speak in the name of religion, those who wrap themselves in religious authority, therefore, rightly or wrongly, are looked upon as moral authorities, and the presumption is that because they are in touch with the lofty pinnacles of religion, which is the source of morality, then they themselves and what they espouse must itself be moral. In the face of such authority making such claims, most people are willing to suspend their criticism and their judgment. And sometimes it is true. Sometimes devoutly religious people are paragons of moral virtue. But just as often they are not, yet the moral aura and cachet of religion leads most people to affirm the virtue of religious belief or authority and displace from the forefront of their minds religion's wicked propensities, or shoo them away as aberrations.

But beyond this, religion is also that phenomenon *par excellence* which places before human beings that which we understand to be sacred or holy. What is often meant by *holy* is something set apart from the ordinary and mundane; something valued intensely and supremely, something felt to be of transcendent importance to a person. As such, that which is holy or sacred, we feel, must be kept free of violation and defilement. In this sense, if I hold a belief or a principle that to my mind is sacred or holy, I seek to protect it from violation; moreover on some level very private, I do not want it touched or invaded by others. The sacred, in this sense, bequeaths to itself a certain exalted immunity and, for many people, respect, in the way in which the invocation of "conscience" invokes a certain respect. If we say that someone undertook an action because she was motivated by conscience to do so, we at first blush are usually motivated to accord the action some respect, even if we end up disagreeing with where that person's conscience has led her. Many people often feel that religion, because it carries sacred beliefs, is worthy of a similar kind of deference and immunity from attack. So we might argue that just as I wish my own highest or most sacred beliefs respected, so I need to approach others with similar respect for their highest or most sacred beliefs, even if I disagree with them. The appeal to sacredness, as the appeal to conscience, invokes respect from others

But is religion truly worthy of such deference and respect? Ought religion, because it touches upon what people feel to be their highest and holiest convictions, be afforded an immunity from the lances of criticism and from invasion simply because it makes such claims? This is the dilemma we face. On the one hand, the culture of tolerance and my own sense of decency propel me toward an attitude of guarded respect, of tolerance. On the other, the real power of religion and the dangers that it poses to my own cherished values of freedom, democracy, and open society, and ultimately to peace, seem so great that perhaps tolerance is a luxury or a courtesy in which we cannot afford to indulge. Perhaps tolerance in this moment is really false tolerance that we practice at the expense of naiveté, and perhaps ultimately self-destruction. Are we to be tolerant toward the religious ideas of others not only when they are merely irrational, but when they are dangerous?

Certainly a person who feels that we should *not* be tolerant is the philosopher and neuroscientist Sam Harris, who with his book *The End of Faith* has won acclaim among rationalists, secularists, atheists, and people of views not much different from ours. Harris's treatise is a powerfully written polemic about the irrationalities and the irrational dangers of religious faith, of which the assaults of 9/11 by the henchmen of Osama bin Laden are the paradigmatic case.

Harris's thesis is, of course, not new. It is the argument that religion not only promotes irrationality, but also urges believers to do evil things, such as kill infidels, commit genocide, and fly hijacked planes into office buildings. What makes his argument both contemporary and urgent is this: given the abilities of small bands of miscreants to wield weapons of unspeakable destructive power, religion in our time is extraordinarily dangerous. Though Harris also condemns Christianity and Judaism, it is the dangers of Islam that should especially alarm us. So Harris reminds us:

> To see the role that faith plays in propagating Muslim violence, we need only ask why so many Muslims are eager to turn themselves into bombs these days. The answer: because the Koran makes this activity seem like a career opportunity. Nothing in the history of Western colonialism explains this behavior (though we can certainly concede that this history offers us much to atone for). Subtract the Muslim belief in martyrdom and jihad, and the actions of suicide bombers become completely unintelligible, as does the spectacle of public jubilation that invariably follows their deaths: insert their peculiar beliefs, and one can only marvel that suicide bombing is not more widespread.

> We live in an age in which most people believe that mere words—"Jesus," "Allah," "Ram"—can mean the difference between eternal torment and bliss everlasting. Considering the stakes here, it is not surprising that many of us occasionally find it necessary to murder other human beings for using the wrong magic words, or the right ones for the wrong reasons. How can any person presume to know that this is the way the universe works? Because it says so in our holy books. How do we know that our holy books are free from error? Because books themselves say so. Epistemological black holes of this sort are fast draining the light from our world.

> There is, of course, much that is wise and consoling and beautiful in our religious books. But words of wisdom and consolation and beauty abound in the pages of Shakespeare, Virgil, and Homer as well, and no one ever murdered

strangers by the thousands because of the inspiration found there. The belief that certain books were written by God (who, for reasons difficult to fathom, made Shakespeare a far better writer than himself) leaves us powerless to address the most potent source of human conflict, past and present. How is it that the absurdity of this idea does not bring us hourly to our knees? It is safe to say that few of us would have thought so many people could believe such a thing, if they did not *actually* believe it. Imagine a world in which generations of human beings come to believe that certain films were made by God or that specific software was coded by him. Imagine a future in which millions of our descendants murder each other over rival interpretations of *Star Wars* or Windows 98. Could anything—*anything*—be more ridiculous? And yet this would be no more ridiculous than the world that we are living in.

This is, needless to say, strong stuff. But just when you thought it was safe to go back into the water, Harris reveals his "take no prisoners" style. For his polemic is not solely directed at those believers whom we might define as religious fundamentalists, scriptural literalists, or fanatics. He has equal contempt, perhaps even greater contempt, for religious moderates. In a way that is reminiscent of the condemnation communists used to launch toward liberals, contending that liberalism does nothing but grease the wheels of, and make acceptable, a system that is unacceptable, so Harris believes that religious moderates stand in the way of allowing a full frontal assault on the irrationality and evil of religion. By promoting a God as benevolent and kind, and religion as a source of goodness, moderates teach us "to respect the unjustified beliefs of others." Harris says explicitly, "I hope to show that the very ideal of religious tolerance—born of the notion that every human being should be free to believe whatever he wants about God—is one of the principle forces driving us toward the abyss."

Though he does not name them, I suspect that when Harris refers to "religious moderates," he means nice, mainline Episcopalians, Methodists, Presbyterians, Reform Jews, and others who promote the values of religious tolerance, ecumenicalism, mutual outreach, and so forth. In this regard, I suspect that we too would take our place in front of his firing squad.

To be clear, Harris's conclusion is that in these times religious tolerance is indeed false tolerance, a prescription for suicide, and his program is one of arousing people to a position of religious intolerance. He appeals to secularists and atheists to take their gloves off and become more militant.

To his credit, Harris spends an entire chapter analyzing the nature of religious faith to demonstrate that faith is self-justifying and often viciously circular in the conclusions that it reaches. He also discusses the nature of belief. We assume, Harris argues, that the beliefs we hold are accurate representations of reality outside ourselves; our beliefs are, moreover, precursors to the actions we take. As Harris notes, if we believe that it is going to rain this afternoon, we make sure to place an umbrella in our hands. Likewise, if we believe that God is real, and God has commanded us to slay the infidel, our belief serves as a warrant and motive for our action.

Since I am both a rationalist and very concerned about the political dangers emerging out of religion, both in the United States and across the global, I found much that was confirmatory of my own views in Harris's powerful and intelligently written treatise. No one, I believe, should assess his arguments as irrelevant, but they are not without problems.

First, I am not sure that if all religion were to disappear tomorrow, a peaceful future would be in store for humankind. Religious apologists, when confronting atheist arguments such as those put forward by Harris, often point to the fact that religion does not have a monopoly on cruelty and bloodletting. The massacres of Stalin and the genocide of Pol Pot were carried out in the name of ideologies that were secular and atheist. The excesses of Papa Doc in Haiti and Joseph Mobutu in the Congo were not religiously inspired, nor were the murderous campaigns of the Shining Path guerillas of Peru or Brazil's death squads or Columbian drug lords. Suicide bombing did not begin in the Middle East, but among Tamil insurgents in Sri Lanka, many of whom were dedicated communists. This is not to say that religion does not inspire violence, and it certainly often legitimates it, but it is to say that Harris's analysis of religion within the matrix of human motivations that cause violence may be too narrow. Moreover, if religion is irrational and delusional, and therefore a secular, atheistic way of life is to be preferred because it is rational and not delusional, then we would expect that the mental health profile of secularists, atheists, and other nonreligious people would be higher than that of religious believers. But I don't think that such a correlation between nonreligious belief and mental health can be empirically found. There are many causes for human beings to act in irrational, nutty, and destructive ways, and religion isn't the only one.

Second, I think Harris's analysis of the relationship of belief to action is, as they say in academia, "overdetermined." The line that leads from our beliefs to our actions is not straight and is often not unbroken. In other words, while I believe that our beliefs *dispose* us toward action, not all our beliefs emerge into the light of day to become full-blown actions. I may believe a multitude of different things, and I do, but not all of my beliefs become actualized. Which beliefs ripen into actions, and which do not, is often determined by factors extraneous to the beliefs themselves. The fact that I believe that it will rain this afternoon may dispose me to take my umbrella, but I may decide not to, for a host of reasons. Perhaps the umbrella is too heavy, or too unwieldy, and on this day I happen to have other packages to carry. Or perhaps there will be no place to put my umbrella when I arrive at my destination. The belief that it will rain this afternoon does not straightaway put the umbrella in my hands, because there are competing beliefs that might win out in shaping my decision.

Likewise, my scriptures and my God may command me to slay the infidel or the idolater, or wage holy war against nonbelievers, yet because of the political and economic circumstances in which I live, and the varying preoccupations of my life, I may feel no special impulse or desire to actualize my religious beliefs and do harm to others. In other words, religious beliefs that commend violence may lead to violent behavior depending on the economic and political circumstances in which religious believers find themselves. At times, those violence-prone edicts will find expression in violent acts; most often, however, they won't because they remain unignited by environmental circumstances.

Moreover, studies have shown that whether religious belief becomes violent or not depends to a great degree on the role of religious leadership. In the hands of religious demagogues, religion can be exploited to turn religious believers toward violence. In the hands of religious leadership of a different kind and with a different agenda, religion can be used for the purpose of reconciliation and peacemaking. Factors such as these leave Harris's treatise, though penetrating and very compelling, not sufficiently comprehensive, nor nuanced. It is the same problem I have with the editorial line of *Free Inquiry* magazine and those centered around Paul Kurtz's project, which has committed itself, out of a stance of rationalism, to exposing and attacking religion as nothing but irrational, harmful, and without any positive social value whatsoever. I certainly agree with the rational critique as far as it goes. But it doesn't go far enough. The problem is that it is too limited. It sees religion almost exclusively from the perspective of religious belief alone and does not take into account the broader sociological, political, and economic milieus in which religious beliefs operate.

With all that said, the problem still remains—where are we to draw the line of tolerance? Clearly for Harris and Paul Kurtz there is no line. The irrationalism of religion and its role as a source of political repression and violence means attacking religion at its source—nothing about it is sacred. Let me throw out several other proposals for consideration.

With relative ease, we can draw a line between public religious action and private religious belief in such a way that we are committed to doing battle with the former while we leave the latter alone. It is my firmly held view that when religion moves into the field of political action, all gloves are off. It becomes a political actor like any other, and religion can claim no special immunity. So when the cardinal makes public pronouncements to overturn *Roe v. Wade*, or Pat Robertson goes on TV to condemn liberals or to call for the assassination of foreign heads of state he doesn't like, or to publicly pray for a hurricane to change course and ravage the godless precincts of New York City, I am equally entitled to enter the political arena and oppose such religiously born public initiatives however I please. Likewise, when Mormons in California underwrote and organized a campaign to support Proposition Eight, which overturned a Supreme Court decision to allow gay marriage, they entered the fray and left themselves vulnerable to assault like any other political actor.

On the other hand, what religious leaders preach to their faithful within the confines of their church or sanctuary is a different story. Here their activity would be respected as private and beyond the reach of my criticism and assault. So in practical terms, if the archbishop supports a street demonstration calling for the overturn of *Roe v. Wade*, I am perfectly within proper bounds, as a political tactic, to launch a counterdemonstration, replete with bullhorn and efforts to drown out the other side. But it would be wrong for me to picket a church in which a priest was conducting a mass, or even preaching to his flock about Catholic teaching on abortion and the need to overturn laws that permit it. Under this approach, with the line so drawn, this would be an impermissible trespass on private, indeed sacred territory, and therefore disrespectful.

Since we are talking about religion, I have a confession. This is the position I have held for a long time. But I have begun to conclude that it may be too indulgent and too tolerant of the other side, and perhaps too easy and "hands off," and so allow a danger to fester that needs to be politically fought now. It is one thing to say that I will take a "hands-off" approach to the private teachings of other religions, but what if those religions preach hate as part of their doctrine, or homophobia? What if they are racist and, as all the major religions are, patriarchal, and espouse the subordination of women? Should we morally allow ourselves the right to invade the sancta of these religious faiths in the service of pushing ahead a political agenda that we feel is necessary because what goes on behind church walls, we sincerely believe, is harmful for an open, democratic, just, and peaceful society? Or should we, in the name of tolerance, refrain from doing so?

Clearly, I understand that there is no such corresponding tolerance coming from the other side. It is a centerpiece of much of the religious Right in this country that the humanist and secular values that I hold most dear are the source of moral degradation and the germ of all that is evil in America. And they condemn my most sacred values in every sphere, both private and public. But, of course, I cannot use the behavior of my adversaries as a standard for my own.

More recently, I have begun to move my wall of tolerance closer to the inner sanctum of the religious beliefs of others. The standard I have used to do so, we might call "the human rights standard." It seems to me that it is not inappropriate, indeed, our times make it necessary, to critique the abuses of religions, their teachings, and their sacred doctrines that degrade the dignity of people, their humanity, and their equality. If certain faiths employ sacred authority to preach and incite violence or xenophobia, or preach homophobia as a sacred duty, or commend the death penalty, or more broadly treat women as less than equals, then it is too much a luxury in our small and globalized world to say that these doctrines, internal to the faith though they may be, are none of my concern as an outsider. I don't think we can afford to look the other way and conclude that these doctrines apply solely to the faithful and therefore are not of our concern. And while not all of these religious teachings will be transformed into deeds, as noted earlier, some of them will be, and they will be used to legitimate destructive actions that will extend far beyond their religious communities of origin. There are times to be tolerant, and there are times to be tough minded.

As for religious beliefs, rituals, and practices that are irrational but have no obvious or clear political potential consequence, these I still have little interest in publicly critiquing, exposing, or combating. If a Christian wishes to partake in the Mass and believes that he is ingesting the body and blood of Christ, or a Jew wishes to observe the Sabbath, or a Muslim prays or gives alms out of religious commitment, I may privately hold that the beliefs that ground these practices, or the practices themselves, are irrational, but I have no interest in doing battle with them. In the first instance, from a pragmatic standpoint, engaging in such practices may actually bring positive ethical value. Faith, or beliefs beyond the facts or the evidence at hand, may sometimes bring beneficent results, and the believer may become a better person because of them. Second, such assault does leave me open to charges of superiority and arrogance, and rightly so. In that sense, and only in that narrow sense, do I give religion a pass, a restricted immunity, if you will. It is here that I part company with Sam Harris and those interested in exposing the irrational elements of religion simply because they are irrational.

In closing, I want to return to the position I articulated a moment ago concerning the critique of religious doctrines and teachings that violate basic human rights. I want to say a few words about tactics.

If we believe that religion has reasserted itself as a political actor in ways that threaten our cherished values of freedom and democracy, and I believe it has, then simply condemning religion for being irrational and proposing that everyone become an atheist or a secular, I contend, is foolhardy, because it is simply doomed to failure. It is here that I also depart from Sam Harris, Paul Kurtz, and others. If we are concerned about the political power of religion in America and in other parts of the globe, and we feel moved to do something about it, then it becomes a question of strategies and tactics. We have to be smart, nuanced, and flexible with regard to how we approach the religions in the service of our goals and purposes. The ends I desire are a world at peace and one in which justice prevails. If people achieve peace and justice through their religious commitments, then so be it. I have no desire to impose an atheist or secular utopia on humankind, which I doubt would be a utopia in any case.

When I talk about tactics, I mean that sometimes it will be right to condemn outright the violative teachings of specific religions, and other times it might be more efficacious to enter into dialogue with those whose beliefs and practices we see as harmful. In my own work, I have found it useful not to spurn cooperation with moderate religionists, as Harris and other militant atheists would suggest, but to work with them toward shared progressive political goals. I do not share the view that religious moderates are merely paving the way for the acceptance of religious extremists.

One mistake that many secularists and atheists make when they think about religions is to see them through ideological and monolithic lenses. In reality, many religious communities are internally diverse, and to paint them with a broad brush as monolithic may make it easier to condemn them, and may make the atheist feel better in the process, but it may not be true to fact, nor politically helpful. In my human rights seminar recently, I was speaking of the Armageddon scenarios and their influence on foreign policy espoused by American evangelicals when one of students politely but confidently argued with me, saying that she is an evangelical Christian and doesn't believe in that stuff at all. It was a necessary corrective. I suspect that behind the homophobic rant of a Pat Robertson or a Jerry Falwell, there are people in the pews who themselves have gay children or may wonder about their own sexual orientation, and may indeed harbor penetrating doubts about what comes down from the pulpit in their names. My point is that we may have political allies among those people whom it is easier to write off, and we might do well to seek them out in the service of political moderation and mutual coexistence.

Let me say in conclusion that no, I don't think that religion legitimately claims much of an immunity. But that said, we should not, therefore, appropriate a license for wholesale condemnation and attack. Rather, in this dangerous political climate, our approach needs to be based on a prudent assessment of what is realistic and what it is we hope to accomplish, while never losing sight of the values of justice, equality, and civil peace, which, from our perspective, ought to be the common aspirations of humankind.

December 2005

The Sordid Campaign To
Deny The Holocaust

Primo Levi, Holocaust survivor, Jew, and humanist, wrote in *The Drowned and the Saved:*

> The first news about the Nazi annihilation camps began to spread in the crucial year of 1942. It…delineated a massacre of such vast proportions, of such extreme cruelty and such intricate motivation, that the public was inclined to reject it because of its very enormity…(M)any survivors (among others, Simon Wiesenthal in the last pages of *The Murderers Are Among Us*) remember that the SS militiamen enjoyed cynically admonishing the prisoners:

> "However this war may end, we have won the war against you; none of you will be left to bear witness, but even if someone were to survive, the world will not believe him. There will perhaps be suspicions, discussions, research by historians, but there will be no certainties, because we will destroy the evidence together with you. And even if some proof should remain and some of you survive, people will say that the events you describe are too monstrous to be believed: they will say that they are the exaggerations of Allied propaganda and will believe us, who will deny everything, and not you."

In the two decades following World War II, we had good reason to believe that Western civilization finally had put behind it the two-thousand-year scourge of anti-Semitism. The period following the war was an era of rebuilding. All eyes and expectations were on a more promising future. It was an age of competing global ideologies: liberal democracy and Soviet communism.

On the American scene, the 1950s and '60s spawned movements that promised to transform the social landscape. Antipoverty programs, the women's movement, the antiwar movement, and, most of all, the civil rights movement kept the sights and the hopes of progressive Americans high. In Eisenhower's day people became more churchgoing, but religious differences seemed to matter less. The ideology of the melting pot held sway. In the 1950s, the sociologist Will Herberg wrote a book on religion in America, *Protestant, Catholic, Jew.* The very title suggested how far the United States had moved from a Christian nation to a society in which Jews were emerging as integral members.

Internationally, ecumenicalism achieved its most important expression in the Second Vatican Council's proclamation *Nostra Aetate,* which rescinded the teaching that Jews collectively were responsible for the killing of Christ. By so doing, it jettisoned the baggage of contemptuous theology that through the centuries had nurtured and legitimized persecution of Jews.

Perhaps most of all, the Holocaust itself led to hope that anti-Semitism at long last had come to an end. The consciousness of the Jew is, in part, archetypally built around social marginality and vulnerability to persecution. This consciousness has been tragically reinforced by centuries of oppression: crusades, forced conversions, inquisitions, forced expulsions, and pogroms. My father was old enough to witness the savagery of tsarist-inspired pogroms in his native Ukraine. These experiences were firmly rooted in his memory. Jewish theology reinforced this consciousness with the teaching that the exile of the Jewish people from the Land of Israel was divine punishment.

The systematic murder of six million Jews—which made the nations of Eastern Europe, except for the Soviet Union, *Judenrein* ("Jew free") and devastated the Jewish populations of Western Europe, destroying nearly one third of the world's Jews—seemed to be the apocalyptic event of historical anti-Semitism, the culminating moment in that long, painful history. The event was so calamitous in its implications that it seemed no one would dare proclaim an anti-Semitic sentiment ever again. Yet after two decades of lying dormant, this oldest of prejudices, this virus of Western civilization, again has awakened and has taken on new malignant expressions.

One of these anti-Semitic expressions comes in the form of a campaign to deny that the Nazi genocide of Jews ever happened. It is contended that if Jews did perish, their numbers were small and they died as normal casualties of war and not because of a Nazi plan to exterminate every Jew who could be hunted down. Despite the testimony of countless witnesses, the minutely detailed documentation by hundreds of historians and the records of the Nazis themselves, who often took pains to document their own cruelty, it is asserted that the gas chambers were not really gas chambers and the systematic annihilation of the Jews is a hoax concocted by a new Jewish conspiracy.

This campaign to deny the Holocaust is a wicked and obscene initiative. It not only brings pain to Jews (virtually all of whom have lost family in the Holocaust) and especially to survivors of the death camps, but, more broadly, it is a dangerous assault on history, memory, and truth. Two factors make this bizarre phenomenon possible. One is the revival of anti-Semitism; the other is a decline in the sense of historical truth. I believe the social conditions that have given rise to Holocaust denial are as important as the phenomenon itself.

Sources of Contemporary Anti-Semitism

There are two schools of thought about the causes of anti-Semitism. The first is that its causes are mysterious and inexplicable: as long as there are Jews, they inevitably will be the focus of a perverted fascination and persistent hatred by the non-Jewish world, and nothing can be done about it. This approach can lead only to a defensive posture in which Jews see themselves forever pitted against an implacably hostile world; it has been used by right-wing Zionists as justification for Israeli excesses such as the massacres at the Sabra and Shatila refugee camps in Lebanon in the 1980s and at Hebron more recently. The second school of thought is that, despite its persistence, anti-Semitism, like racism in general, is explicable in social, economic, and historical terms, and while it may never totally go away, it can essentially be overcome. As a rationalist and a humanist, I believe that all forms of racism can be explained by social conditions. Without that belief we give up on the idea of civilization and cede the ground to barbarism.

What conditions explain the reemergence of anti-Semitism in general and Holocaust denial in particular?

We live in xenophobic times, in which racism, nationalism, tribalism, chauvinism, and particularism have tragically become the predominant foci and motifs of political action. The demise of communism in Eastern Europe has created an ideological vacuum, and xenophobic nationalism has resurfaced to fill the gap. Anti-Semitism, which has a deep and far-reaching history in Russia and other states of the former Soviet Union, is part of that ugly resurgence.

Here at home, though fragmentation has not attained the virulent pitch witnessed in Eastern Europe, we live in the aftermath of the collapse of a political optimism that sustained progressive movements reflecting what is best in the American spirit. Without overarching political ideals to inspire us and bring us together, the door again is open to a politics of small, particularist interests and—when brought to the extreme—racist agendas.

Racism in American today—both white and black—also is fueled by closing economic opportunities and diminishing expectations. Moreover, we are witnessing a wave of immigration unprecedented since the turn of the century. With this influx of a mix of ethnicities, cultures, languages, and races, and the resulting competition for jobs, comes a rise of hate groups and racist ideologies. America has been there before.

Given such tensions, Jews once again have become a familiar target, even as the majority of Jews have become increasingly assimilated into American society. Perhaps, also, because of that. America has provided Jews with opportunities unprecedented in Jewish history, and Jews have made very good use of those opportunities. Though barely 2.5 percent of the population, Jews are prominently represented in numerous prestigious fields, including medicine, law, education, entertainment, publishing, and politics (but not banking, as anti-Semitic canards would have it). It is this very prominence, success, and visibility that, in these uneasy times, make Jews lightning rods for xenophobic hatred. It is one small step from acknowledging Jewish achievement to assuming that it is the result of, and is sustained by, Jewish conspiracies.

Although there are no Jewish conspiracies, the Jewish community in America since and because of the Holocaust has become much better organized and self-protective with regard to its own interests and its promotion of American support for Israel. The prominence of Israel on the world stage, and the perpetual controversy surrounding it, also have become a focus of anti-Semitic assaults. Israel is a nation-state and, as such, is open for criticism, as is any other. But often anti-Israel or anti-Zionist attacks appear to be masks for anti-Semitism.

These brief observations merely scratch the surface; much more could be said about the sources of contemporary anti-Semitism. But I want to discuss an additional denial to gain a foothold.

The Decline of Historical Certainty

We live in sensationalistic times. One example is the triumph of tabloid journalism pandering to the tawdry, the weird, the violent, and the superficial, crowding out the reflective, the intelligent, and the responsible. An extremist will make racist or anti-Semitic utterances, which the media then define as news. When Khalid Muhammad sounds off, that's news. The Reverend Johnny Ray Youngblood, a pastor in Brooklyn who preaches racial reconciliation to a congregation of thousands, we seldom hear about. The journalism of sensationalism forces decent folk to respond to an extremism they would prefer to ignore, thereby giving it a legitimacy it does not deserve. The Holocaust deniers have exploited this strategy.

We live in hedonistic times, in which the desire to be entertained supersedes the desire to be informed. The ways we come to know about our world are reduced to momentary sound bites wrapped in the gloss and titillation of Hollywood productions. Our media culture treats adults like children who cannot swallow reality unless it comes brightly packaged and sugar coated. With information, both current and historical, presented like entertainment, the line separating fact from fiction is becoming increasingly blurred. In our powerfully market-driven culture, this pernicious distortion of reality for profit finds fertile ground among a public that gets its information less and less from responsible sources and more and more from television and the movies.

News reporting, by its nature, never can be objective; it must reflect particular perspectives and reject others. But there was a time when television news reported on issues we might have agreed were important. Today television journalism, for the most part, focuses on the sensational, the salacious, the polemical, the violent, and, increasingly, the imaginary. Turn on the six o'clock news and you will find reports of some fictionalized drama that aired as an entertainment program ten minutes earlier. If reporting on fiction is as news-worthy as reporting on famine in Africa, human rights abuse in China, or the blight of our inner cities, the credulous mind might begin to ask: What is worth knowing and caring about and what is not? What is truth and what is fiction? What is real and what is fanciful?

We live in the age of the docudrama. For the sake of entertainment, facts are deliberately distorted, or gaps in knowledge are filled in with speculation passed off as fact. Television shows portray fantastic scenarios ranging from people abducted by aliens to alleged scientists discovering the remains of Noah's ark. Such shows used to take pains to issue disclaimers, letting viewers know that what they were about to see was make believe. Today, producers and networks seem to be less fastidious. Oliver Stone's film *JFK* presented as historical fact a thor-oughly undocumented and preposterous conspiracy theory of President John F. Kennedy's assassination. Stone's production may have served his ideological and dramatic purposes, but what injury did it do to our ability to discern truth from falsehood? The reality principle is collapsing under the seductive power of the pleasure principle, and a commitment to truth is perilously being lost. This is hap-pening at a time when schools are failing greatly, and the ability of minds, both young and old, to master the art of critical thinking has declined.

Americans never have been a historically minded people. But what is one to make of the fact that 75 percent of students at Ivy League colleges in a recent survey did not know that Abraham Lincoln spoke the words "government of the people, by the people, and for the people" in the Gettysburg Address? In the same survey half the students could not name their two United States sena-tors (*New York Times*, April 30, 1993).

Of course, a knowledge of history is more than a recitation of quota-tions, dates, and events. It is a way to anchor ourselves in the world, develop a sense of values, and chart a blueprint for the future. Without a reverence for history, life becomes superficial, self-interested, hedonistic, shallow, and dumb. Without a sense of history, people become vulnerable to demagoguery and political manipulation. As George Orwell once put it, "Whoever controls the past controls the future."

Historical truth is taking a beating in other ways as well. Multiculturalism, the rightful demand that historical perspectives of minorities and women be factored into the curricula of schools and colleges, is causing conventional interpretations of history to be radically revised. The doctrine of manifest destiny, which from the perspective of European Americans was a triumph, from the standpoint of Native Americans was a calamity. So, some say, was Columbus's landing. History is being reinterpreted to reflect such emerging sensibilities in increasingly politicized college environments.

What all these factors create in the media, the popular culture, and the academy is a climate of confusion and relativism. People are less able to declare with confidence that this is true and that is false, this is a fact and that is not. If they do, such declarations are based less on solid facts and more on empty ideology, rhetoric, and cant.

This contemporary atmosphere of intellectual uncertainty, combined with the ugly climate of reaction and xenophobia now sweeping our society, have created the conditions for the emergence of the insidious campaign to deny that Nazi Germany's systematic genocidal annihilation of six million Jews ever took place. This campaign is nothing more than anti-Semitic hatred gussied up with a patina of academic pretension. But because of the anti-intellectual climate of our times, it is beginning to make itself felt.

Holocaust Deniers: Strategies and Responses

Holocaust denial has become a mainstay of the far right in many countries, including England, Austria, and Germany. It as yet remains a marginal phenomenon, having made the greatest headway in France and the United States. (A recent Roper survey found that 22 percent of adult Americans believe it is possible the Holocaust never happened. Subsequent inquiry revealed, however, that the question posed by the pollster was confusing and resulted in an erroneously high figure.) While most Holocaust deniers can be found in extremist, white supremacist hate groups associated with the Ku Klux Klan, Aryan Nation, Liberty Lobby, and so forth, some are credentialed academics: notably Robert Faurisson, a former professor of literature at the University of Lyon, and Arthur Butz, a professor of electrical engineering at Northwestern University. Together such people constitute, in the words of Deborah Lipstadt, author of *Denying the Holocaust*, "a group motivated by a strange conglomeration of conspiracy theories, delusions, and neo-Nazi tendencies."

While Holocaust denial can be traced back to the 1950s, the current wave comes in new packaging. The trick of extremists these days is to gain influence by looking respectable. Just as David Duke trades in his Klan robes for a business suit, and just as "scientific creationism" is a front by which to work Christian fundamentalist dogma into the public schools, so the anti-Semites of the Holocaust denial movement refer to themselves as "revisionists," implying that they are merely providing an alternative interpretation of the historical record.

By necessity, all historical interpretation is revisionist. Moreover, there was a recognized school of historians called "revisionists," who sought to shift the weight of responsibility for World War I away from Germany and onto America and the other allied powers. This group of historians employed the canons of historical research to reach unconventional conclusions. Holocaust deniers have appropriated the title "revisionist" as if they were part of a legitimate historiographic tradition. They are not. Their methods involve out-and-out falsification, creating "facts" where none exist and ignoring overwhelming and irrefutable evidence that defies their contentions. They refer to their adversaries as "exterminationists," implying that they represent the other side of a legitimate debate. It is an issue no more legitimate than debating whether the earth is flat, but by such strategies the deniers have received more attention than they deserve and have sown doubt in the minds of a segment of an ill-informed and credulous public.

The central contention of the deniers is a complete inversion of what happened during World War II. According to them, the Germans were the true victims and the Jews the victimizers. In Faurrison's words, the gas chambers were a "gigantic politico-financial swindle whose beneficiaries are the state of Israel and international Zionism." If one asks what happened to the six million Jews, the response is that they were deported to Eastern Europe and then made their way across Asia and ultimately to North America. Forced ghettoization is explained as a quarantine to save the German population from spreading disease. For the deniers, only two hundred thousand Jews lost their lives, and certainly not more than a million. Rather than victims of Nazi extermination, those who died were casualties of war, victims of disease or Allied bombings. The gas chambers didn't exist; it would have been technically impossible to murder so many by such facilities. Rather, they were either showers or delousing chambers. If, after the war, Germans admitted to the Holocaust, deniers contend that it was because they had to do so to be accepted back into the family of nations. Deniers are particularly obsessed with Anne Frank's diary, which they claim is a forgery written by her father after the war. And on and on.

The underlying intent of the deniers is the rehabilitation of fascism. If fascism in its national socialist form can be cleansed of the taint of the Holocaust, then the world might conclude that fascism isn't so bad as a political system.

These ideas are crackpot, delusional, totally preposterous, but dangerous. The deniers are attempting to gain entry into the mainstream by cloaking their message with an aura of academic objectivity. They have established computer boards and communicate through international networks. They have appeared on talk shows, representing "the other side of the debate."

Since 1979, one of their initiatives has been the creation of the Institute for Historical Review, which, in imitation of bona fide academic organizations, holds conferences and produces its own journal with the deceptively innocuous title the *Journal of Historical Review*. One has to look twice before realizing that it's a hate rag dressed up to appear respectable.

The Institute for Historical Review is the creation of Willis Carto, also the founder of the Liberty Lobby, with annual revenues in the 1980s of more than four million dollars and its own publishing company. According to Drew Pearson, Carto is a real Hitler fan, and the Liberty Lobby is infiltrated by Nazis who revere Hitler's memory. Carto, according to the Anti-Defamation League, is the most important and influential professional anti-Semite in the United States. Willis Carto's world view is, Deborah Lipstadt writes, encapsulated by three things: contempt and revulsion for Jews, a belief in the need for absolutist government that would protect the "racial heritage" of the United States, and a conviction that there exists a conspiracy to bring dire harm to the Western world. As might be inferred, Carto has almost as much hatred for blacks as he does for Jews. Yet in the deranged politics of anti-Semitic extremism, an alliance has been forged between Butz and Louis Farrakhan, with Butz, according to Deborah Lipstadt, presenting his views on Holocaust denial at a Nation of Islam meeting.

A second strategy by which deniers have attempted to gain access to, and respectability in, the mainstream is to place advertisements in college newspapers, describing the Holocaust as a hoax. This initiative has generated exposure, controversy, and attention. Among colleges whose newspapers have run such ads, with or without editorial comment, are Cornell, Duke, the University of Michigan, Vanderbilt, and Rutgers. Among those that have refused are Berkeley, Brown, Dartmouth, the University of Pennsylvania, Yale, and the University of Wisconsin.

Whether college newspapers should run such ads is debatable. Some have published them, invoking the "light of day" argument: better to exposure this material to public view so people can know and respond to their enemies than to keep it hidden from view. Maybe so. But what is especially troubling is that all the college papers that ran these ads had policies prohibiting the publication of racist, sexist, prejudicial, or religiously offensive advertisements. In short, by masking their anti-Semitism behind a pseudo-intellectual veneer, the deniers succeeded in persuading college editorial boards that they were presenting the other side of a legitimate issue. The Harvard *Crimson*, by contrast, repudiated the idea that ads denying the Holocaust present a "controversial argument based on questionable facts." It refused to print such an ad, declaring it "vicious propaganda based on utter bullshit that has been discredited time and time again." More than "moronic and false," the ad was an attempt to "propagate hatred against Jews."

How to respond to the Holocaust denial campaign is a difficult issue. Several European states and Canada have passed laws prohibiting dissemination of false information that knowingly slanders groups in this way. A student at William Paterson University recently filed a bias suit against a professor for making what he construed to be false claims about the Holocaust. Whether such suits will, or even should, hold up in the United States is arguable.

It will not be long before those who were firsthand witnesses to the Holocaust will be gone. With the death of the last survivor, the Nazi genocide will pass from memory into history. It is the nefarious design of Holocaust deniers to so confound the historical record that future generations will seriously doubt whether such barbarism ever took place.

Both Deborah Lipstadt and the French historian Pierre Vidal-Naquet, who have written books on this subject, maintain that Holocaust deniers ought not to be debated. To do so gives them a legitimacy they do not deserve. But in this age of sensationalist politics, they unfortunately cannot be ignored. They ought not to be debated, *but they need to be exposed* for what they are.

In the long range, all people of good will need to struggle against a hostile social climate to create economic, political, and educational conditions that cause anti-Semitic utterances—indeed, all appeals to racial hatred—to fall on deaf ears. This is a daunting but necessary task. For the near future, I do not hold much hope. For the distant future, I cannot do otherwise.

August 2007

When We Blur Our Boundaries,
We Muddle Our Morals

That American society is facing a crisis of moral values is not merely a rallying call of right-wing propagandists. Note the observations of Harvard Professor Cornel West, a man explicitly identified with the Left:

> America is in the midst of a massive social breakdown (and) cultural decay is pervasive. The erosion of civil society—shattered families, neighborhoods, school and voluntary associations—has contributed to a monumental eclipse of hope and to the collapse of meaning across the country. Civic terrorism—the sheer avalanche of mindless and calculated violence in our social fabric—haunts many urban, suburban, and rural streets.

> Consumer culture—a way of life that spawns addictive personalities and passive citizens—promotes a profound spiritual impoverishment and moral shallowness.

> The culture industries of TV, radio, film, and video bombard Americans with degrading stereotypes—especially women and people of color—and saturate leisure time with seductive images of sexual foreplay and orgiastic pleasures. Never before have Americans been so ill equipped to

confront the traumas of despair, dread, and death, even as so many, especially those among the political and economic elite, ignore the social chaos and self-destruction eating at the core of American society.

Cornel West paints a grim picture, but I think not an incorrect one. Hand in hand with the eclipse of hope and collapse of meaning he speaks of, I would add an erosion of moral values, which he alludes to as moral shallowness brought on by the excesses of our consumer culture.

It's a moral shallowness (we might say a moral absence) which cuts across class lines. It's manifest in crimes without conscience. We fear the thief who steals out of hunger or poverty, but we can at least understand why he does it. We may even hold out the hope that if we abolish hunger and poverty, we will eliminate a great deal of crime. But the mugger, who just as well sticks the knife in our gut as not, and does so without the slightest shred of conscience—such crime makes no moral or logical sense at all, and so the element of fear that pervades our streets and chills our hearts is so much greater.

The executive or politician who operates on the principle of self-interest first, last, and always plays perhaps an even greater role in polluting the moral environment. It's said that Japanese CEOs will often resign if crime or mismanagement takes place on their watch, even if they have no direct involvement with the event. In America, the response seems to be just the opposite: to avoid, evade, and deny responsibility while proclaiming self-protection as the highest virtue. The strategy is to blame others, or place the blame on wider circumstances over which the perpetrator claims he had no control. Or blame it on a disease or an addiction before which the liar, embezzler, molester, or batterer is allegedly helpless. By such a sleight of the hand, moral reality is stood on its head and the moral violator becomes a victim. And if he has enough *chutzpah*, he may even claim that his status as a victim gives him greater moral entitlements, or perhaps greater insight into the social and moral conditions of victimization.

Today, everyone is a dime-store sociologist. In past times we would have identified such a strategy with what it is—a mark of spinelessness and a refuge for cowards. Today, as we all know, with the help of TV and newspaper tabloids, moral violators from all walks of life become objects of fascination and instant celebrities, while their crimes and misdemeanors fade quickly into the background.

The deification of the free market, which was promoted from on high in the 1980s, has spread like an oil spill to befoul the social and moral environment. The highest value of the free market is the promotion of individual self-interest at the expense of others, and so it has become on the moral landscape as well. With the help of the media, we have come to celebrate the malefactor who escapes conviction and punishment through ingenuity and cunning. We applaud him as the true savior who knows how to put it over on the rest of us while blithely forgetting the social misery and destruction he has caused. Anything less would be a sign of weakness.

When was the last time we heard someone in public life who had committed a crime, whether theft, sexual harassment, illicit drug use, or whatever, unequivocally say, "Yes, I am responsible for what I have done, and I am very sorry. But more than merely profess my sorrow, I will accept the consequences of my actions. Not only will I suffer requisite punishment, I will do whatever I can to make up to society and those whom I have hurt for what I have done"? Rather than be refreshed by the moral lucidity of such a proclamation, nowadays such a person would be treated as a type of freak, a masochist, or a fool. Or perhaps we would see him or her as expressing a new take on self-indulgence or narcissism that would land him or her in front of the TV spotlight as the latest oddity.

Uncomfortable with a moral vocabulary, we have replaced it with pop psychology. Every malefactor is transformed into a social worker. If you commit a crime, what you do is feel no shame. You just go for instant counseling, proclaim that you are cured, your addiction or deed behind you, and thrust yourself into the public limelight once more—this time as a social benefactor with a redemptive message to proclaim. Every grisly criminal is a potential culture hero if he is just clever enough or lucky enough to nudge the media spotlight in his direction.

Where have such moral concepts as personal responsibility, guilt, shame, apology, repentance, and restitution gone? They seem to have slipped from our vocabulary. In this feel-good age, we don't like to think this way. This type of moral reasoning leaves us uncomfortable because by necessity it entails making judgments about people's reasoning and behaviors, and we have come to feel that making judgments is a type of taboo; it's simply not nice. Yet the ability to make moral discriminations, especially as they pertain to oneself, is a basis for being a moral person. Making judgments, whether we like it or not, is simply unavoidable. How we express our judgments needs to take into account a sense of tact, timing, and compassion as well as probing reflection on our own motivation, lest we commit the offense of being excessively judgmental. But to abandon the need to make moral discriminations is to abandon morality itself and leaves us prey to the mistaken notion that because all people have a right to their own opinions, all opinions are, therefore, right.

Perhaps we also attribute such moral values to the oppressions of the past; nothing but the vestiges of our biblical, Calvinist, or Victorian heritages to which, in our pleasure-seeking era, we bid good riddance.

Such glib reasoning is a big mistake. I contend that our humanity is tagged to our ability to be moral agents and to hold ourselves accountable for the moral indiscretions we commit. We may be impelled by our drives, our needs, our desires, and an oppressive social condition to violate, abuse, rape, or kill another human being. But our very humanity is vested in our ability to say to ourselves, "I feel with every fiber of my being that I want to lie, steal, rape, or kill, but in the face of all those impulses I choose not to." In that zone between our impulses and our acts, our humanity rests.

Another way of saying this is we must presuppose, except for that small segment of the population that is truly deranged, that all people have the free will to decide what is right and what is wrong, what is respectful behavior is and what is violent behavior. Admittedly, in certain circumstances, the fact that I am drunk or enraged, or a member of a socially oppressed group, may serve as mitigating factors in assessing my legal guilt. But is my view that they should never completely absolve the individual perpetrator from the responsible for his or her actions? To do so is an affront to the moral order on which any civilized society depends. It is also a condescending and offensive assault on the humanity of the person who has committed the act. To say that someone is not responsible for his or her behavior is, to that extent, to imply that he or she is something less than human.

Some may conclude that such reasoning plays into the hands of conservative ideologues. And indeed it may. But I would contend that the notion of individual responsibility, and that every person possesses the freedom and the ability to choose between right and wrong, are ineradicable axioms of the moral life. It's hard for me to see how any society, with the exception of a fascist one, be it a free-market conservative, social democratic or communist society, would survive if it assumed that its members were not responsible for their behavior.

As rooted in the human experience as it is, the ability to think morally and ultimately to behave morally is a function of social conditioning, with education being one of the most important conditioning agents. While I don't believe we can suppress our moral sense all together, whether morality is strong or weak is dependent on a lot of factors in the culture.

If this is the case, how has our society gotten to the point where it is today?

This is a question that is as complex as it is urgent. Needless to say, there are many theories, some overlapping, others competing. This morning I want to share my analysis of what I believe is one extremely pernicious factor that contributes to the erosion of moral sensibilities. It is a market-driven phenomenon that insinuates itself into the popular culture and thereby into the consciousness of the masses of Americans. It has informed the way we think, and, to the extent that how we think affects how we act, it has informed our behavior and especially our moral behavior as well.

Let me explain what I mean. Basic to our process of thinking is the fact that we tend to think in categories. As we grow out of infancy, we become aware of what is me and what is not me. When we say that we *understand* something, what we are really saying is that we have the ability to organize our chaotic thoughts into a coherent pattern that stands out against the background of our experiences that are yet to be organized, and so remain confused. Basic to our thinking is the ability to say "this is this" and "that is that" and the two entities are in some sense distinct from each other. I've already noted that our capacity to think morally is dependent upon our ability to make moral discriminations; that is, to say "this is right, that is wrong; this is good, that is bad."

This is very simplistic, but I think our ability to obtain clarity in our thinking has in great measure to do with this ability to show how varying ideas and concepts, in effect, are distinct and differ from one another.

Having said that, I agree that novelty and creativity in our thinking emerge when we see underlying patterns of commonality in things that at first glance we hold to be different. This is especially true of artistic perceptions. The artist may even deliberately blur the boundaries between distinctive entities, as when Picasso, for example, has a human face emerging from a geometric object. I suspect Picasso is implying there is a commonality between the geometrical form and the human one that is most creatively and playfully expressed in this way. But artistic expression is a special type of endeavor, and I want to put it aside for the sake of this discussion. My concerns are social and don't touch upon the internal issues of art.

The point I make is that, for at least the past twenty years, we are expressing in the popular media a deliberate blurring of what were previously understood boundaries between different categories of cultural concern. I want to provide several examples of what I mean.

The first that comes to mind is the emergence, if not triumph, of tabloidism in print and especially TV journalism. One could argue, and I would argue, that the primary purpose of the news is to provide information that we cannot otherwise gather for ourselves, in order to enable us to become more astute and effective citizens within a democratic society. In this sense, the news traditionally has been primarily serious and sober stuff. To be sure, newspapers have long had entertainment, society, and gossip columns, along with comics and crosswords. But the point to be made here is that entertainment was kept separate from news reporting. Today, in a free-market mania to boost ratings, and hence advertising revenues, the line between what is news and what is entertainment is deliberately erased.

Debate on health care is news, as are issues of foreign policy, economic trends, human rights, etc. The fact that Sharon Stone is taking a shower with Sylvester Stallone is not news, nor are endless reports on what Michael Jackson wears, or who was seen with whom, or who had what for breakfast. Nor is it a legitimate function of the eleven o'clock news to provide a report of some fictionalized show that was aired on the same network two hours earlier. The danger isn't only that bad, crass, superficial journalism will drive out the good, which it is amply doing. By homogenizing news with entertainment, the message is conveyed that there is no difference between the two, or that one is as important as the other. All truths, what's important and what's not, become relative. If all one knew about the world were derived from such sources, the power of discrimination needed in order to make important decisions as a citizen in society would be dumbed down and hopelessly blurred. And so it has become.

The effects of tabloidism are leaching into more serious domains as well. In the arena of serious literature, the lines between truth and fiction are being blurred. An article written for the *Baltimore Sun* and reprinted in the *Record* of Hackensack a few years back noted the following:

> It's obvious that the tabloidization we see in television and newspapers is affecting books as well. Even serious journalists, if they want to get $300,000 or $400,000 advances, have to come up with the kinds of revelations that only a few years ago would have appeared only in the *National Enquirer.* And the standard of what is definitive biography has changed. We didn't need to know all about James Joyce's sex life ten years ago, and now we do.

The author cites Joe McGinniss's six-hundred-page biography of Ted Kennedy, *The Last Brother.* In the book, McGinniss, who interviewed Kennedy, often speculated on what the senator thought and felt.

And on Bob Woodward's recently published book, titled *The Agenda,* the writer notes, "A recent book about the Clinton White House opens with an August 1991 scene between Bill and Hillary Clinton in bed, discussing whether he should run for president. The book is written as though the author was there himself, transcribing the couple's pillow talk conversation."

The point, of course, is that he wasn't. The need to entertain is increasingly superseding a commitment to truthfulness and a loyalty to facts.

Returning to the visual media, there's a proliferation of so-called docudramas, in which, for the sake of entertainment, historical events are merged with a heavy dose of fiction. So one doesn't know what really happened and what is make believe.

In the *New York Times* of April 30, 1993, reviewer Michiko Kakutani cited Oliver Stone's *JFK* as a particularly nefarious example of this phenomenon and noted the following:

> Many…young people, like many of their elders, get their history from movies and television, media that are taking increased liberties with the truth, routinely blurring fact and

fiction, and distorting real events to make dramatic or ideological points…The willingness to mix up fact with speculation encourages people to confuse verisimilitude with reality, and the tendency shows no sign of abating.

Given that Americans' historical consciousness is already so weak, this type of manipulation of the truth is potentially very dangerous. Indeed, she ends the article with Orwell's ominous warning: "Whoever controls the past controls the future. Whoever controls the present controls the past." Again, such deliberate blurring relativizes the truth and erodes the ability to make cognitive distinctions between what happened and what didn't happen; what is true and what is false.

Another powerful phenomenon is the ever-proliferating TV talk shows, which in their grab for audiences are becoming increasing more bizarre. I suspect that an appeal of talk shows is related to the pleasures of voyeurism, since confession of one's private thoughts, feelings, and fantasies is what they are primarily about.

The argument has been made that these shows serve a beneficial purpose in that they expose to the light of day previously hidden or denied social problems, such as domestic violence, depression, various kinds of addiction, rape, and so forth, which can now be more adequately addressed. I suppose this is so.

But I also see considerable social harm in these endless exposés of the underside of the human condition.

First, they blur the boundaries between what is appropriately public and what should be private discourse. I believe that civility is ultimately dependent on keeping reasonably separate the public and private spheres. I certainly think that we should find outlets for our pains, our fantasies, our sense of victimization, but these expressions should be guided by appropriate time and place considerations. The place to talk about these things is with one's friends, lover, spouse, psychotherapist, or clergyman, and not before an audience of millions of anonymous TV viewers. Public exposure of these very personal matters, I think, models a self-indulgence that cheapens the import and value of such confessional conversations.

More importantly, these shows serve to further relativize moral values. First we hear from the rape victim. Then we hear from the rapist, who narrates his story, telling us about his abused childhood and informing us about how he is now in therapy. The professional expert provides his insight and the audience applauds. What we have just witnessed is the leveling of moral responsibility. Whatever moral reprobation is due to a man who has committed such an abominable crime is dissolved by the alchemy of modern-day psychobabble. The moral has been totally transformed into the psychological, and with it our ability to make moral decisions between victims and those who victimize.

Conceptually related to the vulgarity of the talk show has been the transformation and status of pornography in the popular culture. I don't want to discuss in this context such current debates as whether viewing pornography is *ipso facto* an assault on women, or whether the arms of state should be employed to censor it, however important these discussions are. I want to make a different point.

It seems to me that a particularly harmful aspect of pornography is that it has seeped its way into popular media—and the movies—while masquerading as something else. Smut is smut, and there was a time when every twelve-year-old boy knew what was and what wasn't pornography. What seems to be destructive is the prominence and intensity of the titillation factor in what is passed off as standard TV and movie fare. When dramas, such as soap operas, or comedies are essentially masks for sexual innuendo and stimulation, the boundaries are again blurred between legitimate drama and the pornographic. This, in my view, creates a confusion, which leads ultimately to greater harm than if pornography is socially and culturally defined as such. I am not saying that what is pornographic and what isn't is easily defined. My point is that the limits are being deliberately pushed, and the line between pornography and what is not pornography is being blurred for the sake of higher ratings and greater box office revenues. A multitude of viewers may disagree as to whether what they have just seen is pornographic. But I bet that every TV and Hollywood producer knows exactly what he is doing and what kind of appeal he is attempting to generate when he airs a show or produces another sleazy film.

My own view is that pornography is essentially a male preoccupation that is not going to go away. I think the better approach, as with other manifestations of the underside of human interest, is not to repress, which I think over time is impossible, but to contain. Pornography belongs in the red-light districts, and in milieus segregated for the pursuit of those interests, where everyone at least understands what it is about. The confounding of boundaries degrades moral values and does the most harm.

Finally, I come to a somewhat different, but related issue. It has to deal with authority and relations within the family. Here I am moving onto closer, more personal ground.

My father was born in 1903 into a different world. He was an Eastern European gentleman and businessman who dressed the part. By looking at his appearance and social demeanor, there was little doubt that he was an adult, and children were children. The difference between the generations was clear and distinct. The 1960s, of course, changed all that, especially in modes of dress. My parents never wore dungarees, nor did they ever sit on the floor.

I am not implying for one nanosecond that I would ever want to return to the rigidity, formality, and aloofness that marked and divided the generations before the social revolutions of the 1960s. The efforts by middle-aged baby boomers to be more youthful, more spontaneous, and more in tune with their children are, for the most part, much to the good.

My point is more nuanced. Perhaps in many households too much was given away. In yielding the formality of older generations, perhaps what was given up also was a sense of parental authority.

I believe in authority, but not in authoritarianism, which is arbitrary authority. Perhaps the two are somewhat confused, and that is part of the problem. I believe in authority that comes with experience, with age, and, when appropriate, with one's situation or status. To be sure, authority can be criticized, and overthrown when it's abusive. But I believe that society and families need authority, and children especially do. Perhaps in giving up the appearance of our parents' generation, some who became parents themselves also gave up their sense of empowerment and authority, which their children badly need, particularly to be assured that they live in a structured and protected environment.

Children need parents to be their parents, not their friends. To forgo that role is again to blur boundaries that serve to foster moral development. Perhaps these are among the most important boundaries of all, and among the most difficult to sustain.

The point that I have been trying to make has been implied in what has gone before. If our culture has powerfully blurred the distinctions between fact and fiction, truth and make believe, should there be any mystery as to why more people seem to have difficulty in bringing clarity to their moral reasoning and distinguishing right from wrong? I think not.

In closing, let me say that I have no simple antidote to the pervasive problem I have been unfolding. As Cornel West implies, the moral shallowness we experience in American society is tied to massive economic and social forces that lie beneath it. We need to work hard to ensure that those institutions that give meaning, hope, and purpose to life, such as schools and work and family, are strong and secure.

We need also to stand against the currents that threaten to cheapen our lives and dull our moral sensitivities. We need to reanchor ourselves to those timeless values that our intuition tells us make life meaningful: the search for the truth and the respect for the humanity of others, and our own. And then we need to teach our children well.

October 1994

Reclaiming The Enlightenment

A cting on the entitlements that "the Laws of Nature and of Nature's God" had given to the American people, Thomas Jefferson wrote in 1776, "We hold these truths to be self-evident, that all men are created equal, that they are endowed by their Creator with certain unalienable rights, that among these are Life, Liberty, and the pursuit of Happiness."

Eighty-seven years later, between ten thousand and twenty thousand people gathered on the fields of Gettysburg to hear President Abraham Lincoln give a speech that lasted no more than three minutes. Though rumors have persisted that Lincoln wrote the 272 words of the Gettysburg Address on the back of an envelope in a momentary flash of inspiration, the truth is that he thought long and hard, not only about the composition of that brief address, but the historic role he intended it to play. For in writing the Gettysburg Address, Lincoln consciously was attempting to fulfill the unfulfilled promises that Jefferson had proclaimed in the Declaration of Independence. Whereas the birth of the nation heralded, but left unrealized, the equality of all men, the Civil War and the emancipation of the slaves rededicated the nation to "a new birth of freedom," a democratic government "of the people, by the people, and for the people."

And it was almost exactly a hundred years later, standing before the Lincoln Memorial on August 28, 1963, that Martin Luther King echoed the words of Jefferson and Lincoln when he said:

> Five score years ago, a great American, in whose symbolic shadow we now stand, signed the Emancipation Proclamation...

> But one hundred years later, we must face the tragic fact that the Negro is still not free. One hundred years later, that life of the Negro is still sadly crippled by the manacles of segregation and the chains of discrimination...

> In a sense we have come to our nation's capital to cash a check. When the architects of our republic wrote the magnificent words of the Constitution and the Declaration of Independence, they were signing a promissory note to which every American was to fall heir. This note was a promise that all men would be guaranteed the unalienable rights of life, liberty, and the pursuit of happiness.

> It is obvious today that America has defaulted on this promissory note insofar as her citizens of color are concerned. Instead of honoring this sacred obligation, America has given the Negro people a bad check; a check which has come back marked "Insufficient Funds." But we refuse to believe that the bank of justice is bankrupt. We refuse to believe that there are insufficient funds in the great vaults of opportunity of this nation. So we have come to cash this check—a check that will give us upon demand the riches of freedom and the security of justice.

These three examples of timeless American oratory, coming from the eighteenth, nineteenth, and twentieth centuries, respectively, all reveal a common thread running through them and share common values.

They address themselves to the sturdy values of equality, justice, freedom, and the promises of a progressively unfolding and more bountiful future.

These ideas of justice, equality, freedom, and progress, ideas that frame the modern world and our modern consciousness, did not come from nowhere.

Jefferson did not himself create them, nor did Lincoln, nor did King. They inherited these ideas from the glorious outpouring of thought, creativity, and discovery known as the European Enlightenment.

The Enlightenment was that radical awakening to the power of the human mind. It was a movement that flourished in the century between the Glorious Revolution in England in 1688 and the French Revolution in 1789, but it really extended for a hundred years before and almost a hundred years after that latter date.

What was the Enlightenment? Let's put it this way. If you had lived in medieval Europe, the world around you would essentially be unknowable and unknown. Even if you were among the rare individuals who were educated, you would have little sense of history and almost no grasp on how the world works. The world would confront you, in and of itself, as an inscrutable mystery, and all mysteries would ultimately be explained as an expression of God's will. Yours would be an authoritarian world governed by the power of God, his church, and his monarchs, who ruled by divine decree.

That changed in the seventeenth century, when men such as Galileo, Kepler, and, most of all, Isaac Newton created modern science. With the age of science came the extraordinary discovery that human beings could actually use the power of their minds and their reason to decipher how nature works. The planets, which to the medieval mind were embedded in crystalline spheres and propelled by the power of invisible angels, in the seventeenth century saw those angels replaced by the laws of gravitation and celestial mechanics.

The Enlightenment brought another remarkable discovery. Not only was nature scrutable to the human mind, but nature could actually be transformed to make life better, perhaps even happier, for humankind. Reason could be harnessed to scientific discovery, and scientific discovery led to applied technology.

In the minds of Enlightenment philosophers, reason and inquiry were directed to not only the natural but also the social world that we inhabit.

If there were laws that governed how nature works, perhaps there were analogous laws that determined how human beings function in society. Political philosophers such as Jefferson believed that there were. And just as Newtonian laws are part of nature, so there are basic rights that are inalienable from and natural to human beings, just as a person's shadow is inalienable from him or her. And according to Jefferson and those of his ilk, it is the role, indeed, the very purpose of the state and government to protect those natural rights.

The period of the Enlightenment gave us modern science, but it also gave us the modern political world we enjoy. It overthrew absolute monarchs and replaced them with the democratic state, where power and legitimacy do not come from the king above but from the people below.

The Enlightenment was a heady and exhilarating time. Its temperament was one of skepticism, secularism, and cosmopolitanism. It extended from Edinburgh to Naples, Paris to Berlin, Boston to Philadelphia. It sought to replace ignorance with knowledge, superstition and illusion with reason, authoritarianism with democracy, degradation with dignity, the childhood of humankind with its maturity, traditional religion with secularism, divine will with natural law. But most of all the Enlightenment cherished freedom—freedom to inquire, freedom to know, and freedom from political tyranny.

The Enlightenment boasted such geniuses as the Scotsmen David Hume and Adam Smith, the Englishmen John Locke and Jeremy Bentham, the Germans Gotthold Lessing and Immanuel Kant, the Italian Cesare Beccaria, the Frenchmen Montesquieu, Rousseau, and Voltaire, and the Americans Benjamin Franklin and Thomas Jefferson, among dozens of others. These *philosophes*, as they were called, preached ethics and free trade, tolerance and universalism, democracy and revolution, human dignity and humane punishment for criminals. While most of these figures did not abandon their belief in God, they relegated God to the austere and impersonal role of Grand Architect of the universe, while they moved to the forefront of their concerns the radical and progressive improvement of human society, and employed reason, science, and political freedom as the vehicles to get us there.

If we enjoy the fruits of science and medicine and a lifespan of seventy-five years, if we have come to cherish liberty and the concept of rights, if we enjoy a skeptical approach to life and value the free mind—in short, if we are willing to defend our modern way of life, with all its pitfalls, challenges, and tragedies—then we need to thank the philosophers, scientists, inventors, and artists too of the era of the European Enlightenment.

An appreciation of the Enlightenment is directly relevant to us as Ethical Culturists also, for Ethical Culture and its humanism are assuredly children of the Enlightenment. Felix Adler was educated in the best German universities, which in the nineteenth century were the intellectually freest and most proficient in the world, and resonated with the spirit of such Enlightenment figures as Hegel and Kant. Indeed, Adler was an indirect disciple of Kant, and his Ethical Culture, his primary emphasis on ethics, and his attack on traditional religion were built on broadly Kantian principles. In its commitment to ethics, dignity, democracy, free inquiry, universalism, and reason, Ethical Culture has remained loyal to the legacy and spirit of the Enlightenment.

Despite its glories, the Enlightenment is under deep attack today as it has been for at least the last twenty years. There are even those who believe that it was a grand historical mistake, and in some unimaginable way argue the world would have been better off had it never occurred. The attack on the Enlightenment is most evident in academia and among intellectual social critics, but, as is often the case, what goes on in the ivory tower often parallels what transpires in the culture as a whole, and even plays a role in precipitating cultural attitudes.

The attack on the Enlightenment is manifested in the so-called culture wars that have been raging in the universities. Should students study and revere only the classical texts of "dead, white, European males" who were primarily Enlightenment figures, or should they study in addition, or instead, the texts of writers from the non-Western world? More importantly, which texts are more worth studying, and how would we know whether they are or are not? The attack on the Enlightenment is manifested in a renewed respect given to religion, and to those beliefs that fall short of rational criteria. Fifty years ago, many educated people in the West would have looked at religion as a medieval superstition and a relic of the premodern age. Even if they would not have said so, they would have felt sympathy for Voltaire's call, *"ecrasez l'infame"*—"erase the infamous thing." Today in the name of tolerance, we feel a need to abide sincerely rendered points of view no matter how counterfactual or, from a rational point of view, preposterous they may be.

In the West, equality, including equality between the sexes, is a salient Enlightenment value. "Equal pay for equal work" easily rolls from our lips. But when we confront women in Muslim countries who wear the veil and profess that they choose to do so as an authentic expression of their cultural and religious traditions and beliefs, what happens to our commitment to gender equality? Perhaps a confidence that we Westerns would have had fifty years ago is thrown off balance when we encounter deep-rooted cultures that are not Western and never passed through the liberalizing screen of the Enlightenment. The Western Enlightenment project is forced to question its own premises when confronted with what has come to be known as "cultural relativism."

And the attack on the Enlightenment is manifest in disillusionment with science. Fifty years ago, science was applauded as a messiah that drove progress and would improve life for all, as it had for three hundred years. But with the piling high of toxic waste, global warming, and nuclear weapons and debris that will be around forever, science has fallen off its pedestal. So little regard is there for the importance of science and its truths that we even now in 2003 have a president of the United States, George W. Bush, who claims to be a "creationist" and does not believe in the theory of evolution, even though evolution is one of the foundational pillars and principles of modern science on which the scaffolding of virtually all contemporary science is built. Some in this country may applaud it; for most others, it is probably a matter of indifference. Some believe in evolution, others in creationism, just as some prefer chocolate ice cream while others favor pistachio. It's just a matter of taste and opinion all the way down. A blanket of tolerance, or one might argue "false tolerance," trumps any claim to learned authority and knowledge, scientific or otherwise.

Some see in the attack on the Enlightenment a devaluing of knowledge and learning generally; a devaluation of ideas and facts and their replacement by opinions; and the transformation of politics into culture and learning into a form of entertainment, authority into celebrity, and the pursuit of objective knowledge into subjective feelings, with all of these changes blessed by a mantra of tolerance.

Why the disillusionment with the Enlightenment? Why the attack?

There are two main sources—one historical, demographic, and factual; the other intellectual.

Critics make an interesting and important observation. While white, Christian, European men of the seventeenth and eighteenth centuries were professing universalism, equality, tolerance, justice, freedom, humanity, the dignity of human beings, and all those enlightened values, they were at the same time conquering the world, enslaving nonwhite people, subjugating women, with few exceptions despising Jews, and otherwise engaging in imperialism, colonialism, and genocide. Indeed it is true. Virtually all the luminaries the Enlightenment we can evaluate by our standards as racist, male chauvinist, anti-Semitic bigots.

When it came to women, the men of the Enlightenment equated humanity with the capacity for reason, and women, they argued, did not have enough of it. Hence, the defense of continued patriarchy and male dominance. The amiable David Hume and the ethically obsessed rationalist Immanuel Kant, in their correspondences, had vile things to say about Africans. Voltaire was a polemical anti-Semite, and Thomas Jefferson, who penned the immortal words that "all men are created equal," at the same time owned, bought, and sold human beings who happened to have come from Africa and have dark skin.

In order to seal their point, those who despair of the Enlightenment will pose the following question: Which was the most highly educated, rational, enlightened society of the twentieth century? The land that cherished Goethe and loved Beethoven? The answer is midcentury Germany. And what were the fruits of all this rationalism, high culture, education, science, and technology? The fruits of all this, they conclude, was the creation of a cult of death, wherein science, education, reason, philosophy, technology, and bureaucracy were marshaled in the service of creating killing factories dedicated to systematically murdering with greatest efficiency the largest number of people in the quickest period of time at the least cost. Where does the Enlightenment lead? The Enlightenment leads to and ends at Auschwitz.

But how could this be? How could Thomas Jefferson look into the face of a black man and not quite see a human being? How could this contradiction abide?

Here we need to take an intellectual turn for a moment. The great mistake of the Enlightenment, so its critics argue, is that it dedicated itself to that belief that there is some kind of objective truth out there that we can discover through the dispassionate use of our reason. Moreover, the Enlightenment was hung up on abstract concepts, such as universalism, which have no real existence. The Enlightenment preached ideals that don't exist in the real world, and therefore was blind to those concrete facts of people's lives that motivate them. For example, the Enlightenment taught respect for "humanity in general" while overlooking the fact that there is no such thing as a "human being in general," or a universal human being, just as there is no such thing as a flower in general. There are only French people, Italians, Africans, Jews, etc. By glorifying an abstract ideal that doesn't truly exist, the men of the Enlightenment equated that ideal with themselves, the dominant group of white, educated, Christian, European men. The ideal standard became their standard for what was excellent, indeed superior. By contrast all other types, be they women, blacks, Jews, or whatever, were deemed by varying degrees to be inferior to those professed standards of excellence. Behind the rationale of universal values, there resides a justification for male dominance, imperialism, the derogation of all people who fall short of European ideals. Despite its stated pretension of universal humanity and equality based on that universal humanity, the high-minded values of the Enlightenment really function as a mask to hide the power of the interests of those putting forward those ideals. Ask a French sculptor in Paris in 1780 to make a bust of a "human being in general," an ideal category that is not found in reality, and the chances are that his bust will look very much like a French *man*. He will simply identify the ideal type with himself, thus setting in motion a hierarchy that implies that all others are lesser and inferior types.

The intellectual basis of this argument is that there is no such thing as objective truth or even objective facts that are somehow outside of the interests of those who are proclaiming those facts. All statements of facts, it is maintained, are really made in order to push forward the power interests of those who are making them. There are no universal truths, only socially created assertions of power masquerading as universal truths. There is a feminist adage in this regard that says "objectivity is really 'male subjectivity.'" So when Jefferson proclaimed "all men are created equal," what he really meant was "men like us—those who share our values, our skin color, our privilege, our habits, and our way of life," and not "the other."

This unmasking of the pretensions of Enlightenment is propelled by facts on the ground and the experiences of other people and other cultures that we have. We truly live now in a multicultural world in which we bump up against people who not Western. What makes this contact different from the eighteenth and ninetieth centuries is that we are confronting non-Western peoples not as subordinates or slaves, but as equals who are challenging the presumptions of the West by claiming that their cultural values are not only different from ourselves but are as authentic as ours. Who in the United States before

September 11, 2001, even thought of the Muslim world? But now we can't help but think of it, and take it very seriously.

This challenge coming from the non-Western world is essentially new, and it is a cause for us in the West to reflect on our basic values. Such reflection has no doubt created a crisis of self-confidence that the West has had in itself and in the Enlightenment.

One response to the challenge coming from the realities of multicultural-ism is the growth of tolerance in the face of diversity. To a great extent, this has been a very good thing. Americans, I believe, are really trying hard to overcome their long-standing prejudices, and I think there are really tangible successes. It is no longer in good form to make fun of fat people or people with handi-caps, or to enjoy circus freak shows. No longer could a Father Coughlin spew his gutter anti-Semitism to three million avid radio listeners, and the Ku Klux Klan, once an organization of three million people, can today claim barely three thousand. I, for one, believe that the mainstream reaction to Muslims in America after 9/11 could have been much worse had it not been for the work of the so-called "cultural Left" and its often derided commitment to "politi-cal correctness." The noted American philosopher Richard Rorty has written that the cultural Left, with its emphasis on tolerance for diversity, has helped to "reduce sadism" in American life, and I think he is right. To some extent I concede that the attack on the Enlightenment and presumed superiority of its values growing out of the West have been chastened and softened as a result of our unavoidable encounter with people who are different. And to some extent I admit that that has been a good thing. But only to an extent.

The question I ask is, to what extent do we take the value of tolerance? At what point does a commitment to tolerance morph into a position in which you stand for nothing at all? At what point do we conclude that there are no universal values, that all values are really local values, and accede to a cultural relativism in which all things are permissible in its name?

If my Enlightenment-derived morality causes me to oppose the death pen-alty, am I to conclude that it is appropriate for me to oppose it in the West, but ignore it when it is applied to Muslims by Muslims on the grounds that Islamic law allows it and it has always been a part of Muslim culture? What about the amputation of limbs for certain crimes? Is this a matter of cruel and degrad-ing punishment when applied in the West, but acceptable in the Muslim world if a case can be made that it is part of Muslim practice going back fourteen hundred years?

When it comes to women's equality, am I to accept all forms of oppression of women because that oppression has been time honored and sanctioned as an authentic part of a traditional culture, even when women themselves voluntarily accede to it? When it comes to distinctive headgear probably, wearing veils maybe, but barring women from work and assigning them to the home exclusively to be uneducated breeding machines, no, my universalism does not accept that. My commitment to universal values, to Enlightenment values, proclaims that all people want and need to have enough autonomy in life to make their own choices; all people want to be free of coercion and free of gratuitous pain inflicted upon them. The arguments for cultural relativism and for tolerance for me do not extend so far as to violate what I believe to be universally true.

Placing myself at variance with some academic colleagues, I continue to believe in the Enlightenment project and its values of reason, rights, dignity, equality, and justice as universal values that in some sense are binding on all people. Clearly different cultures will express these values differently, but in some sense they remain in principle the same. This is sometimes referred to as "pluralism." In short, I believe in tolerance and I believe in respect for diversity, but not without limits. Although it is very unpopular to say so these days, I believe that some ways of life are better than others. And ways of life in which people preserve a range of autonomy, in which they have the freedom to remain in a community or leave it, are better than a way of life in which people are the objects of authoritarianism, coercion, and the infliction of unwanted pain—even if these realities are sanctioned by the cultures of which they are a part.

Those who condemn the Enlightenment and its universalism and its abstractions make at least two mistakes. While it is true that the universal values of humanity and equality professed by the men of the Enlightenment may have served in part as a mask to deny those very principles to those who were not like them, this is not all that those principles have done. Jefferson, who proclaimed that all men are created equal and then, as a conflicted hypocrite, violated that principle by keeping slaves, did not therefore invalidate the importance and inspirational power of the very principle he proclaimed. Those black people and women whom Jefferson excluded from his democracy were able to use his very own words to agitate for the freedom and equality that he himself had denied them. And people everywhere for generations have used that sturdy Enlightenment ideal that "all men are created equal" to argue for their freedom and equality wherever they may be. The principle has a power to transcend its own application in any historical period. Indeed, despite the claims of cultural relativists, when people find themselves oppressed, they will argue against their oppression using terms of freedom, equality, and justice that are very much like those first articulated by the creators of the European Enlightenment, for indeed I would argue that those values are universal.

The second mistake that those who knock the Enlightenment make is the assumption that cultures are somehow monolithic, that there is a Muslim culture, or an African culture, or a Latino or Jewish culture. But this is assuredly a naïve, romantic, and false understanding of what a culture is. Cultures are not monolithic phenomena. Rather they are products of what Cornel West calls "radical hybridity." Culture is a dynamic, not a static reality. There are Muslims to whom enlightenment values are foreign, and others who accept and applaud them. In African tribal cultures, there are women who will submit to female genital mutilation as an acceptable initiation rite into their community, and there are other women who will attempt to escape it and condemn it as a brutal, barbaric expression of patriarchy. In my class at the United Nations University for Peace, there was a Pakistani student who fully supported the program of human rights and was particularly upset about the way women are treated in his country. Was he less of a Pakistani, or not a real Muslim, because he held these views? We should not be so quick to say so.

My own view is that we in the West may have given away too much in the name of tolerance, and that by holding on to the values of equality, justice, and universal dignity and rights as we understand them, we may actually have more allies in other cultures than we initially realize.

We live in a world in which political power in this country and elsewhere is increasingly in the hands of religious literalists, fundamentalists, and fanatics, and it isn't OK. And we should not be afraid to say so. We live in a world in which even educated people believe in alien abductions and astrology over astronomy and all kinds of related irrational nonsense, and it isn't OK. And we should not be afraid to say so. We live a society in which the middle class is dwindling, the rich are increasingly privileged, and economic justice is in short supply, whether one is white or black or Latino, male or female. We live in a world in which two billion people subsist on less than two dollars a day, and it isn't getting better, and it isn't OK. We live in a world in which millions are infected with AIDS, slavery flourishes in Africa and Asia, women are bought and sold as part of vast economic sex trade, children are condemned to drudgery as lifelong indentured servants, and barbaric wars rage on. These moral evils remain evil regardless of the cultures that perpetrate them and regardless of the cultures of those who suffer them. In order to create a moral world, we need to reclaim a sturdy foundation of universal justice and equality, and the universal dignity of all human beings, and state it out loud without apology and with confidence.

If we are to care about these conditions, and long to see them overcome, then we need to rededicate ourselves to the enlightened ideals on which the modern world has been built: to knowledge, to freedom, to basic human rights, to justice, to equality, to dignity, to those universal values that make for human decency, even nobility. Not for some people, but for all.

January 2003

Religion, Ethnicity, Identity, And Ethical Culture

In the years since the assault on the World Trade Center and Pentagon, the feelings I had on the day of the attack have been confirmed: the collective psyche of Americans has been indelibly changed. Whether fear of continued terrorist attacks on American soil is hyped for political purposes or not, the attacks have brought a continuous low-level anxiety into American society, which, of course, is exactly what terrorism is designed to do.

Why elements of Islam have emerged at this time to engage in warfare with the West can be explained by its own specific causes, which are open to ongoing debate. It's a crucial debate to have. But I want to discuss a much larger phenomenon, which reaches out to touch not only Islam but other world religions as well. The phenomenon I want to examine with you shapes American society also, and therefore reflection on it, I think, is worthy of our effort.

Islam is not the only religion today in which violence is committed in the name of religion. In India, Hindus have unleashed terrible assaults on Muslims, who comprise about 15 percent of India's population and have a history in that country going back many centuries. In Sri Lanka, the peace has been dashed, and a horrible civil war between the Hindu Tamil minority in that country and the Buddhist majority has flared up again in a place that visitors used to refer to as a paradise. Hizbollah, an Islamist Shiite group in Lebanon, assaults Israel with its arsenal of thirteen thousand missiles. In Gaza, Hamas, a Sunni Islamic group, lobs its generally ineffective but continuous stream of missiles into central Israel. On the West Bank, fanatic Jewish extremists have essentially held hostage the more moderate Israeli majority in reaching a mediated peace agreement with the Palestinians, and still attack Palestinians in the their midst with impunity. In Iraq, despite disclaimers that the violence has morphed into a civil war, Shiite militias kill Sunnis and vice versa with incredible ferocity. In Nigeria, the largest country in Africa, sporadic violence occasionally flares up between Muslims in the north and Christians in the south, and on and on.

If we broaden the character of group violence beyond religion to include ethnic strife, the list gets much longer. In the past fifteen years, we have heard about the Serbian genocide against the Bosnian Muslims, eight hundred thousand Tutsis slaughtered by Hutus in Rwanda, and a quarter of a million Arab Muslims killing non-Arab Darfurians in Sudan. And these are just the mass killings that make it into the news. They are merely the tip of the iceberg.

The violence of the Cold War, which pitted the Soviet Union against the United States and which was pursued through hot wars carried on by proxies in Latin America, Africa, and Asia, has, of course, disappeared with the end of the Soviet Union. Yet no sooner did we see the end of that forty-five-year bilateral strife, with nuclear annihilation hanging over our heads, than we see the emergence of religiously and ethnically based violence.

We can ask, what is going on here? What conditions and what ideas enable this to happen? Though, as mentioned, each specific conflict has its own dynamics, we can well ask whether there is a common denominator to warfare done in the name of one's religion or ethnic group. I want to answer that question by bringing it home to American society and what has been going on in our society for the past forty years or so. Though the United States has not experienced ethnic or religious violence coming from within American, we have become very divided along the lines of religion, especially, and ethnicity, as witnessed in the backlash against immigrants who are coming here.

To some extent, what we are experiencing here, I believe, has application elsewhere in the world.

Up until about forty years ago, and before the emergence of the black power movement, the reigning ideology of American identity was that of the "melting pot." One came to America as an immigrant, and for the most part left one's Old World identity behind. Your ethnicity would melt into a new American identity, which would bear scant resemblance to where you came from and the habits of the past. What black power did was to expose the "melting pot" as a masked form of Anglo dominance to which minorities had to conform and which for blacks, by virtue of their skin color, was an impossible and humiliating goal.

In our time, the ideology of the melting pot has been greatly challenged by the ideology of what has come to be called "diversity" or "multiculturalism." What has spurred the popularity of multiculturalism has certainly been the meteoric wave of new immigrants in the past fifteen years or so, the largest such wave since the last great influx of Eastern Europeans between 1881 and 1926, the time when my mother's parents and my father came over. This time the immigrants come from more exotic places, such as India, Pakistan, and Korea, and have darker skins, as is the case with South Asians and Latinos, who make up the largest group. Today, in California, with a population of more than thirty-three million people, non-Latino Caucasians are a minority. The complexion of America is certainly turning darker, and with new immigrants come new ethnic folkways and habits, languages, and religions.

Western European nations, which, unlike America, have historically not been countries made up of immigrants, are also experiencing new waves of immigration from Asia, the Middle East, and Africa. This is totally new in the European experience and challenges each of those countries to develop new frameworks and policies. It has caused them to redefine the notion of their national identities. Each country is grasping for its own solutions of how to deal with the rapid influx of minorities in their midst. Some of the minorities are very large. It is estimated that one half of all residents who now call London home were born outside of England, and in France, 10 percent of the population is Muslim. Riding on the Paris subway is now almost indistinguishable from riding the New York subways.

It is the brute fact of people from different cultures now living side by side that has helped spur the emergence of the doctrine of multiculturalism, and has made it necessary.

I want to speak for a while about multiculturalism, because I must confess I harbor a deep-rooted ambivalence about multiculturalism, and I am troubled because I think it has been, and is, the spawning ground for some ominous problems that beg for much more thorough examination.

At its best, multiculturalism has been a very good thing. It has attempted to overcome negative and bigoted stereotypes of people from ethnic and religious groups other than one's own, through fostering understanding of other cultures and thereby making them seem less alien, and therefore less threatening. At its best, it has generated at least tolerance and sometimes genuine acceptance and appreciation across ethnic and religious lines.

I have seen it in action. I teach very gifted students in the Hunter College honors program. My class of young people are amazingly ethnically diverse, with Russian, Uzbek, Ethiopian, Indian, Haitian, and Egyptian young people, among others, representing an almost equal diversity of religions. It is quite common to see in the same class yarmulkes and hejabs as well as standard Western dress. What impresses me greatly, and I find tremendously satisfying, is that these students seem to take it all in stride. They seem relaxed with the environment of diversity and, as best as I can tell, they see it as normal and take it for granted. I think it is the way we would want it to be.

But I believe that there is a flip side to the ideology of multiculturalism that is not good. If multiculturalism has succeeded significantly in banishing negative stereotyping of ethnic groups, it has also accomplished something else that I think sends us on a slippery slope toward danger.

On the negative side, multiculturalism has created a general fetish with group identity, whether ethnic identity or religious. It has encouraged people, both in the United States and beyond, to define themselves by a single identity, be it Latino, Muslim, evangelical, Jewish, Hindu, black, or whatever. If you ask people who they are, I think it is increasingly common for people to identify themselves by their ethnicity or their religion, and my point is that there is something in the air that encourages them to do so. When this type of self-identity becomes a person's dominant or even *exclusive* way of understanding himself or herself, it by necessity must frame how a person sees others, that is, in mutually exclusive terms.

I need to explain what I mean in greater detail. Humanist that I am, I do not think that ethnicity will ever disappear. It may change its substance and its form, but I don't think that it will go away. I believe that it is simply not possible for people to build a sense of their inner identity around the abstract concept of universal humanity, or of a "person in general." People need to build their identities around concretes, which are going to be specific, indeed culturally or ethnically specific; around specific language, customs, food preferences, stories, a style of humor, etc. I think it is an anthropological given that people are socialized within smaller groups, which helps to mold their identity and give them a sense of themselves.

We live in a time, however, when I think that this fascination with ethnic group and religious identity has gone over the top and has been overly romanticized. At times, it seems as if there is a mad rush for people to jump on the ethnic and religious bandwagon. There is a certain empowerment and enchantment with the notion of group identity, be it Italian, Irish, Puerto Rican, Native American, or whatever, especially if you come from a historically oppressed group. But when this sense of group or ethnic identity is raised to the level of one's exclusive identity, I think that it partakes of a fallacy that can, and at times of inflammatory political circumstances does, turn malignant and violent.

I need to explain what I mean. To the extent to which a person feels that his or her ethnic or religious identity is his or her exclusive identity, to that extent he or she is seeing the world from the perspective of self over against an "alien other." The "me" and the "not me." My exclusive identity as an evangelical, a Jew, a Muslim, an African American, or whatever sets the stage for drawing the lines between those who are like me, part of the in group, and those who are irredeemably outside my circle and different from me and those like me. The lines of exclusivity have been drawn, and when political tensions increase, in the worst cases, conflict and violence between religious and ethnic groups can be the result.

My point is that there is something about our times, ideologically, that impresses upon many people the need to couch their identity in these exclusive ethnic and religious terms.

My argument is that there is something crude in this fetish over religious and ethnic identity that is not true to the way in which people are actually socialized in the modern world. For such people there seems to be the understanding that their ethnic identity is sort of a cosmic given, something they need to discover and grow unto as a type of self-realization. But I think that this is true only to a small extent, and is primarily untrue.

Closer to reality, is the fact that identity is not monolithic. It is not exclusively this or that. It cannot be reduced to a single element, be it ethnic or religious. The truer reality is that the identity of any single individual is itself highly complex and multiple. We carry within us many possible identities, *and it is within our power to choose which elements we want to play up and which we want to play down.*

It is sort of instructive, and I think liberating, to engage in a meditation in which we ask ourselves, who am I? And the honest answer is that we are not any one thing, but a complex of many things. So, using myself as an example, what are the elements of my identity? They are at least the following:

I am a male Caucasian, American of East European ancestry, a Jew, humanist, agnostic, Ethical Culturist, middle class, nonconformist, progressive, heterosexual with a commitment to the rights of gays. I am an English speaker with an appreciation for foreign languages. I am a religious leader, academic, university professor, writer, reader, public speaker, insatiable schmoozer, scholar, social critic, internationalist, traveler, bicyclist, camper, aficionado of the wilderness, an activist, community organizer, human rights advocate, civil libertarian, a pragmatist who is also a dreamer and idealist, father, grandfather, brother, husband, and on and on. My point is that my identity is not reducible to one thing, but a consortium of many things. But most importantly, within a broad range it is within my power to choose to put any of these identifiers in the forefront of my identity and to place others in the background. In other words, my identity and yours is not a determinism that you or I are fated to live out, but it is, moreover, a matter of choice. Our identity, in great measure, is not something that we solely inherit. It is rather something that we, within broad limits, create. So if you ask me, which community do I belong to? The answer is I belong to many communities, and I have the power to cross lines and move from one to the other. Certain types of multicultural or communitarian think-ing that are very popular these days proclaim that one ethnic identity must be the principle, dominant, or exclusive identity that molds a person's values and ethics and a sense of the self. True, the ethnic or religious culture that one is born into may exert a strong influence on who the person is. But to be an influ-ence is not the same thing as to determine a person's identity. A person still has a range of choices as to how he or she wishes to identify himself or herself.

But there is a second hidden fallacy in the notion that a cultural or ethnic community into which a person is born has to dominate or determine his or her identity. Just as an individual's identity is multiple and complex, even more so is that true of so-called cultures, either ethnic or religious. From the outside other cultures, be they black, Jewish, Sikh, Muslim, or evangelical Christian, might all seem uniform and monolithic. But this kind of reductionism is silly and it's wrong. All one has to do is enter into that so-called community, and what usually becomes strikingly dramatic is how diverse from the inside such ethnic or cultural communities really are. In fact, so diverse, that their members are often at each other's throats. If, for example, a person says he or she is a Jew, Latino, or Muslim, that, in and of itself, says very little about that person's values.

If someone is identified as a member of the Jewish "community," this alone tells me almost nothing about him or her, certainly nothing about which I can feel confident. Is that person a pious believer or an atheist? Left wing or right wing, or politically apathetic? That person could hold an almost infinite range of values across a very wide spectrum. Is that person a Hasidic Jew whose entire life is to live by divine commands and who attempts to close himself off from the world and outsiders as much as possible? Is that person a modern orthodox Jew who lives by divine command but also embraces large elements of the secular world? Is that person a Reform or Conservative Jew, or is that person a contemporary Israeli whose identity is national and who also is antireligious? Or is that person totally secular, someone whose Jewish identity is far in the background and whose commitment to radical, left-wing politics means everything? Or is that person a Sephardic Jew from North Africa, with customs far apart from anything familiar to Westerners? Anyone who knows anything about the Jewish world knows that it is incredibly and often acrimoniously diverse, with hundreds of hairsplitting options, many of which have little in common with each other across a whole spectrum of options. In other words, to say that a person is shaped predominantly by his or her ethnic culture or religion is to overlook the wide range of choices within that culture.

If I know a person is a member of the Latino community, that again tells me nothing about that the person. Is he a wealthy right-wing Cuban businessman in Miami, or a Salvadoran *campesino* with a strong indigenous heritage; a fascist in the Argentine military or a communist revolutionary in Peru? Is that person a lapsed Roman Catholic in Mexico, or an enthusiastic Pentecostal in Guatemala, or a secularist in Uruguay? Or is that person a third-generation

United States citizen with a Latino surname, living in New Jersey, married to a Norwegian, and not speaking Spanish? Latinos all. But to conclude that therefore they comprise a common culture or share common values in all but the most attenuated sense is counterfactual and preposterous.

Even people in traditional or tribal cultures in undeveloped parts of the world cannot be reduced to or be assumed to have common values. In a particular African tribe you may find women who will accept genital circumcision as a necessary way to affirm tribal identity and become marriageable. And in the same culture and "community" you will find women who will denounce it as an unacceptable form of patriarchy and as a form of barbarism, and they will attempt to escape it.

Perhaps more relevant today is the question of Muslim identity, which we in the West tend to see through ideological and monolithic lenses. There are 1.3 billion Muslims in the world, and the diversity in that population is immense in every which way. Sure, there is a fringe of violent extremists and terrorists who win adherents. Some Muslims are terrorists and they are dangerous and the threat is real, and we need to deal with it. We know that and it needs to be taken most seriously. But we make a great mistake if we take the part for the whole. It is contrary to fact to see Muslim people exclusively through their religious identities. Indeed, the majority of the two million to seven million Muslims in America are not mosque affiliated, and there is no reason to believe that their religious identity is the primary way in which they see themselves or is of very great significance to them.

In France, where problems with the large Muslim minority make news, the situation on the ground may not be as bad as the headlines suggest. A vast majority of France's Muslims support France's republican values and care little for jihadism. A 2004 poll reported that 90 percent of France's Muslims said that gender equality was important to them. Sixty-eight percent support the separation of church and state, and French Muslims attend mosque at no higher rates than Catholics and Protestants go to church, or Jews to synagogue. The government's 2004 law to ban head scarves created a lot of controversy in the international press, but French Muslims have long seen it as a marginal issue, and 71 percent reported in 2004 that it was getting too much attention. There were riots among Muslim youths in the Parisian suburbs in November, 2005, but those riots had nothing to do with yearnings for a worldwide caliphate and everything to do with France's socioeconomic problems. My point of these few examples is that if a person says he or she is Muslim, it doesn't necessarily mean that religion is the sole or dominant element that determines who he or she is or what he or she values or how he or she acts. If we think that it does, then we have cut out all Muslims with the same cookie cutter. We have established crude boundaries between us and them, the lines have been drawn, and conflict becomes all the more possible. Of course, Islamic extremists have done exactly the same thing. They are obsessed with the evils of the West, which reveals a type of enduring colonial mind-set. Muslim terrorists could hardly exist without the West. When Osama bin Laden demonizes "the West," I sometimes wonder, who is he talking about, Che Guevara? Albert Einstein? Leonardo da Vinci? Martin Luther King? Adolf Hitler? Marilyn Monroe? Westerners all, but with nothing in common. It is reductionism on all sides that sets the stage for an "us or them" mentality and for civilizational violence.

Parenthetically, I believe that when dealing with Islamic terrorism, we would do much better in putting less focus on the Islamic religion, which can be used to support both violence and tolerance, and much more focus on the political and economic realities that let demagogues exploit religion for nefarious purposes. For example, Indonesia, which long had a more tolerant variant of Islam, was beginning to move in a more anti-US, jihadist direction. But that movement changed course after the generous and effective relief effort launched by the United States in the wake of the tsunami.

A far better understanding, and one that is in short supply today, is to recognize, as my teacher of many years ago, Cornel West, once said, that every culture, every ethnic and religious group, is a product of "radical hybridity." Especially in this globalized world, where instant communication, the Internet, and global trade have caused cultures to interpenetrate each other, there is no such thing as a pure culture. Every cultural identity, and every individual identity, is a hybrid, a mixture, which opens up an array of options.

Where does all this lead? I think that in these times, which have made a fetish of ethnic and religious identity, there is real saving value in recognizing that reducing people to their ethnicity or religion primarily and seeing ourselves and them through that lens can be dangerous. Far better to embrace a cosmopolitan ideal. Far better to embrace and promote an idea that people in great measure have the freedom to forge their own identities out of their own experiences and choices. Far better to embrace the idea that people and groups are highly differentiated and complex, and that we have the freedom to move across boundaries of ethnicity and religion to build relations with people on the basis of shared values and interests. Seeing that the boundaries of ethnicity and religion are not impregnable walls but can be made porous, and should be, can be a true foundation for mutual cooperation and peace.

In closing, I would like to say that as small as it is, I think Ethical Culture has gotten it right. Its philosophy has kept alive the ideal that people need to move outside the boundaries of ethnicity and religion to appreciate and embrace the universal humanity that resides in all people. The richest life, Ethical Culture proclaims, is lived in the zone between the universal and the particular. By keeping that ideal alive, we work to break down the walls that divide us. And in doing so, we can be a voice for peace at a time and in a world that sorely needs it.

September 2006

Religion And Religious Violence

September 11, 2001, was perhaps the single most horrifying day in American history. It initiated an open-ended war on terrorism that is still with us, and it is serving as the Bush administration's justification for another war that our nation will probably soon initiate.

These are frightening times that have brought near to home an enemy that two years ago was at most marginal to our thinking and our lives. The times we are in raise many murky questions that leave us unsettled.

We in the West have been rudely awakened to the world of Islam and the violence and hatred against us that are perpetrated in its name. More than one sixth of humanity is Muslim, yet we Westerners know virtually nothing about Islam. Ignorance, of course, breeds fear. It raises questions of whether Islam is characterologically a violent religion or not. Whether it is intractable. How broadly and deeply hatred of the West permeates the Islamic world. Whether Islam and democracy are incompatible. Whether peace and mutual coexistence are possible or whether a protracted clash of civilizations is just beginning to heat up.

How we answer these questions will either cause us to feel deeply fretful and anxious about the future or will enable us as a nation to plan new strategies and serve as a basis for optimism and hope.

As crucial as these questions are, I want to focus on a broader question in order to deal indirectly with the issues above. It is a question that underlies these distinctive questions that we may be asking about Islam. The broader issue I wish to discuss is how religion relates to violence in general and terror in particular.

I have often suggested that one needs to be cautious in talking about "religion" in general, as if there were such a thing. There are multitudes of religions, interpreted in countless ways by billions of people. They differ remarkably in beliefs, practices, values, and everything else. Moreover, the religions are often expressions of ways of life, of cultural modes of being, which cannot be organized so neatly into discrete packages we call "religion" as we think of it in the West. To talk about "religion" is to discuss an abstraction. Nevertheless, there may be distinctive modes of religious thinking that cut across the different religions, especially when religious thinking becomes extremist. It is that religious extremist mind-set that I want to focus on.

Before I do, I can't resist mentioning a dangerous condition in this country that has permitted religious extremism here at home to gain more influence than leaves me comfortable.

For the past two decades American society has had a love affair with religion. There has been a great deal of anxiety about moral and social breakdown in this country—drugs, crime, abortion, divorce, sexual permissiveness, teenage pregnancy, pornography, failing schools, etc. Though there are undoubtedly many social problems we face, anxiety over these issues has been fueled by conservative and ultraconservative leaders who have told us that religion provides the only cure. The underlying problem is secular, godless values—secular humanism, if you like—for which a return to God and religion is the only response.

This proreligious propaganda has resulted in a popular belief that religion can only be good. In turn, this sunny view of religion has allowed right-wing religious demagogues in our country to make the most moronic and vile pronouncements, clothe them in the sanctity of religion, and thereby leave them almost invulnerable to public criticism and attack. So a few years ago, when Pat Robertson on his TV show prayed that a hurricane be diverted from the shores of North Carolina and strike instead the evil precincts of New York City, nary a criticism was raised. Without much reflection, such a hateful pronouncement is something that no one over the age of six ought to believe. Yet people such as Robertson are considered to be serious religious thinkers after whom the media fawn, and who therefore are deemed worthy participants in the public debate on a whole range of issues.

George W. Bush's faith-based initiative, which would give tax money directly to churches to do their social services, is the political high-water mark of this notion that religion is totally good and the savior of our social ills. But imagine the unthinkable consequences if this ill-conceived program had been in place before September 11. There is good evidence that certain mosques were being used as fronts to raise and then ferry donations to support terrorist groups in the Middle East such as bin Laden's. Had this program been in place, it would have meant that US government money—your tax money and mine—would have been used to underwrite those terrorist operations directed at destroying American society itself. We would have helped bankroll that very assault. Charitable choice has received a lot of opposition, in great measure from the churches themselves, but it remains a very dangerous force.

Just this morning I read that the George W. Bush administration is giving demonstration grants to Pat Robertson's Operation Blessing, which will then redistribute these funds directly to his various religious institutions. Robertson, in addition to being a dangerous bigot who has written about international conspiracies involving Jewish bankers, at first opposed charitable choice when he learned that federal monies would be given to Muslims, the Unification Church, and other religious groups, not merely evangelical Christians. Clearly Robertson is prepared to sell his convictions for thirty pieces of silver, and it seems without too many pangs of conscience.

There is an effort to Christianize America, or at a minimum to religionize this country, an effort that comes from many sources and entails many strategies. It has shifted the lines of religious allegiance so that Jews, Catholics, and Protestants, who three decades ago were mutually inimical, have been brought together on their conservative wings to form an alliance against the forces of liberalism and secularism. At the heart of this nefarious campaign is the concerted effort to destroy the Jeffersonian wall of separation between church and state.

I can identify three major sectors of American society that in an overlapping way sustain this campaign. At the popular level there are the conservative Protestant churches, the religious Right, and their allies among conservative Catholics and Orthodox Jews. On the academic level, there are conservative intellectuals such as Richard John Neuhaus and Yale Law School's Steven Carter. Neuhaus has made the claim that since organized prayer was removed from the schools, the public square has been rendered naked of guiding values that only religion can supply. Carter has argued that religion has become marginal in American life, though from my point of view I barely know what he is talking about, since American society is simply saturated by religion.

Neuhaus and Carter have given great respectability to the argument that a secular government must, perforce, be hostile to religion, and so we badly need government to support religions, which brings me to the third group, comprised of politicians and jurists.

Three justices of the Supreme Court, Rehnquist, Scalia, and Thomas, do not believe in the separation of church and state. They are joined by noted political leaders, Joseph Lieberman among the most articulate. What these individuals affirm is a doctrine of nonpreferentialism. That means that government may actively support and financially underwrite religion as long as it does not prefer one religion over another. This doctrine overturns more than fifty years of Supreme Court reasoning on the relation of church to state. And in a major act of historical revisionism, it firmly contradiction the principles held by James Madison, the father of our Constitution, Thomas Jefferson, and the other Founding Fathers, who believed firmly that the role of the state was to preserve rights, among them life, liberty, and property, period—and not to foster divine salvation or shape morality.

It is this doctrine of nonpreferentialism that justifies such dangerous initiatives as charitable choice and school vouchers, even seemingly petty ones such as crèches and menorahs on public lands. Friends, the wall separating church from state is being aggressively torn down brick by brick, and that ominous act of destruction is fueled in the sanctuaries of the conservative churches, and I include among them broad swaths of Orthodox Judaism.

All this is sustained by a climate that sophomorically and uncritically makes the assumption that religion can be nothing but a positive resource that works only for the social good.

I trust that we humanists do not have such a sunny view of human nature or of religion, which is, by our lights, a human creation.

There are certain humanists, I realize, who are allergic to religion. I am not one of them. If religion inspires awful deeds, it also inspires very noble ones. There is simply no way one can explain the work of Martin Luther King without reference to his deep commitments in the black Baptist faith; nor Gandhi's faith and inspiration as a devout Hindu. The ability of the people of Le Chambon, a village in France, to unite to rescue imperiled Jews during World War II under the watchful eyes of the Nazis was inspired by their Protestant faith, in fact a rather fundamentalist kind.

And religious apologists will often turn on secularists with the evidence that Stalin's massacres and the Khmer Rouge's killing fields were the outgrowth of secular ideologies gone amok. Such indictment is not so readily dismissed.

But humanists have long appreciated that much of humankind's sorry history of bloodletting has been fostered by religious motives and justified by religious sanctions.

In the first century BCE, the Roman poet Lucretius said, *"Tantum religio potuit suadere malorum!"* ("How many evils does religion inspire!"). It was Voltaire who, during the European Enlightenment, declared *"Ecrasez l'infame"* ("Crush the infamous thing"), referring to the Christian church and its irrational superstitions. Such have been the rallying cries for militant atheists, rationalists, secularists, and humanists over the ages who have appreciated the destructive power of religion and ecclesiastical authority. They would point to the religious hatred and bloodletting of the Crusades, the Inquisitions, the wars of the Protestant Reformation, and a multitude of other historical and contemporary wars sanctified by religious faith. Those who have killed and died in the name of religion compose one of the sorriest of phenomena in the career of humankind. The terrorist assaults coming now with the sanctions of Islam are but the latest in the history of the malignant underside of religion.

But like apologists for religion, such antireligionists, I believe, often grossly simplify and caricature religion, in this case in order to condemn it. The story of the relationship of religion and violence is much more complex and can't be properly understood divorced from the economic and political climate in which religion finds itself and operates.

We live in a time of religiously inspired terrorism. But it needs to be mentioned that not all terrorism is religious. Much is strictly political and secular. The Shining Path guerillas in Peru engage in terror, as do the Basque separatists of Spain. The purges of Stalin and Pol Pot were not religious. Death squads in El Salvador and Brazil are not composed of religious terrorists. And many of the bombings by Americans in the Vietnam War were terroristic attempts to deter villagers from harboring the Vietcong and North Vietnamese troops. Yet the ends here, again, were political and not religious.

But what is it about religion that can and does lend itself to violence? After all, all the major faiths espouse the values of peace, brotherhood, love, and compassion as the ends toward which they reach. In the three monotheist faiths, God is a loving God whose love is to be emulated by his earthly devotees as among the highest ends and purposes of religious devotion.

While promoting the supreme values of God's goodness and human peace, the great religions, Christianity, Judaism, Islam, Hinduism, and even Buddhism, are committed to values of absolute justice and are strewn with images and myths that are saturated with conflict, violence, and war. Apparent in myths of all historical religions is the divide between believers and unbelievers, the saved and the damned, those who are blessed and those who are accursed in God's eyes. If one is so moved and committed, one can find in sacred scriptures and traditions God's justification for murder, apocalyptic strife, even genocide. We should be smart enough about human nature to know that if one has a grudge, one can always find justification within one's religious texts or traditions to act out one's anger and revenge, and do so in God's name and with God's blessing. It is this underside of religion that is smoothed over these days, and such a move is both intellectually untenable and very dangerous. Religion can be employed in the service of good or evil, and it is very misleading and wrong to deny it.

I have long been upset with what I perceive to be a dereliction of honesty by religionists who are moderate and who refuse to take responsibility for their extremists and fanatics, who do their despicable deeds in the name of those faiths. It does no good, and I believe it is too facile, for moderate Christians, Jews, and Muslims to say in the face of violence committed in the name of those religions, "These acts of violence are not really Christianity, Judaism, and Islam, because this is not what our faith teaches." Well, your faith does teach those things, and you can't so readily dismiss them.

Almost all religion exists on a continuum from liberal and tolerant to fanatic and xenophobic, and it is dishonest to glibly claim innocence by asserting that those who do evil in your name are somehow not related to your faith and that it does not justify violence. You may believe that your faith comes from a pure and perfect God. But all religion must pass through the minds, interests, and impulses of human beings, who are anything but pure and perfect. Clothing your own belief and faith in the sanctity of religion does not give the practitioner of religion a magic ticket that bootstraps him or her out of the human condition. Even if religion comes from a good God, men still interpreted and will corrupt it out of their own impulses, interests, and needs.

In this regard, we need keep in mind that Islam has no monopoly on religiously sanctioned violence. In the past fourteen hundred years, far more violence has been committed in the name of Christianity than in the name of Islam. Even today violence and terror are sanctioned by Christianity—by both the IRA and the Protestant minority in Northern Ireland. In our country, a radical fringe of the antiabortion movement justifies its killing of abortion providers in the name of a brand of fundamentalist Christianity. Much of the antigovernment militia movement, which is now happily in decline, was inspired by the so-called Christian Identity movement, a lurid anti-Semitic, antiminority cult that proclaims that Anglo-Saxons are the true chosen people and those claiming to be Jews are imposters and the descendants of Eve mating with Satan. They also hold that we need to replace the United States with a Christian republic. This was the theology behind the Aryan Nation movement in this country. It was also a creed that inspired Timothy McVeigh in his bombing of the Murrah office building in Oklahoma City in 1995. Though it received scant press coverage, McVeigh had contact with a commune called Elohim City on the Texas-Arkansas border. He read their literature. What is better known is that he was inspired by a book called the *Turner Diaries*, which served as a blueprint for the Oklahoma bombing. This book, which was a favorite of the militias, is based on Christian Identity ideology.

Historically, there has been little terrorism in the name of Judaism, in great measure because the number of Jews worldwide is very small, and for two thousand years Jews have been an imperiled minority without political power.

With modern Israel, that has changed, and we see the emergence of right-wing fanatics who kill in the name of Judaism. In 1994, Baruch Goldstein, a Brooklyn-born-and-raised doctor, entered the Muslim side of the Tomb of the Patriarchs and massacred more than thirty Muslims at prayer in Hebron on the West Bank. He is revered as a hero by many of his compatriots. Goldstein had been a follower of Rabbi Meir Kahane. In Kahane's theological notions, the modern secular state of Israel is anathema, Jewish possession of the West Bank is biblically sanctioned, and the presence of non-Jews is a humiliation. Kahane's religious vision was one of "messianic catastrophism," in which the

Messiah will come in great conflict in which Jews triumph and praise God with their successes. In short, human actions will bring cosmic results, an idea that has long been a staple of right-wing Jewish theology. Nor should we forget that Yitzhak Rabin's assassin, a young man by the name of Yigal Amir, justified his murder of the prime minister on religious grounds, stating that he had no regrets and had acted on orders from God. In part, Amir's act was sanctioned by militant rabbis, who referenced Jewish law that permits the destruction of a "pursuer" if need be to save one's life. Rabin was labeled such a pursuer on the grounds that he was willing to cede territory to the Palestinians that would put Jewish lives in danger, and a religious sanction was neatly found.

We tend to think of Hinduism as a nondogmatic, inclusive, and relatively tolerant religion. Yet for the past twenty years, Hindu nationalists have gained tremendous influence and political power in India. There has resulted an intensification of Hindu-Muslim violence and the killing of Christian missionaries in India. In 1992, thousands of Hindus mobbed the city of Ayodhya in northern India, and despite the efforts of thousands of police to stem the violence, the mob utterly destroyed the Babri Mosque, sacred to Muslims, on the grounds that the Indian god Ram was born exactly on that spot.

Buddhism is perhaps the most pacifistic of the great religions. But its record on violence is not totally clean. In Sri Lanka, Buddhist nationalism has helped sustain a lengthy and bloody civil war with the minority Hindu Tamils, who are seeking an independent state. And in what has been the most ominous of terrorist attacks in modern Japan, the Aum Shinrikyo, a Buddhist cult mixed with Christian Armageddon elements, was responsible for dropping the deadly nerve gas sarin in the Tokyo subway. That attack in 1995, which killed twelve and left over fifty-five hundred injured, some permanently, was frighteningly easy to pull off.

And now we come to Islamic terrorism. The recent list of attacks against both Islamic states themselves and the West is large and growing: from the Egyptian Islamic Group, which assassinated Sadat in 1981 and killed foreign tourists at Luxor in the 1990s, to the state-sponsored terrorism of Iran, to the Hamas and Islamic jihad groups on the West Bank, Hizbollah in Lebanon, and the incredibly brutal and terroristic civil war sustained by Islamic fundamentalists in Algeria. And then there are those directed at American targets: the first attack on the World Trade Center, in 1993, inspired by the Egyptian cleric

Sheikh Omar Abdel Rahman, who preached out of a mosque in Jersey City, an attack that paved the ground for the assault of September 11; the bombing in Riyadh, Saudi Arabia, in November 1995; the Khobar Towers near Dhahran in June 1996; the bombings of the US embassies in Tanzania and Kenya in 1998; and the USS *Cole* in Yemen in October 2000. Bin Laden's Al Qaeda group has been implicated in all of these assaults, and of course, the recent unspeakable attack on American soil.

Without creating an equivalence among all these acts of terror, are there, nevertheless, some things that the religious mind-set, when brought to extremes, bears in common across the various religions?

I believe there are:

Religion is the human preoccupation *par excellence* for focusing the mind on absolutes. Religion speaks to good and evil, insiders and outsiders, holiness and defilement—often in terms that are categorical and uncompromising. There are believers who are sanctified by God, and there are infidels and heretics who are accursed by God. And we need to remember that nothing commands like one's commanding God. The stage is set by religion for justifying hatred of the other, namely xenophobia. In religious terms, the despised outsider is not only hated by me, but by God, the Author and Governor of the universe. To expel, oppress, or kill the outsider is therefore to do God's work in his name. Religion speaks also to divine justice, which is absolute justice. While this principle can often lead to the most ennobling idealist ends, as the career of Martin Luther King has shown, the divine call to justice can also lead to the most wicked of deeds.

Religious scriptures, as mentioned, are strewn with violence, military defeat of enemies, and even genocide. Crucial to this violence is that it is *holy violence* that takes place on the cosmic plane. An expression of this violence is cosmic war, which is usually an all-or-nothing proposition.

I remember in high school reading the Greek epic the *Iliad*. You might recall that while the Greeks were battling the Trojans on the earthly plane, the gods of Olympus had their favorites. The Trojan War was going on on two levels—between the Greeks and the Trojans on the level below, and between Athena and Hera and the other gods on Olympus.

War becomes holy war when the battle you are fighting against your enemies is a battle for God's cause, the absolute cause, the eternal cause. What you are acting out on the mundane field of action is a replica of a struggle that reaches up to heaven and is sanctioned by it.

Read the Christian book of Revelation and you will see a phantasmagoria of violent images in which the followers of Christ are saved and the followers of Satan and the Antichrist are thrown into pits of fire and suffer eternal torture. These are the end times, the final judgment, when Christ, the alleged Prince of Peace, has no trouble damning unbelievers to never-ending agony. Jerry Falwell and Pat Robertson love this stuff. It is the type of scriptural authority that allows you to hate people you don't like with total impunity. With God on your side, hate can take a holiday from the sense of responsibility, self-reflection, and hesitation that hateful attitudes usually inspire in more mature individuals. Killing another human being is difficult. But if you are righteous in this extreme way, it can become a guiltless act. The more you hate in God's name, the more sanctified you become. In the biblical mentality, vengeance is often a righteous act.

In the Hebrew Bible, the book of Joshua is mainly devoted to God's demand that the Hebrews take over the land by literally wiping out entire towns and peoples. It is ethnic cleansing with divine sanction.

The most beloved of sacred Hindu epics, the Bhagavad Gita, has the God Krishna disguised as a charioteer urging King Arjuna into battle for the conquest of the world.

In times of peace, among more sophisticated and sober interpreters, these texts are read allegorically and symbolically as tools by which to spiritualize life in the service of seeking the highest.

In times of strife, oppression, and desperation, in the hands of fundamentalists, they are read not symbolically, but literally, and the consequences can be deadly. That is what fundamentalism means: religious scripture is understood literally, without allegory, without symbolism, and without humor.

Another essential component of many traditions is sacrifice, usually of an animal but sometimes of a human being. Sacrifice is an act of killing. When applied to human beings it can elide with a concept of self-sacrifice, of martyrdom made holy in response to oppression.

Religious terror on the world stage is as much symbolic as it is strategic. It is theater. The purpose is to demand attention, all the while infuriating and humiliating its victims. For the perpetrator it supplies a heady dose of the exhilaration of power in the midst of conditions that have made one relatively powerless. Its goal is to dramatically impose one's issues on the global stage, even if victory on the plane of politics is only a remote possibility.

And so this brings us to Islamic terrorism. The question of the moment is whether there is anything distinctive to Islam, beyond these generic characteristics of the fundamentalist mind-set that makes it especially incorrigible.

If we, the lay public, are confused about this, it is not our ignorance alone that breeds this confusion. Those who study Islam are sharply divided on his issue.

In one camp there are those Islamicists who will point to the fact that Islam, unlike Christianity and Judaism, never experienced the Enlightenment, which has had a secularizing and liberalizing effect. They will point out that Mohammed himself was not only a religious prophet but also an administrator and military man, and that much of the early history of Islam involves military conquest. Scholars in this camp will point out that Islam is totalistic in the sense that there is no separation between the religious and political realms. The idea of an independent secular realm in which politics can function simply doesn't exist in Islam. In Islam, since everything is religious, this ensures that force, when it is used, is used in the name of religion. They will point out that although Islam provides a secondary, though protected status for "the People of the Book," that is, Jews and Christians, those outside these faiths are labeled "unbelievers" and "infidels" and have no such protections at all. They either accept Islam or are out to death. Most scholars who have studied the "shari'a," or Islamic law, have concluded that Islamic law is incompatible with modern notions of human rights. This is because the modern idea of human rights is secular in origin, originating from social contract theory, whereas in the Islamic concept of rights, rights come only from God. All these factors and more add up to a concept of Islam that is essentially intolerant, immune to secular ideas, and antimodern.

There are those Islamicists who say otherwise. They claim that this understanding of Islam is simply too static. They will point out that Islam, like all religions, changes its contours based on political and economic circumstances and needs that have little to do with the religion itself. Christianity, throughout its history, has been virulently intolerant at times, and in other epochs has fostered tolerance. In Islam, for example, the concept of *jihad*, which means "struggle," sometimes has been interpreted as an internal spiritual struggle of the individual believer. When Islam is under political distress, *jihad* will be given a more literal and militaristic interpretation. They will point out that the Koran places great value on peace, brotherhood, and tolerance; that the spread of the faith must not be by coercion; and that there have been historical periods when Islam exhibited great tolerance toward both other Islamic sects within the faith and non-Islamic peoples. They will point to the fact that Islam is anything but monolithic. That it spans more than fifty countries and many languages and ethnic groups. That it is tremendously diverse and differs from place to place and time to time. What makes segments of the Muslim world prone to violence is not that Islam is inherently violent, but that certain economic and political circumstances allow extremism to arise, and that these circumstances are relatively new and not consigned to Islam alone. In the final analysis, Islam is what Muslims say it is. And how Islam, or any religion, is interpreted is a product of political, economic, and social factors that themselves are not religious.

Though I am not a scholar of Islam, I suspect that the second interpretation is closer to the truth. In the broadest sense, religion itself does not cause violence, but becomes violent when ignited by a felt reality of oppression and humiliation.

So to the payoff question: Are we now engaged in a war against religion? Against Islam? I believe the answer is yes, but only one virulent, extremist expression of Islam. But to say that is not enough. It is to understand that that extremist expression of Islam also has roots in historical, economic, and political discontents that are widespread in the Islamic world.

An analysis of those discontents must await another time. But I think it is generally correct to conclude that for much of the last century, there has been among Muslims a growing discontent with what is called "secular nationalism," that is, a state and society built on secular premises. It is argued that in imitation of the West, the Islamic world has tried the model of the secular state—all but a minority of Islamic countries have secular governments of some kind—but this model derived from the West has failed to deliver the goods. What it has delivered are self-seeking, corrupt, often military dictatorships that keep themselves in power while they oppress their people and subjects. And these potentates, whether in Egypt, Saudi Arabia, or previously in Iran with the shah, are kept alive by American aid for American interests.

In many ways the West has won, and the masses in many Islamic countries grow more desperate. Under such realities, there is logic in the appeal to their own Islamic roots as sources of pride and power. And those who have violent agendas can and do bend and exploit the Islamic religion for their purposes.

If the war against terrorism, which I believe must be fought, is going to be long, then the battle against the conditions of despair that serve as the context for terrorism is going to be much longer.

In the final analysis, it depends on our faith in democracy. It is a faith that people everywhere yearn for participation in the political and economic affairs by which they can govern and control their own lives. This is true in the Islamic world as well. And it must be noted that democracies seldom nurture terrorism. The antidote to terrorism is democracy.

Though it is a long, complex story, I think we as a nation need to take a harder look at the Islamic world—not just at its leadership at the top, but at its people below. We need to get to know it and the aspirations of the people who live in that world, not to exploit it or remake it in our image, but, in time, to develop a policy that will help others to govern themselves free of oppression. By so doing, we will assist in undermining the temptations that turn religion into a force for violence and hate.

October 2002

Prudes And Libertines: Politics, Religion, And Polarization

My title comes from an important, indeed superlative book entitled *American Grace: How Religion Divides and Unites Us*. The book, published in 2010 and coauthored by Robert Putnam, a professor of public policy at Harvard, is an exhaustive on-the-ground survey of American religion and its relation to social trends and to politics.

A central concern of the authors is trying to explain the degree of religiosity expressed by the American people and how religion is changing. A prevailing trend they document is how religion has waxed and waned generally since the end of World War II, and how it has done so among different sectors of the populations and within different denominations.

The authors assert that over the past fifty years, American religion has undergone, so to speak, a shock and two aftershocks. The Eisenhower years were conservative ones, and masses of Americans went to church as a matter of probity. It was what patriotic Americans did, especially in the face of godless communism. Though it is now hard to believe, in those years, the majority of Americans in the pews were Democrats and many Republicans did not attend church. But I'll get to how religious affiliation, or the lack of it, has become aligned with each of the major political parties later on. At this point, it is best for the authors to speak for themselves. They write:

> Our argument in brief is this: While change and adaptability have long been the hallmark of American religion,

over the last half century the direction and pace of change have shifted and accelerated in three seismic phases. Since the 1950s, one major shock and two aftershocks have shaken and cleaved the American religious landscape, successively thrusting a large portion of one generation in a secular direction, then in reaction thrusting a different group of the population in a conservative religious direction, and finally, in counterreaction to that first aftershock, setting yet another generation of Americans in a more secular direction. Just as an earthquake and its aftershocks can leave a deep fissure in physical terrain, so too this religious quake and its pair of aftershocks have left a deep rift in the political and religious topography of America.

And after the quiet of the Eisenhower years, what was that initial earthquake that started American religion listing and reeling and quaking? As you might have guessed, it was the 1960s, which culturally extended itself into the early '70s. It was the age of drugs, sex, and rock and roll. It was also, as you might remember, the era when some religiously radical theologians ushered in the "death of God" movement, and the query "Is God Dead?" made its stark appearance on the cover of that venerable American icon, *Time* magazine.

The impact of the 1960s on American religion was, indeed, seismic. While in the 1950s, religious seminaries were booming, by 1971, 40 percent of all clergy surveyed said that they were considering changing their profession. Sales of religious books dropped by a third. Mainline Protestant churches became demoralized. In the Catholic Church, American trends were supplemented by the liberalizing effects of Vatican II. Though the number of Catholics remained constant, the number of people attending Mass dropped off precipitously in the 1960s.

While church attendance in the '60s didn't change much for people over fifty, the drop-off among twentysomething people was very great. Among those eighteen to twenty-nine, those who went to church weekly was 51 percent in 1957. In December 1971, it was 28 percent. The drop-off figure among black youth (and African Americans are the most devout ethnic group in America) was even greater than for whites. In 1952, 75 percent of Americans said that religion was "very important" to them personally. By 1978, that figure had fallen to 52 percent.

The crisis in confidence in religion that people experienced in the '60s encouraged many people to go it alone. And so we saw a variety of religious experiments, from the Age of Aquarius to Jesus freaks, Scientology, Zen, est, Esalen, transcendental meditation, and the Unification Church. That was the religious shock.

The first aftershock has lasted for more than forty years and is as close as the 2012 presidential campaign. From the time of the Scopes trial in 1925, the huge evangelical Protestant subculture was for the most part quiescent and apolitical. Whatever political influence there was, was carried forward by a few national notables, Billy Graham being the most well-known. But he was the exception. Jerry Falwell gave sermons in the early '70s admonishing his flock to stay away from political action, on the grounds that the secular world was corrupting and was the realm of the devil. Though it is hard to believe, there were even evangelical ministers back then who supported a women's right to have an abortion. Most evangelicals were and are Baptists, and historically Baptists have had a pretty good history of supporting church/state separation, harkening back to Roger Williams of Rhode Island. Having an abortion was a matter of individual conscience and not the state's business. Not anymore.

In the late '70s, with the founding of the Moral Majority, evangelicals came out of their apolitical closet, and the American political landscape since then has moved very far to the right. So far to the right that what we previously thought of as the lunatic fringe now occupies the base of the Republican Party. As evangelicals became politicized in the 1970s and flexed their political muscles through the '80s, they also grew numerically.

This growth was due to demographic factors, such as a high birth rate, by the success evangelicals had with regard to keeping their children in the fold, and by winning converts. Converts then came to evangelical churches in part because they were shrewd organizers and robust marketers of their faith. But beyond these factors, evangelicals have long found the general culture to be threatening, and especially the culture of the '60s. And in their common fears they found solidarity and strength. Among the elements that disquieted them have been the legacy of Great Society liberalism, the civil rights movement, and in particular efforts during the Carter administration to remove government tax exemptions from all white "academies" and colleges. Some argue that changing gender roles have upset the patriarchy that is deeply embedded in conservative religious theology, and we need also cite Supreme Court decisions that widened the gap of church/state separation and removed prayer from the public schools. All these trends have no doubt played their part in augmenting and politicizing the evangelical subculture in America.

But the one area of concern that was no doubt most powerful in creating this aftershock was what evangelicals perceived as the moral decadence and sexual permissiveness of mainline society. Abortion, pornography, nonmarital sex, and homosexuality were all hot-button issues in the 1960s. And as the majority of the society moved in a more liberal direction, conservatives felt more challenged, and more threatened, if not besieged. But within the context of sexual issues, Putnam and his coauthor, David Campbell, have been able to document that the issue that was most upsetting to evangelicals was not homosexuality, or even extramarital sex. It was the sanctioning of premarital sex, which quickly became almost normative in the culture. As the authors state:

> The norm regarding premarital sex does encapsulate an astonishingly rapid change in intimate mores, as a well-defined cohort of young people, four fifths of whom accepted sex before marriage, charged into a population of their elders, four fifths of whom rejected that principle—literally a revolution in traditional moral views at a pace certainly unprecedented in American history.

It was this collision of tectonic plates along the fault line of premarital sex that created the first great aftershock coming in the wake of the 1960s and thereby generated the evangelical backlash with all the reactionary politics it has brought with it.

If opposition to premarital sex was a main factor in the growth of evangelical Protestantism and its political power in the late '70s and '80s, it is not the factor that has sustained it. Rather, since the mid-1980s, it has been opposition to abortion and a deep-seated anxiety over homosexuality as expressed politically through opposition to gay marriage. But something else has changed on the religiopolitical landscape in the past twenty-five years. And that is that these central political issues have also become the basis of affiliation with our two major political parties. In other words, religion has become partisan.

Throughout American history, Americans divided themselves trenchantly along religious lines. Protestants hated Catholics and feared Catholic power, and Catholics hated Protestants, and both pretty much hated the Jews. Many Protestant Americans saw Catholicism as a dark cult with the pope conspiring to dominate American society. As a young boy, I can personally remember when John Kennedy, while campaigning to be our first Catholic president, had to bend over backward, over and over again, to tell the American people that if he were elected president of the United States, his highest loyalty would be to the Constitution and not to the pope in Rome. Protestant ministers, led by the famous Norman Vincent Peale, led a campaign to oppose Kennedy's candidacy on the grounds that a Catholic president could not help but be a lackey for the Vatican.

But these antediluvian religious boundaries in American society began to dissolve in the mid-'70s and political loyalties became radically reshuffled. Today, the very religious are part of a coalition that unites conservative Protestants with conservative Catholics and orthodox Jews. On the other side of the divide are mainline religious moderates, liberals, secularists, and people professing no religion at all. But as abortion and opposition to gay marriage became pivotal issues, the Democratic and Republican parties became identified with one position or the other. And so, the more deeply religious you are, the more you identify with the Republican Party, and if you are mildly religious or a secularist, you identify with the Democrats. In other words, religion has become politically partisan with greater polarization than at any time in American history, at least since the Civil War. The only exception to this, and it is a considerable exception, are African Americans, for which the opposite pertains. By most religious indicators, blacks are the most devout ethnic group in America. But they are also most reliably members of the Democratic Party. However, as it pertains to the white majority, as the polarization has gone on longer and has become more entrenched on the Republican side, it has become more extreme.

Though it hasn't fully formed as yet, what we are seeing aspects of on the right is the resurgence of misogyny. A centerpiece of all conservative religion, whether it be Christian, Jewish, or Muslim, is patriarchy, which travels fist in glove with a yen for hierarchy, tradition, order, and control. For conservative religionists, control over women, and especially control over women's sexuality, harkening back to times when women were property, has been a major preoccupation. We see glimmers of it on the political landscape, I believe.

We have seen state legislatures trying to mandate invasive transvaginal sonograms for women wanting abortions. Then there is the issue of contraception, which hasn't been a political issue for fifty years.

The several attacks we have seen on contraception have been reignited by the Catholic Church and defended in particular by aspiring presidential candidate Rick Santorum. It was the Obama administration's initiative to require religiously affiliated institutions, but not churches, to cover contraception for their employees, which opened the door to this retrograde condemnation of birth control. Though 98 percent of all women have used birth control, Santorum's position is that it is immoral. No intercourse except with the intent to procreate. While he can claim fealty to his church's position, one senses that behind this birth control fracas is, again, a discomfort with women's sexual freedom. It is women's sexuality, never men's, that becomes the focal point of political and social concern. Rush Limbaugh may be a crude and boorish media clown, but he wouldn't take the liberty of calling a decorous young law student who supports contraception a "whore" and a "slut" unless he felt that there was an audience, perhaps a large one, who is ready to receive such defamatory drivel.

Behind this assault on women's sexuality, I again see looming a long-deferred discomfort with the cultural earthquake of the 1960s. It's as if those who felt besieged by the changes of that period took their discomforts and went underground to have them resurface forty-five years later. Indeed, those who constitute the hard core of religiously conservative Republicans are overwhelming white and older, old enough to have experienced the 1960s firsthand. As hideous as it is, I don't believe that this new misogyny will go very far. The horse is long out of the barn, and the status and freedom of women too deeply entrenched in our culture for there to be a reversion to early times and previous norms. I predict that this assault, vested in the Republican Party, is so contrary to the interests of women, who comprise half of the electorate, and to many men of more egalitarian values, that it will in time burn itself out. But as Thomas Jefferson so wisely and correctly warned us, "The price of liberty is eternal vigilance," for this assault on women is very disquieting.

The unholy alliance of the Republican Party with religion of a very conservative kind has caused the Republican Party to hemorrhage, as I believe it should. I do not think that this crazy marriage of extremist politics and extremist religion will last for much longer. Though the moment looks dark, and indeed menacing, there are reasons to believe that the future will be brighter because it will be more moderate. Beneath the din of the racket we hear coming from religion and politics, there are undercurrents aborning that don't make the news, but will, I believe, soon emerge to transform the landscape in a more benign direction.

Which brings me to the second great aftershock. If the first aftershock was the emergence of the Christian right in reaction to the earthquake of the 1960s, then the second aftershock is the reaction of the younger generation, the so-called millennials, to the fusion of religion and politics that lies at the heart of the Republican Party as we have been discussing it. It is this reaction and other dynamics on the religious landscape that I now want to look at.

In the 1950s, when surveyed, 95 to 97 percent of Americans stated that they belonged to a specific religious denomination or tradition. Inversely, in the '60s, only 5 to 7 percent said they had "no religion," and this number remained static until the early 1990s. Then something began to happen. The number of people claiming to have no religious affiliation began to rise meteorically, so that today, more than 16 percent of the American population claims to have no religious affiliation. The number of so-called nones is larger than the African American population, or larger than the Jewish, Muslim, Hindu, and Buddhist population put together.

The major explanation for this explosion of people declaring "no religion" is generational. For those young people coming of age in the 1990s and 2000s, the numbers are staggering, now hovering around 25 to 30 percent of this cohort. What is also interesting is that as they age, they seem not to become more religious, using affiliation with a denomination, again, as the benchmark of religiosity. This means that as the population ages, the older sector of the population, only 5 percent of whom say they have no religion, are being replaced by a cohort of which more than 25 percent say they have no religion, thus massively driving the entire American population in the direction of no religion.

At the same time growth among evangelicals, who increased their ranks in the 1970s and '80s, began to slow down to the point where evangelical

Christianity has stopped growing. In the mid-1980s, evangelical twentysome-things outnumbered people of the same age claiming no religion by a ratio of two to one. Today, those figures have almost been reversed, so that today's "nones" in their twenties outnumber evangelical youth by a ratio of one and a half to one.

Politically speaking, the new "nones" are drawn from the center and the left of the political spectrum. Their growth corresponds to the strength of the religious Right when it reached its high-water mark, indicating that the rise of disaffection from organized religion is a backlash against the religious Right. Indeed, when asked, such millennials state that they are turned off to religion because of its identity with right-wing politics and its issues, finding religious people judgmental, hypocritical, and insincere. In other words, they conclude that "if this is what religion means, then I don't want any part of it."

When we look at specific issues, we find, perhaps surprisingly, that the new "nones" are somewhat more conservative than the boomer generation on the issue of abortion. They have not backtracked, however, on premarital sex. But the issue in which there is a real shift, in fact an issue that almost defines this generation, is their comfort with homosexuality and their support for gay mar-riage. This may not only be a backlash against the homophobia of the Christian Right, but may reflect that this younger cohort came of age when gays have been depicted positively in the media and through much of the popular culture.

One can never predict the future, but we may provisionally conclude that as this younger generation ages, it will mitigate the political power of religion, especially the Christian Right, and inject greater tolerance and less extremism into our political life. This demographic shift, as implied, is a source of hope.

As a footnote, I need to mention that even with the numbers of those declaring "no religious affiliation," that does not mean that this growing cohort of the population is comprised of atheists or agnostics, who remain no more than perhaps 4 percent of the population. Indeed most "nones" still retain reli-gious feelings, may see themselves as "spiritual," and may occasionally even go to church. But by definition, they do not identify with organized religion. The payoff, again, is their relationship to a more liberal politics and not the texture of their belief or nonbelief.

There are other dynamics that loom on the horizon and can inspire us with hope for a more benign future. Though they get drowned out in the cacophony of religious polemics, quiet changes are going on in the religious landscape that are very worthy of our consideration.

The prevailing reality is that American society is fluid, and America is becoming more pluralistic. Here is what I mean. Traditionally, religious identity was a matter of inheritance. Your religion was the religion passed down to you by your parents. This age-old reality has radically changed in our lifetime. Increasingly, religious identity has become a matter of choice. Surveys have found that today at least one third of all Americans—and that number is rising—identify with a religion other than that they were born into. In other words, they have switched. This means several things. As religion increasingly is based not on the authority of tradition, but on personal autonomy, religious affiliation and identity have become more unstable, and the religious marketplace has become more fickle and more volatile. Rather than doing one's duty to God, the causes of religious affiliation are more grounded in personal needs and wants. Hence, on the supply side, churches and their clergy have to become more entrepreneurial in order to attract and retain members. Perhaps as much producers and entertainers than purveyors of the word.

This may make religion a more superficial affair, but my point is that the great increase in religious switching has also made people more tolerant of religious differences and more tolerant of people who hold to a different religion. In short, religious boundaries are not as important as they used to be. This tolerance is reflected in religious attitudes. When asked, 89 percent of Catholics, 82 percent of mainline Protestants, and 100 percent of Mormons say that non-Christians can find salvation and go to heaven. They affirm this conviction often in defiance of the official theological positions of their churches. Perhaps closer to our theological interests, 87 percent of Americans agree that people without a religious faith can be good Americans. This, despite the marginalization of atheists. And in a finding that takes two thousand years of ingrained prejudice and hatred and stands them on their head, when Americans are asked what their favorite religious group is, the response is Jews.

But perhaps even more consequential than religious mixing is the contemporary reality of intermarriage in American society. Studies show that roughly half of all married Americans are married to someone who came from a different religious tradition. What this signifies is that extended families have become increasingly religiously pluralistic. Two out of three American families have at least one extended family member who is of another religion. Adding to the diversity of religious acquaintanceship, the average American reports that he or she has at least two close friends with a religious affiliation different from his or hers. The result is that Americans increasingly have gotten to know people who are religiously different from themselves, have been able to develop warm feelings about them, and have been able to accept them into the tapestry of our national community.

The payoff of all this religious pluralism should be clear. It is much harder to be a bigot toward people who are not of your religious persuasion if your best friend is one, or your favorite cousin is such, or if you are married to one and your child carries with her, at least in part, your spouse's religious heritage. The result of all this inter religious mingling, marrying, and friendships is a more tolerant society and a less hostile one.

I will close by citing the words with which the authors I have relied on end their magisterial study. Putnam and Campbell write:

How has America solved the puzzle of religious pluralism—the coexistence of religious diversity and devotion? And how has it done so in the wake of growing religious polarization? By creating a web of interlocking personal relationships among people of many different faiths.

This is America's grace.
And, I would add, may it be our future.
April 2012

Humanist Heroes

Our Martyr: A Eulogy For Giordano Bruno On The Four Hundredth Anniversary Of His Execution

Each person and each community defines itself by certain myths or stories. As individuals we may think of ourselves as kind and sensitive, strong and headstrong. We may see ourselves as victors in the struggles of life or as victims of life's injustices. We may fancy ourselves as battlers or as passive recipients of what life has in store for us. We may see in our life stories people who are self-confident or people who are halting and hesitant. Or maybe both. To say that each person defines herself or himself within a story or myth does not mean that such self-understanding is false. It is merely to say that since we cannot understand our lives by dissecting all their myriad details and experiences, we have a natural tendency to fuse these details together into a story line. In short, each person lives in his stories, in his narratives.

As it is for individuals, so it is for groups. As Americans we have a self-image as hardworking, productive, democratic, and freedom loving. Christians have their self-understanding, Jews theirs, Hindus their own. So does the community of Met fans, Yankee fans, Democrats, and Republicans. Democrats comprise the party of compassion and egalitarianism; Republicans, that of opportunity combined with individual initiative, etc.

The myths that groups have of themselves serve many important purposes. People sharing a common story are bound together because of that story. Commonly held myths locate people in the larger scheme of things. They bind people to larger values and define for them their place in history. People are inspired by the myths they hold. Ultimately the images and narratives we have of ourselves serve as sources of empowerment and dignity.

As Ethical Culturists we are humanists, and a question we can ask is, what are our collective myths and stories? The most compelling answer I can give is that our story is the glorious struggle for, and expansion of, freedom and the free mind over the ages. It's a powerful story, it's an ennobling story, and it is our story.

While we can debate endlessly whether people are happier today than they were in ages past, one area where we can point to moral progress with great pride is in the expanding circle of freedom. Throughout the centuries humankind has succeeded in moving the locus of human authority, both intellectual and political, away from sources outside the individual to increasingly situate it in the individual himself or herself.

In other words, the career of humankind has been the slow march toward greater freedom and the inclusion of more and more people within that circle.

Most of this progress has taken place within the past four hundred years and seems to accelerate as we move closer to our times. The markers are clear to see. In the modern era we have replaced authoritarian kingdoms with democracy. We have, with notable exceptions, abolished slavery. We have enfranchised women. We have developed an ever more refined conception of human rights. We have created great documents to objectivize, universalize, and safeguard those rights. We have seen the empowerment of labor and, in our times, the dramatic civil rights movement, which has sought and greatly achieved the enfranchisement of minorities. We have seen the circle of inclusion widen even more to subtend the disabled, gays, and other members of the human species who share our humanity but have been excluded from a full enjoyment of their rights and freedoms.

Our story is this slow march of human freedom. It is the expansion of personal autonomy. It is the triumph of increased tolerance. It is the widening of the circle that invites more of us in to share its fruits.

Side by side with the development of political freedom and upon which it has been built has been the story of the unfettered mind through the ages. The seventeenth-century philosopher Spinoza had said that "a man should be able to think what he wants and say what he thinks." In Spinoza's Holland, the most tolerant nation then existing, it was still not safe for "a man to think what he wants and to say what he thinks."

The triumph of the free mind has resulted from a long, hard, incremental struggle taken on by men and women, alone or together, who had the will and the courage to see beyond the conditions under which they lived. They were able to hold out a vision of human beings guided not by the limitation of their conditions, but inspired by a broader view of human possibilities.

The story of freedom is a story of struggle. To win even a small victory in that struggle, these visionaries often had to run afoul of the powers that be and advance their cause at the peril of great risk, and often sacrifice. We can count among them Socrates, Erasmus, Galileo, Spinoza, Darwin, Frederick Douglass, Elizabeth Stanton. In our own time, Gandhi, Martin Luther King, Andrei Sakharov. There are hundreds of other men and women, famous and totally unknown, who have engaged in quiet, steadfast acts of courage.

To add a bit of realism to this drama, one has to note that many heroes of the free mind whose legacies of courage we today enjoy were not necessarily nice human beings. Often they were terribly troubled and obnoxiously stubborn in the pursuit of their own truths. Some who advanced freedom did so for motives that were set in other directions, perhaps self-interested ones, that were not so magnanimous at all. Yet they are part of the story also. Human beings and history are complex. It was Immanuel Kant who so aptly observed that "out of the crooked timber of humanity, nothing straight has ever been made."

I want to bring to light the life of a man who added a piece to that slow struggle for the free mind. And though he was one of the most brilliant personalities of his time, he has been greatly lost to history. He was an Italian who flourished in the sixteenth century. He was a creator of that glorious period of human expression we know as the Renaissance. His name was Giordano Bruno. And though he is greatly unknown to Americans, he remains a folk hero to an untold number of Italians who herald him as an icon in the struggle for the free mind against the forces of authoritarianism, which, in the case of Bruno, was the authority of the Church and the papacy.

I want to talk about Bruno before the end of this year (2000), since I felt the calendar would never afford me a better opportunity. For Giordano Bruno was put to death in the year 1600. February 17 marked four hundred years since his execution.

Bruno was not a humanist in the modern sense, nor was he even a scientist, though he wrote broadly on scientific issues. To claim that he was our martyr is, therefore, a stretch, an exaggeration I allowed myself in the search for a catchy title. Bruno was rather a champion of the unrelenting free mind and the stubborn pursuit of truth. And in that sense his story overlaps with the humanist story.

Bruno lived in complicated, tumultuous, and unstable times. We can see the Renaissance as a period of transition between the Middle Ages, which came before it, and the Age of Science, which it prefigured. It was a period in European history that lasted roughly from 1350 to 1600.

The Renaissance, which began in the Italian city-states, marked a rebirth of interest in the Roman and Greek classics, with their characteristic emphasis on humanity as expressed in a cultivated understanding of literature and art. The Renaissance marked the beginning of modern trade and the growth of cities and secular pursuits that characterize the modern world. It was an era unparalleled in artistic genius, great literature, and inventive science. We associate with it names such as Raphael, Michelangelo, Petrarch, Alberti, Masaccio, da Vinci, and others.

Politically, it was a time of the emergence of competing city-states, warfare, power grabbing, and intrigue. A young Florentine by the name of Nicolo Macchiavelli wrote a brilliant treatise called *The Prince*. It was a handbook on how princes could best retain their power in an age when to sit on any throne was risky business. What is noteworthy about *The Prince* is that it makes scant reference to the authority of religion, except to say that the virtues the prince needs to retain power oppose the values taught by the church, namely humility and piety. *The Prince* is considered to be, therefore, the first secular treatise that foreshadows the coming of the modern world.

The Renaissance was a complex time that blended disparate elements in a cauldron of creativity. It was a time that mixed humanism with religion, man with God, science with a fascination with magic, astronomy with astrology, and the power of the state with the power of the church. It was time in which the unparalleled supremacy of the church as both a religious and temporal power began to break down and was challenged by the competing forces, most of all the Protestant Reformation.

Into this world, Giordano Bruno was born in 1548, near Naples and in view of Mount Vesuvius. His father was a soldier, and at a young age he became a Dominican monk. Bruno's independence of mind was evident early. He refused to place pictures of the saints in his cell at the monastery and refused to give the right answers to questions his teachers posed. In 1576, Bruno was formally accused of heresy and fled from Naples. He spent the rest of his life traveling through Europe, spending seldom more than two years in any one place. His life became almost an uninterrupted, unbroken stream of persecution, much of it brought on by his own provocation of the authorities with whom he also sought to ingratiate himself. He first went to Rome but, finding that no safer than Naples, he went to northern Italy and then crossed over into Switzerland and lived in Geneva, where John Calvin had not much before set up a city-state as a center of the Protestant revolt against the church. Geneva at the time was a haven for Catholic heretics, but Bruno's enthusiasm soon turned to disappointment. He had written a pamphlet criticizing the errors of Calvin's successor. He was arrested, briefly imprisoned, and released after he confessed his guilt and agreed to have all copies of his book destroyed.

Bruno fled Geneva as he had Naples three years earlier. He then traveled through France, visiting Lyon, Avignon, and Montpellier until he found a teaching position in Toulouse. Two years later, for reasons probably other than persecution, he went to Paris, where he taught theology at the famed university and made several friends, including Henry III, king of France.

Bruno became known as a brilliant lecturer and famed practitioner of the lost art of mnemotechny. Mnemotechny, or the art of memory, was a respected skill that had its origins in the occultism of the Middle Ages. It was related to magic because it was felt that the experience of the adept reflected the whole universe within the context of his own mind. It also gave its practitioner knowledge of the divine mind. It was a revived form of Gnosticism. In this sense, those who mastered the art of memory were considered to be inspired and have special powers. Bruno believed his teachings on the art of memory were among his most important contributions, and it reflected what to us is the strange admixture of rationalism and the occultism that was characteristic of much of his thinking. Bruno was an exponent of the hermetic tradition, which blended Greek mythology and Egyptian religion with the mystical elements of neo-Platonism, all in the name of Christianity.

Early in 1583, Bruno relocated once again, this time to England, where he lived at the French embassy. While in England, Bruno met Queen Elizabeth, about whom he had positive things to say. He taught at Oxford and while there produced his most important philosophical works. Though he spent only two years in England, where he befriended the poet Philip Sidney, it was Bruno's most creative period. He wrote dialogues, philosophical treatises, plays, and poetry. It was the time in which he developed his theories about the universe.

Bruno was the first major defender of Copernicus's theory that the sun, and not the earth, lies at the center of the solar system. In this sense, he was a bridge between Copernicus and Galileo, who would soon be able to validate Copernicus's theory through telescopic observation and his own discoveries in physics. Though Galileo never mentioned Bruno, it is possible that he was silent because he feared the repressive power of the Inquisition, which in a few decades would submit him to trial and house arrest.

Bruno did far more than support the Copernican theory. He advanced ideas that would make any twentieth-century space buff proud. Among the doctrines he proclaimed and defended was that universe was not closed, but infinite in time and space. He speculated that the stars were individual worlds, like our own, and were inhabited by beings much like ourselves. He promoted the idea that in an infinite universe, there was no absolute direction, but that the positions of heavenly bodies were relative to one another. He wrote extensive books defending these ideas, which in their time, but not ours, were both novel and radical.

Much was religiously at stake here. The religious authority of the Catholic Church was in great measure bolstered by its claims to be authoritative in all branches of knowledge, especially philosophy and what became known as science. And the prevailing philosophical authority for the church was Aristotle. If Aristotle said a person had two livers and three lungs, a person was believed to have two livers and three lungs.

What Aristotle did say was that the sun, moon, and all heavenly bodies revolved around the earth, the center of God's creation. They were embedded in crystalline spheres and revolved in perfect circles, which suggested a perfect, closed, and rather small universe.

Copernicus's theories confounded that divine blueprint and thus upset the church's teaching about God's creation and plan for humankind. It dethroned humankind, the jewel in the crown of creation, from its privileged central position. The notion of an infinite universe, as put forth by Bruno, was particularly upsetting in its implications. If the universe were infinite, where was there a place for an infinite God? Indeed, in a way that preceded Spinoza, Bruno even speculated that God and Nature comprise one identical substance that assumes two different forms. This idea, often defined as pantheism, that is, that God is in everything, is very un-Christian and very heretical. These ideas were literally hundreds of years ahead of their time and particularly threatening to church authority.

It did not help that Bruno had no respect for the authority of Aristotle, even proclaiming that the Aristotelians of his day were boring pedants. He denounced Aristotle in terms that were both vehement and sarcastic—this in an age when what one said publicly, no less taught, was often tightly controlled. Bruno sought to replace Aristotle with an eclectic and creative mix of an imaginative philosophy of his own making.

But that was not all. While in Britain, Bruno published treatises that favorably incorporated the mystical insights of the Jewish cabala. He preached a philosophy, moreover, which intensely questioned such doctrines as the virginity of Mary, the significance of the Mass, and the Crucifixion. He challenged a belief that the Trinity embodied three separate persons, and in this sense he expressed broadly Unitarian leanings. Bruno went even further. In satires that he wrote while in Britain, he not only poked fun at the pedantry of academics he did not like, but criticized what he saw as superstition in both Roman Catholicism and Protestant Christianity.

Bruno returned to Paris and, unable to find employment, left for Germany in what was the final phase of his wanderings. He went to Wittenberg and then Marburg, where he fell again into conflict with the ruling Protestants. He went to Prague and finally, in 1590, he went to Frankfurt, then Zurich and Frankfurt again, writing, publishing, and stirring up trouble all the while.

While in Frankfurt, Bruno received two letters of invitation from a young Venetian aristocrat to come to Venice to teach him the art of memory. Perhaps because Venice was an independent city-state in some competition with Rome, Bruno felt it would be safe to return to his homeland. This student, named Mocenigo, became dissatisfied with Bruno's teaching, and betrayed him to the Inquisition in Venice.

Bruno was thrown into prison and repeatedly interrogated about his philosophy. Witnesses were brought to confirm Bruno's heresies. Yet the nature of the Inquisition was such that an accused, who could be brought up on charges on the basis of the say-so of a single individual, was allowed no lawyer to defend himself, nor any right of cross-examination. Bruno was accused of many acts of heresy, including denial of Christ's divinity, the mythical character of the Bible, belief in universal salvation, and cosmological speculation, such as the plurality of worlds and the infinity of the universe. He was also accused of lavishing too much praise on Queen Elizabeth.

Bruno was left to rehearse over and over again his life story and the beliefs that comprised his complex and difficult teachings. Very naively, Bruno believed that his views were ultimately compatible with the teaching of the church, and that if he had an opportunity to plead before the pope, he would surely be exonerated of the charges against him.

His interrogation in Venice went on continually for almost two years, until the Grand Inquisition claimed jurisdiction and had him extradited to Rome. For eight more years he was kept in a dungeon and threatened with torture. Rather than seek reconciliation with the church, after six years he admitted that he was guilty in the eyes of the authorities. He was offered his freedom if only he would recant his beliefs and agree to repent. But Giordano steadfastly refused to do so, and so sealed his doom.

His eight inquisitors declared him to be an "impenitent, pertinacious, and obstinate heretic" and condemned him to be burned at the stake, to be followed by the burning of his books. When the verdict was declared Bruno was reported to have responded, "Perhaps you who pronounce my sentence are in greater fear than I who receive it."

On February 17, 1600, with considerable pomp, Giordano Bruno was led to the stake in the Campo di Fiori, the Field of Flowers, in Rome. Given an opportunity at the very end to deny his own beliefs before the authority of the church and in the face of death, he one last time refused. And so Giordano Bruno was committed to the flames, having become, ironically, a martyr, not to a church which produced many martyrs, but to the power and glory of the free mind that we today, four hundred years later, so prosperously enjoy.

In 1889, a monument to Giordano Bruno was erected in the Campo di Fiori at the location at which he was executed. And I am told that today it is a place where small children particularly like to gather and play.

A final question remains as to the place that this somewhat obscure and complex thinker holds in the history of ideas and the march of freedom.

As implied, though Bruno was a very early and courageous defender of the Copernican theory and had many amazingly prescient things to say in the area of cosmology, it would be wrong to see him as a scientist, as some do. His interests were not really scientific; he engaged in such speculations to push ahead his philosophical and religious interests, which, as noted, found their roots at least partially in mysticism and magic.

But on second thought, Bruno's universe, corrected for its magical and spiritualized elements, did reflect in many ways the cosmology that was to arise in the seventeenth century in the Age of Science. In that sense he was a Renaissance forerunner of the modern era. It is not always a rigorous scientific method that pushes science ahead, but rather the deployment of a creative and fertile imagination. No less a figure than Einstein once noted that in the discovery of new ideas, imagination is more important than intellect. Giordano Bruno, thinking and writing at the predawn of the scientific era, fulfilled Einstein's observations.

Bruno was the first thinker to advance the idea of an infinite universe, as opposed to a closed and cramped one—a belief that persisted for almost two thousand years through the authority of Aristotle. By breaking down Aristotelian authority, he was able to open the human mind to a sense of an infinite universe that sets no limits to human reason. Rather, this sense of infinity created a great incentive for the expansion of human reason, which was so profitably employed by the thinkers of the European Enlightenment.

And lastly, Bruno was the first major thinker to engage in thinking in a way that was independent of the authority of religion, theology, and the church. In other words, with Bruno, thought itself became independent and free of authoritarian shackles or religious purposes to constrain or guide it. We usually think of Rene Descartes doing this and name him the father of modern thinking and philosophy. But Giordano Bruno flourished as a freethinker almost a century before Descartes, and so gains an important place in the modern revolution.

Throughout the seventeenth century, the heretical ideas of Giordano Bruno were too dangerous to entertain or be associated with. But with the coming of the eighteenth century, he was discovered by the Romantics, most of all Samuel Taylor Coleridge, who admired the breadth and freedom of his imagination.

And though Giordano Bruno may not ring a chord of recognition in us today, he certainly did to our country's greatest poet, who was also the most powerful bard of American freedom we have ever had. In praise of a figure whom Walt Whitman saw as a spiritual ancestor of his own, he said:

> As America's mental courage is so indebted, above all current lands and peoples, to the noble army of Old-world martyrs past, how incumbent on us that we clear those martyrs' lives and names, and hold them up for reverent admiration as well as beacons. And typical of this, and standing for it and all perhaps, Giordano Bruno may well be put, today and to come, in our New World's thankfulest heart and memory.

November 2000

The 350th Anniversary Of Spinoza's Excommunication And The Creation Of The Modern World

The year 1656 may not loom large in the annals of Western history, but perhaps it should. For it was in that year, on July 27, to be exact, 350 years ago, that a precocious twenty-four-year-old man was excommunicated from Amsterdam's Jewish community. It was the fate of Baruch Spinoza to become a revolutionary figure who charted the philosophical and political blueprints that laid the basis for the creation of the modern world. In some sense, his thinking was a hundred years, and even two hundred years, ahead of its time, and though Spinoza lived his entire life within the seventeenth century, much of his thinking remains relevant to us today. It is my intent to try to show how.

Of the more than 280 edicts of excommunication proclaimed by the elders of the Amsterdam Jewish community in the seventeenth century, the wording of Spinoza's was by far the most virulent and condemnatory. He was accused of "abominable heresies" and "monstrous deeds." But what those heresies and deeds were remain unknown. Barring the discovery of some newly found manuscript or letter, the reasons for his excommunication will remain a mystery and no better than a matter of speculation for intellectual historians.

It was sometimes presumed that Spinoza's excommunication, and the many others proclaimed by the elders of the Amsterdam synagogue, was an example of the sheer authoritarianism and close mindedness of a backward and benighted community. But this assuredly was far from the truth. The

Amsterdam Jewish community was comprised, to great degree, of respectable middle-class merchants and businessmen. It was an urbane community whose residents had connections to their Christian neighbors and the wider world. It was by no means a ghetto. For example, Saul Morteira, the chief rabbi of the Amsterdam community, was a graduate of the University of Padua, worked at the Louvre, and was conversant in Latin. Rabbi Manasseh ben Israel, another religious leader of the community, had been a painter, a friend of Rembrandt, who for a while lived in the Jewish sector and traveled to London to meet Oliver Cromwell to plead for the return of the Jews to England.

While the Jewish community was sophisticated and reasonably well off, it was nevertheless insecure and faced two great challenges, one from without and one from within. It was these challenges that caused the community to employ the threat of excommunication as a tool to ensure that its members lived orderly lives. Though Holland in the seventeenth century was a haven of tolerance, the Jews who migrated there still understood that they were the guests of their Calvinist hosts. Therefore, the Jewish community had to demonstrate that it was religiously proper, since any deviance from religious propriety threatened the security of the community as a whole. Secondly, the majority of Amsterdam's Jews were recent immigrants from the Iberian Peninsula. In the seventeenth century, the Inquisition was still alive and well in Spain and Portugal. During the Inquisition, Jews were forced to leave Spain and Portugal, suffer the pain of death, or convert to Catholicism. Many converted and lived openly as Christians, but secretly continued to engage in Jewish rituals, however attenuated, and sustain an underground Jewish identity. These secret or crypto-Jews were referred to as *marranos, conversos,* or "New Christians," and they were always in danger of discovery by the Inquisition because of the suspicion that they would secretly attempt to convert Christians to Judaism.

By coming to Holland, these secret Jews could live their Jewish identities openly and freely and out of danger. But after generations of living as Christians, their Judaism was very much alloyed with Christian rituals and habits. Their Judaism had been badly corrupted and many aspects of Jewish life forgotten. So it was the role of the leaders of the community to help restore appropriate and normative forms of Jewish religious observance, and they used, again, the power of excommunication to put the community in order.

Miguel d'Espinosa, Baruch Spinoza's father, was one such *marrano* who emigrated from Portugal to Holland in 1623.

Most of the bans of excommunication, many for minor infractions, were for brief durations. And with appropriate acts of penance and a contribution to the synagogue, the excommunicates were restored to the community. What differentiated Spinoza's excommunication was not only its severity, but the fact that, having been expelled from the Jewish community of Amsterdam, Spinoza never looked back.

What was especially noteworthy in Spinoza's case, which goes to the heart of my address, is that having left the Jewish community, Spinoza never converted to Christianity, nor became a member of any religious community at all. He became, rather, a freestanding, independent citizen of the Dutch Republic. In this sense, Spinoza became the first modern person in Western history.

Throughout the Middle Ages, every man and woman was inseparably a part of a religious community, and his or her identity was rooted in that fact. One was a member of the Christian, Islamic, or Jewish communities, and there was no such political animal as a person who stood alone aside of his or her religious community.

If there is anything that is emblematic of modern life, it is the idea of individualism: that we have identities that are ours alone and that politically we can be individual and free citizens of the nation-states in which we live. By choosing to live outside of any religious community, either Jewish or Christian, Spinoza embodied the modern concepts of self and citizenship, which today in the West we take for granted.

But there was a second way in which Spinoza represented, indeed ushered in, the modern world. In a time and place in which religion reigned as a pervasive and all-powerful force in the public and private lives of men and women, Spinoza articulated a philosophy and commended a way of life that were radically secular, and therefore profoundly heretical to the sensibilities, beliefs, and values of the people of his time. Indeed, he either had to write his philosophical treatises anonymously or ensure that they were published only after his death.

What did Spinoza stand for, and what was his philosophical contribution that made him a revolutionary figure in the history of Western thought?

Joseph Chuman

First and foremost, Spinoza, in a way that was totally uncompromising, stood for a life grounded on reason. More than any philosopher before or since, Spinoza advocated a life based on reason, and it was the rigorous employment of reason that, he believed, was the only way to establish our moral freedom and our happiness. When we talk about "freedom" in Spinoza's thought, we have to be careful to understand that he meant by freedom something extremely specific that can be grasped only by understanding his philosophy as a whole.

Though Spinoza's thought is sublimely difficult to understand and remains subject to continuous debate and interpretation, what I will venture to do is to provide the barest outline of his philosophy, in order to provide a glimmer of his contribution to creating the modern world, as I have put it.

Spinoza wrote eleven books, two of which are pillars in the canon of Western philosophy. His masterpiece is his *Ethics*, in which he lays out his technical philosophy of reality, that is, his metaphysics. The second goes by the inelegant name of the *Theological-Political Treatise*, in which he articulates his philosophy of the modern liberal state and makes a powerful case for religious tolerance and individual freedom of thought and speech.

Let it be said that the *Ethics* is an exquisitely difficult book. Not only is it written in Latin, it is written in a Latin that is so dry that it ensures that no one could ever write a line of poetry or fiction using that language. It is also written in a style that was not uncommon among philosophers of the period. To write his masterpiece, Spinoza used a style that is referred to as "the geometrical method." If one looks at the *Ethics*, ones sees that it is written in the manner of a geometrical proof, replete with definitions, axioms, propositions, proofs, and corollaries. Each proof follows with airtight logic from the one before it, and Spinoza's entire treatise holds together as an interlocking, logical whole. Indeed, the structure of his *Ethics* is emblematic and descriptive of his philosophy of reality; reality, he argues, is comprised of an infinitely large, seamless chain of causes and effects that are logically put together with the absolute flawlessness of mathematical and logical theorems.

In the *Ethics*, however, Spinoza uses the method and vocabulary of the medievals to reach totally radical, heretical, and thoroughly modern conclusions.

For example, it was a mainstay of religious thought, appropriated and asserted by Spinoza's earlier contemporary, René Descartes, that reality is comprised of two fundamental and totally separate substances: thought and matter, or we might say spirit and body. Or, in a theological vein, there is God, the Creator, who is totally spirit, and then there is the creation, which is material, and the two are totally different substances. Spinoza at the beginning of the *Ethics* demonstrates that the existence of two totally different, independent substances is a logical impossibility, and logic demands that there can only be a single substance, not two.

You might be saying, so what? But the consequences of this seemingly innocuous and technical declaration could not be more far reaching. By demonstrating that reality is made of only a single substance, not two, Spinoza is dispassionately but radically concluding that God and his creation, which Spinoza called Nature, are one and the same thing. From the Christian and Jewish perspectives, this is heresy. So if you ask Spinoza, what do you call reality? He says you can call it either "God" or "Nature" (*Deus sive natura*) and it is exactly the same thing. Spinoza was later called "a God-intoxicated man" because in the *Ethics* he continuously refers to God. But if we understand, by God, Nature, then we can just as well see Spinoza as an atheist.

We usually think of God as infinite, and indeed Nature is infinite, because for Spinoza there is nothing outside of Nature. We think of God as omnipotent, and for Spinoza, Nature is omnipotent, because there is no force greater than Nature. But Spinoza's God is radically different from the God of Christianity or Judaism. For one thing, Spinoza's God has a body, that is, the material universe. In conventional religious belief this is heresy, because God is understood to be pure spirit. For Spinoza, God or Nature is also austerely impersonal, as indeed Nature is impersonal. God does not judge us, reward us, punish us, or care about us. As Spinoza says, "Those who endeavor to love God cannot hope that God will love them in return." God is also eternal, not in the common sense of existing forever, but in the more philosophical sense of being atemporal, that is timeless, without time, outside of time. And where did God come from? For Spinoza, God or Nature is the one stand-alone, independent substance. God, for Spinoza, is self-created, the one and only thing which is not brought into existence by something outside of it, because there is nothing outside of it. God, says Spinoza, is a cause of itself; the Latin phrase is *causa sui*. In short, God or Nature is a single, infinite, interlocking, unitary system logically organized according to—for lack of a better term—what we can call natural laws.

Such laws are ultimately knowable by the power of human reason in the way in which the laws of logic or mathematics are known by reason. Divine categories inclusive of God's will, God's judgment and love, God's morality, and God's miraculous abilities and the special creation of the world and man are replaced by Nature, sublimely impersonal, deterministic, and austere. In conventional religion, we know God's intentions by reading scripture. In Spinoza's philosophy, we get to know God by getting to know the world and how Nature is structured and operates. When Einstein was asked whether he believed in God, his response was, "I believe in the God of Spinoza." Einstein believed in the God of Spinoza because he believed in a universe that was rationally organized and deterministic—and, he added, because Spinoza's God is not concerned with the fate and action of human beings.

This is a point that needs to be emphasized. While God or Nature is totally free, in the sense that there is nothing external to constrain it, Nature is constituted and organized in a totally deterministic way. Within Nature there is no freedom. Everything within Nature is caused and can be rationally explained by antecedent causes and reasons. Other than God or Nature itself, there is nothing, ourselves included, that is not brought into being and explainable by antecedent causes. Spinoza's universe is a billiard ball universe in which the existence, motion, and behavior of every object in it is caused by and can be rationally explained by antecedent causes and reasons. And we are no exceptions.

By claiming that we are part of Nature, Spinoza was proclaiming another heresy. In the Christian and Jewish scheme of things, human beings are not merely a part of Nature. We are special and we are unique because we are created in the divine image and we possess a soul. For Spinoza, this presumption is a sheer illusion. It is a mistake born of ignorance, and the inadequate use of our reason. It is a fantasy. Man, for Spinoza, is a part of Nature and governed by the laws of Nature. As he says, "Man is not a special kingdom within a kingdom, but man is part of the kingdom of Nature." Such a proclamation was, needless to say, far ahead of its time. It is one thing for Darwin to make the claim that man is a totally natural being and nothing but a natural being in the nineteenth century. It was quite an extraordinary conclusion to draw in the middle of the seventeenth.

Locating man as a totally natural being lies at the heart of Spinoza's system. This is because his ultimate aim in the *Ethics* is to demonstrate how human beings can wrest from Nature, however determinate it is, a modicum of freedom, and in the process of attaining freedom we can achieve happiness. Freedom, for Spinoza, is a prerequisite for happiness, for the person who is enslaved, either politically or emotionally, cannot be happy. To be free for Spinoza is to assert our power. For Spinoza, freedom, power, and happiness go together. But to achieve emotional freedom, which is the point of the *Ethics*, we need to have a correct understanding of where we fit in the scheme of things, and we have to have some understanding of the emotions. In Spinoza's philosophy, in a tradition that goes all the way back to Aristotle, an increase in our knowledge brings an increase in our power. And to increase our power is to increase our pleasure and our happiness.

Book 3 of the *Ethics* is devoted to his theory of the emotions, which is too detailed to explain in summary form. But this much is essential to where Spinoza wants us to go. Spinoza claims that there are two types of knowledge. The first way in which we know things takes the form of images we create in our minds as a result of things that happen to us. Stimuli impinge upon us and we create images in our minds. We are told a story, we are taught a lesson, we see an object such as a tree, and we develop the image of a tree in our minds. As a result of these experiences, the mind forms certain images, whatever they may be. The second form of knowledge results from an internal process of mind, which we can identify with the processes of logic and mathematics. When I arrive at the conclusion that $2 + 2 = 4$, the processes by which I arrive at that conclusion are not based on stimuli I receive from the outside world. It is a thoroughly interior mental process. Furthermore, and most importantly, the truths of logic and mathematics have a compelling certainty about them that no knowledge or ideas gained in any other way can have: that $a^2 + b^2 = c^2$ is an eternal, indisputable truth and gives us certainty in a way in which nothing else can. Knowledge that comes through the senses, Spinoza tells us, is uncertain knowledge; it is befogged and often inaccurate. Such knowledge that comes through our senses, he refers to as "imagination," and it results in what he calls "inadequate ideas." But through the use of reason and reason alone, as we apply reason in mathematics or logic, we gain what Spinoza calls "adequate ideas," which are the higher and totally accurate form of knowledge. That $2 + 2 = 4$, or a triangle has three sides, is a certainty that is absolute and for which there can be no doubt. For Spinoza,

Nature in its deterministic majesty is immanently so organized. Just look at the laws of physics, for example, wherein the physical universe is explicable in rational and logical principles that grip the mind with their absolute truth.

He gives us an example of what he means by the two types of knowledge. When we look at the sun, he says, according to our senses, we conclude it is a small disk maybe two hundred yards away. But we can correct that inadequate idea through an understanding of the laws of physics, which tells us that the sun is a very large object millions of miles away. Reason is the vehicle that corrects our inadequate ideas. And replaces them with adequate ideas.

The same kind of lawfulness can be applied to our emotions, for our emotions are natural phenomena, as are the motions of the planets and the stars. When it comes to our emotions, we experience both pain and pleasure. We experience pain when we are the passive objects of some stimulus that impinges upon us. Someone is angry at us, and we feel hurt. We feel jealous. We lose something we love. Spinoza believes that we suffer the pain of negative emotions, what he calls "passions," because we do not have an adequate understanding of ourselves. But if we can gain an adequate idea of the causes of our hurt by gaining a clear and rational understanding of ourselves as to what makes us feel as we do, we can gain some mastery over our emotions; we can move from being a victim of our emotion and achieve a sense of freedom and power. In short, for Spinoza, knowledge, in this case correct self-knowledge, leads to freedom from what he calls "the bondage of the negative emotions." Spinoza believes that our emotions are determined and as necessary as is any physical object in nature. But by understanding that necessity, we act according to our own nature, we identify with our own nature, we are one with the necessity of our nature, and therefore become free. Through correct understanding, we are no longer compelled from the outside, which is the opposite of freedom. But to be self-determined is to be a cause of ourselves, so to speak, and is to achieve freedom. We are free only when we act in accordance with the requirements, the laws, of our own nature.

Some people, not incorrectly, have seen Spinoza as a very early precursor to Freud, for it is the assumption of Freud's psychoanalysis that knowledge of what makes us who we are and what causes us to suffer as we do is the vehicle toward liberation from our psychic pain, from our negative emotions.

But Spinoza takes his concept of freedom and the happiness that it produces one grand step beyond this notion of psychological freedom. Remember that God is Nature, and since we are part of Nature, we are also in some sense part of God. (Needless to say, this was also a great, monumental heresy.) In that sense, when we gain correct knowledge of ourselves as natural beings whose makeup is as lawful and as necessary as the stars, the planets, and everything of which the universe is comprised, to that extent we get to know God also. We gain a correct understanding of where we stand in the deterministic order of nature. For Spinoza adequate ideas and correct knowledge are a source of joy. The highest good for Spinoza, the greatest happiness, is what Spinoza refers to as the "intellectual love of God." When we can gain an intuitive grasp of the order of Nature and our place in it, and gain a sense of the universe as a grand, timeless, unified system, accessible in its basic outlines to our reason, we have achieved the highest form of happiness. Spinoza's final, glorious vision is like that of a poetically inspired physicist who, upon unlocking the mysteries of Nature, is enraptured and awed by the grandeur and order of the universe. It is then that we contemplate reality, not with a focus on immediate preoccupations or particulars, but with a focus upon reality from the very long view. We see the universe, as Spinoza puts it, *sub specie aeternitatis*, from the standpoint of eternity—that is, in its necessary, harmonious, timeless grandeur. We grasp the big picture. The end of life, Spinoza proclaimed, is the realization of human freedom through knowing where we fit in the chain of causal necessity, and knowing how the reality we encounter could not be different from what it is. By studying the laws of Nature, in a sense, we get to know the mind of God, because God himself is identified with the rational, deterministic, indwelling structure of Nature. And when we possess this knowledge in a flash of intuitive insight, we have achieved a type of this-worldly beatitude.

Clearly not everyone can achieve this rarified insight. For as Spinoza tells us at the end of the *Ethics*, "All things excellent are as difficult as they are rare." But if people cannot achieve this grand appreciation of Nature, Spinoza's philosophy lets us know that it is because of ignorance, not because human beings are tainted with sin or are in any sense evil, for, difficult as it is, this type of mastery through knowledge and self-knowledge is possible within the human condition.

Spinoza's technical philosophy as laid out in the *Ethics* becomes the basis for his political philosophy, and here too he was far ahead of his times. If happiness built upon freedom is the ultimate end of human life, then the political state must be one that enables people to live in freedom in order to seek their happiness.

Spinoza lived in a century in which Europe drenched itself in the blood of the wars of religion. And in Spinoza's day, religion continued to have tremendous influence over the political lives of people. His *Theological-Political Treatise* was devoted to decoupling religion from the state, so that the state could be organized in the most rational and practical way, in a way that maintained both security and freedom. In other words, he advocated a secular state, divorced from religious influence.

His strategy to render the state free of religious influence was nothing less than extraordinary. It was to demonstrate that the basis of religious authority, that is, the Bible, both Jewish and Christian, is riddled with contradictions, is not founded on reasonable premises, and is a pile of superstitions not worthy of our belief. He potently argues that the prophets of the Old and New Testaments did not make their religious pronouncements based on reason, but rather that they were ignorant men who had vivid imaginations and a strong moral sense and spoke to primitive folk in a language that they understood to manipulate them into obedience in the service of doing good. As philosophers, Spinoza believed, we understand this function of the ancient prophets and do not regard their writings as making any claim to literal truth. It should be noted that Spinoza was the world's first biblical critic, and his detailed critique of the Bible came two hundred years before the emergence of modern biblical criticism, which took off in the early nineteenth century in Germany.

The state has to be based on premises other than religion. The state, according to Spinoza, needs to provide order and security first of all. If the state is repressive, if it attempts to prevent people from believing as they will, the state will only invite rebellion and disorder. Therefore, a rationally governed state will be a tolerant state. It will be one in which, as Spinoza said, "every man will think what he likes, and say what he thinks." Spinoza believed in democracy, but it was a democracy that would not meet our contemporary standards. He believed that a democracy in which there were property qualifications was the least likely to interfere with individual freedom. He believed that universities should be free of government control, and that there should be no established religions, but that churches should be supported by their own believers. He was a very early proponent of the separation of church and state. It was the condition of tolerance that maximized freedom, a condition in which Spinoza believed people could most pursue their happiness, which for him was the end of life. And it was the function of the state to provide for these conditions.

What was Spinoza's legacy, and in what way is he relevant to us today? In a certain sense, Spinoza did not have any formal disciples. His philosophy, especially as elaborated in the *Ethics*, was too hot to handle, too radical. In intellectual circles, to be called a "Spinozist" was to be branded an atheist, with all the evil connotations that that implied. But, in another sense, as the title of my address implies, Spinoza laid the groundwork for the creation of the modern world in which we live. In his philosophy, one can see the emergence of individualism, of secularism, of free thought, of political tolerance, of the separation of church and state, of the idea that man is naturally fitted with sufficient resources to govern his life without benefit of supernatural support or intervention. And most of all, we see in Spinoza the significance of the scientific paradigm and the importance of reason. These values are the pillars of the modernity that we enjoy, and Spinoza was a father of them all.

Spinoza, who lived in the seventeenth century, was clearly an early architect of the European Enlightenment, which gave birth to the idea of modern democracy. In 1683, six years after Spinoza's death, when circumstances in England became too treacherous, the philosopher John Locke moved to Amsterdam, where he lived for five years before he began to publish. According to philosopher, Rebecca Goldstein, in her book *Betraying Spinoza*, there is no doubt that while in Amsterdam, Locke conversed with people who knew Spinoza personally as well as his ideas, including his political thought. John Locke, of course, was the major influence on Thomas Jefferson and the creation of American democracy.

In a broader sense, Spinoza was an apostle of the liberation of human beings from the shackles of ignorance, superstition, and the political forces that suppress the free mind. And it is in these commitments that I believe he makes his most relevant contribution to our times.

We live in age characterized by an extraordinary outpouring of unreason. The continuing power of counterrational religious ideas and their influence on our political culture, 350 years after the time of Spinoza, would no doubt be baffling to him if he were to return. It is baffling to many of us also.

If nothing else, Spinoza remains a powerful icon to the importance of reason in our personal and public lives. We who are naturalists, humanists, and freethinkers are Spinoza's intellectual children. We need sources of inspiration. We need heroes. In Spinoza's thought we can find the inspiration to carry on the project of the Enlightenment, a project that is severely challenged at this moment. How this challenge is met will determine the fate of the values we most cherish.

November 2006

The Religion Of The
Founding Fathers

The American humorist Will Rogers once said, "Nothing changes like the past." That observation is undoubtedly true. All history is seen through the lens of the present. All of us, no matter how objective we think we are, shape the past with the tools of our present interests, political, ethical, and otherwise. We want a past that will validate our current values and beliefs.

As distressing as it is to countenance, America is now engaged in a great culture war, and the focus of that war is on the place of religion in public and political life. While religion has always been a powerful force in shaping American values and politics, in the past thirty years, with the emergence of the Christian evangelical subculture into the political realm, America has become stridently divided against itself. Throughout most of the twentieth century, religion was considered primarily a private affair. But since the ascent of Jerry Falwell's "Moral Majority" in the late 1970s, religion has come out of the closet with repressed energy, seeking to impose its values on the faithful and those outside the faith, that is, on you, me, and all Americans. Today, religion has become a powerful actor, and many people express their political interest in the name of religion and religious values.

The lines of separation in the culture wars generally pit American Protestant evangelicals and fundamentalists, together with their conservative Catholic and some Orthodox Jewish allies, against political liberals, religious moderates, secularists, and humanists. Geographically, the culture wars unite religious conservatives in the American South, Midwest, and mountain states against the putative elites who reside in the Boston-to-Washington axis and on the West Coast.

Religious conservatives are profoundly dissatisfied with the current state of America. Their agenda is, of course, well known to us. They seek to end a women's right to abortion, and some are even attacking all forms of birth control. They wish to restore prayer to the public schools, which means their specific denominational prayer. They want to ensure that abstinence is the only form of sex educational allowable. They have cut funding to international family planning groups in Africa that promote condom use as a form of birth control and disease prevention. They want to replace the teaching of evolution, which is the central pillar of biology, with so-called scientific creationism and intelligent design theory. They want to ensure that Jews return to Israel in order to jump-start the Second Coming of Jesus as a prelude to Armageddon, and the damning of everyone other than themselves to eternal torment. They are generally uncomfortable with the status of women in society and want to return women to the home and to a position of subordination to their husbands. They seek to drastically curtail, if not end, government entitlement programs, and advocate coping with social dislocations through private charity alone. They want to see the federal judiciary staffed with ultraconservative judges. But the biggest canopy that stretches over all these initiatives and values, and that gives them unity, is the destruction of the secular character of American government, and the desire for the United States to fulfill its alleged mission as a "Christian nation" with an explicitly Christian government.

At the ideological center of the culture wars, whose context is religion, is strident conflict over how to interpret the sixteen words at the very beginning of the Bill of Rights: "Congress shall make no law respecting an establishment of religion, or prohibiting the free exercise thereof." Thomas Jefferson famously noted that the relationship between the establishment clause and the free exercise clause is such that it creates a wall of separation between church and state. This interpretation was reconfirmed in a 1947 Supreme Court decision by Justice Hugo Black, and this understanding remained judicial doctrine for the next forty years. But religious conservatives and their secular allies have a different interpretation. Many will agree that the religion clauses bar the establishment of an official American church, like the Church of England, but they will argue that this is all the religion clauses prevent. For them, it is perfectly desirable for government to use all its power, including the power of the purse, to actively support religion. They say that government should support all religions equally, but their actions indicate that they don't really mean it. It is clear that they want and seek government privilege for their religion—conservative evangelical Christianity.

A crucial aspect of this battle is to enlist the Founding Fathers as allies. The contention of the Christian Right is that the founders of the republic were pious Christians just like themselves, and because they were such, it must follow that they wanted the American government not to be secular but to support the Christian religion. For Pat Robertson, Jerry Falwell, Randall Terry, Timothy LaHaye, and other stalwarts of the Christian Right, religious pluralism is anathema, the separation of church in state is a lie perpetrated by the political Left, the Bible is the foundation of our republic and its founding documents, and the Founding Fathers, such as Washington, Jefferson, Madison, and others, were committed Christians who never intended that God, religion, and Christianity should be removed from governmental discourse and affairs of state.

But is this a correct reading of the religious beliefs and intentions of the Founding Fathers? That is the issue under discussion here, and, as I have tried to show, it is anything but merely academic. I have read quite a bit on the issue, trying to bracket my own biases in favor of intellectual integrity and objectivity, as far as they can take me.

The issue of the religion of the founders is not, at first glance, as clear as one might wish, and this is true for many reasons. First, there were many founders of the American republic, and these different men believed different things about religion. Second, all of them were undoubtedly Christians, and most of them attended church with some regularity. So, if one merely glances at the outward form of their behavior without peering beneath the surface, one can superficially come away with the impression that they were indeed pious Christians. Third, the waters are muddied because the United States, as it has historically evolved, has had a mixed and complex relationship to religion. What I mean is that we can tease out two traditions that characterized early America. One of these traditions, of which the Puritans were the exemplary proponents, is deeply imbued with religion. The Puritans came to this country on a religious mission to establish "a New Jerusalem in a New World" and to create "a city upon a hill." Their intent was clearly to establish a Christian nation, a Christian commonwealth. To that end, they established a theocracy in Massachusetts and Connecticut. Their Congregational churches were supported by tax levies, and those not belonging to the church were deemed heretics. In the Puritan Fundamental Orders of Connecticut, their founding charter, they made clear that their government rested on divine authority and pursued godly purposes. It is also important to remember that of the thirteen original colonies, nine had established churches; Massachusetts's lasted well until into the 1830s. This thread intertwining religion with American society has continued to endure and has become more or less pronounced in various historical epochs. And when the Christian Right today talks about its commitment to restore America as a Christian nation, it is most likely that this colonial experience, which harkens back to an era of established churches, theocracy, and the hegemonic role that religion played in public and private life, is what it has in mind.

What the Christian Right conveniently forgets is another strand of American history. When George Washington took the oath of office as our first president, swearing to "preserve, protect, and defend the Constitution of the United States," he was pledging to support a totally godless Constitution, for the US Constitution deliberately and self-consciously, and after rigorous debate in the convention that gave it birth, nowhere mentions the word "God" and only references the word "religion" once, and here negatively. Article VI of the Constitution proclaims that there share be "no religious test" for public office. This was a very radical move in those days, considering that many of the states had religious tests for public office. But Article VI was nevertheless enacted over public fears that the government would fall into the infidel hands of Quakers, Papists, Mohammedans, and Jews.

But what did the Founding Fathers believe, and how did their beliefs shape the relationship between church and state that has long been a foundation of our political life? Again, different founders believed different things. Samuel Adams, Patrick Henry, and John Jay were orthodox Christians. Adams, for example, though a father of the American Revolution, was, in a spirit that would make Jerry Falwell proud, a critic of what he saw as a decline of morals in late eighteenth century America. Adams was admiring of the Puritans and wanted to see a type of Puritan restoration in post-Revolutionary America. But, as traditional in their Christianity as some of the founders were, others, in particular

Thomas Paine, Benjamin Franklin, George Washington, John Adams, Thomas Jefferson, and James Madison, had very different religious beliefs, which made them similar to one other, as each at the same time sustained his own creative views on religion. First let me discuss what they had in common.

Although these founders were all Protestant Christians, they were Christians of a very special type. All of them were profoundly influenced in their thinking by the European Enlightenment. The Enlightenment was that extraordinary historical epoch that saw the birth of science and the creation of the modern world. It has come to be known as the Age of Reason. At the center of Enlightenment thought was the revolutionary idea that nature behaves in ways that are lawful, and that the powers of human reason can actually be employed to discover those laws. The towering figure of the Enlightenment in this regard was the scientific genius Sir Isaac Newton, who discovered, among other things, the laws of gravitation and who created the basis for modern physics. While Newton himself was traditionally religious, his contributions to science and to ways of thinking had a profound effect on theories of truth and on religion. As a result of the scientific revolution, educated individuals began to develop a skeptical approach to matters of belief, including religious beliefs. To be held with conviction and integrity, beliefs had to meet the test of reason. This rational frame of mind, combined with the appreciation that nature behaves with regularity in accordance with natural laws, ushered in a new religious perspective known as deism.

What was deism? Deism was a religious movement that flourished primarily in England, but also in France and in the American colonies. It was short lived, lasting from the early eighteenth century to the early nineteenth. Deism was not a separate religion or sect, nor did it develop its own form of worship or religious ceremonies. It was rather a system of belief that was expressed within the Christian context. Grounding themselves primarily in nature, reason, and the scientific world view, deists professed a belief in God as the Creator of the universe, who, having brought the universe into existence, wound it up with Newtonian laws, as one would wind a watch, and then actively went into retirement from the world, as the world unfolded according to those divinely imbued laws. The universe of the deist was an austerely mechanistic one in which the laws of nature revealed the mind of God, and in which studying nature, i.e., God's creation, took the place of divine worship.

So one could worship God as the Creator, one could admire his creation with awe, and, for the deist, God was providential because he had set in motion the unfolding of future events at the Creation. But for the strict deist, God was sublimely impersonal; the expectation that God would intervene in human affairs was implausible, and because deists believed in the regularity of nature, miracles made no sense.

What should be clear is that deists sustained a critical approach to the major articles of faith of traditional Christianity. Supernaturalism was suspect, and beliefs such as divine revelation, the incarnation of Jesus, and the resurrection were held by many deists to be nothing more than benighted superstition. Even prayer, for deists, had to be radically reunderstood in order to be acceptable. For many of them, religious ritual of any type made little or no sense.

Deists, also believing that their natural religion was essentially the purest religious expression, held that Christianity, and by extension all historical religions, were corruptions of what religion truly is and should be. In this sense, deists were neither atheists nor antireligious. They were rather what one might call religious "restorationists," that is, they were attempting to restore religion to its pure, essential, uncorrupted state.

A hallmark of a deist was how he or she referred to God. He or she almost never spoke of God as "the God of Israel" but in terms that were remote, impersonal, and austere. So God was referred to as "the First Cause," "the Creator of the Universe," "the Divine Artist," "the Grand Architect," "the God of Nature," "Nature's God," "the Divine Providence," and so forth. Within the 1,323 words of the Declaration of Independence, one finds the words "Creator," "Nature's God," "Divine Providence," and "Supreme Judge," thus clearly revealing the deistic frame of mind that underlies it. The thinkers of the Enlightenment saw reason as a force for human liberation—liberation from political and ecclesiastical tyranny, and liberation from ignorance and superstition. And deism was the religion of reason *par excellence*, which they employed in great measure to strip away what was arcane, mystical, and mysterious in orthodox Christianity. It is this commitment to reason, to nature, and to skepticism that lay at the heart of the religious beliefs of major founders of the republic. I would also argue that this commitment to deism and the progressive values on which it stands—reason, nature as orderly, enlightenment—directly influenced the creation of the documents on which the United States is founded. In other words, there is a direct link between the religious beliefs of the major Founding Fathers and the political principles that brought the United States into being. Rather than being based on Christianity, as the religious Right would have it, "the United States of America is the first example of government erected on the simple principles of nature," as John Adams put it.

If Paine, Franklin, Washington, Adams, Jefferson, and Madison were all deists, they did not all hold their views to the same degree and in the same way. In almost all cases, their deism was amalgamated with Christian beliefs to a greater or lesser extent, at least in form, if not in substance. In his recent book, *The Faiths of the Founding Fathers*, the historian David Holmes divides their beliefs into distinct categories. Among them are the categories of "radical deist," "Christian deist" and "Unitarian Christian."

Of all the major founders, Thomas Paine was the most religiously radical. Although he was no atheist, Thomas Paine, in his famous treatise *The Age of Reason*, launched an attack on Christianity for being an aggressively negative force in human history, and on the Bible as no more worthy of credence than the mythology of the Greeks and Romans. In a profession of his own deistical faith, Thomas Paine famously wrote, "I believe in one God, and no more; and I hope for happiness beyond this life. I believe in the equality of man and I believe that religious duties consist in doing justice, loving mercy, and endeavoring to make our fellow creatures happy." This is not atheism, but it is not Christianity either, and Paine was shunned for his religious radicalism even by many of his co-revolutionaries, Jefferson and Madison being exceptions.

Benjamin Franklin was born into a strict Calvinist home, but by fifteen had become a type of deist. Franklin seldom went to church, but he felt, as did Washington, that religious belief and affiliation could have a positive influence on civic virtue and public order. In his values, Franklin retained elements of his strict Puritan upbringing, as expressed in his commitment to honesty, hard work, and thrift, but he clothed those values, as an adult, in very different beliefs. Franklin was a type of freethinker who did not, unlike Tom Paine, feel it necessary or wise to polemicize against the faith of others. He personally believed in a benevolent Deity, but felt that the most important way to express one's religious beliefs is by doing good to one's fellow man. Morality, for Franklin, was at the heart of religion. Five weeks before his death, a Congregationalist minister queried Franklin about his religious beliefs. He said,

Here is my Creed. I believe in one God, creator of the universe. That he governs his world by Providence. That he ought to be worshipped. That the most acceptable service we can render him, is doing good to his other Children. That the Soul of Man is immortal, and will be treated with Justice in another life, respecting its conduct in this. These I take to be the fundamental principles of all sound religion.

Franklin, though somewhat ambivalent about his religious beliefs, was very clear that virtue in religion needs to be put before orthodoxy, and that vital religion needs to veer away from dogmatism and toward inclusion and tolerance.

George Washington was born into the established Episcopal Church of Virginia. He seems to have been an avid churchgoer all his life, especially when he was in cities and had easy access to church. As mentioned, he also believed that religion informed morality and insisted on having chaplains in the Continental army. When president, he had no trouble calling for official days.

But there were also strong deistical tendencies in Washington's religious life. In accordance with the behavior of deists, Washington was never confirmed in the Episcopal or any other church, nor did he ever participate in the rite of Holy Communion, the most important Christian rite and the one in which the Trinitarian character of God is most explicit. In fact, in his correspondence, he always refers to God in the remote, magisterial terms used by deists—"the Grand Architect of the Universe," etc. Moreover, Washington seldom mentions Christianity specifically, and almost never mentions the name of Jesus Christ. Washington belonged to the Masons, a fraternity that was attractive to deists. But most important, and certainly most important for our thesis, Washington's views veered toward religious freedom—not tolerance—and religious inclusion in the new republic. As you probably know, Washington allayed the fears of the Jewish minority when he famously wrote to the Hebrew congregation of Newport, Rhode Island, that the United States is in no way founded on the Christian religion.

John Adams was a Unitarian and, like Washington, but even more so, was a frequent participant in church. Unitarianism, which became very influential in eastern New England among the elites, was not like the humanistic Unitarianism of today. Unitarianism in the eighteenth century remained highly ritualistic, cerebral, and very Christian in its forms and rituals. It represented, however, the liberal wing of New England Congregationalism and was very much influenced by the rationalism of the Enlightenment. In this sense, Unitarianism greatly overlapped with what we might call "Christian deism." To that end, it softened the doctrine of predestination, the depravity of man, and, as its name implies, was anti-Trinitarian. This meant that Jesus was not the same as God, and so for many Unitarians Jesus remained the paramount moral exemplar, but was not divine. Divinely inspired, but not God. In the spirit of the deists, Adams declared, "God has given us reason to find out the truth and the real end of our existence." It was this commitment to reason that caused Adams to hate narrow-mindedness, oppression, and intolerance.

I'll end this survey with a brief look at the religious thought of Thomas Jefferson. Jefferson was the greatest and most far-reaching product of the Enlightenment that America had produced, though his religious views were complex and not so easy to tease out with pristine clarity. But of the founders, no one had more confidence in reason and its ability to usher in an optimistic future for humankind than did Jefferson.

During his college years at William and Mary, Jefferson devoured the writings of the great Enlightenment thinkers, and he became one himself. At his home in Monticello, Jefferson kept statues of Francis Bacon, John Locke, and Isaac Newton, the three luminaries of the Enlightenment, whom Jefferson referred to as "the three greatest men who ever lived."

Unlike many of his peers, Jefferson knew French, so he could read the French philosophes such as Voltaire, Rousseau, Diderot in the original. The French deists were far more radical than their English counterparts, and it is this identification with French ideals that got Jefferson into a lot of political hot water later in his career. Though he became a religious radical himself, Jefferson remained outwardly a formal member of the Episcopal Church throughout his life and enjoyed going to church to hear a good sermon.

Like Adams, but unlike Washington, Jefferson was extremely curious about religion and theology. But unlike Adams, he did not believe that religion was necessary for the sustaining of public morality and virtue. He believed that human beings have an innate moral sense and that even atheists could be moral.

Jefferson admired the person and morality of Jesus, but it was a Jesus whom he refashioned in his own terms. Jefferson had little use for the Old Testament, which he thought was riddled with superstition and a vengeful God. And when it came to the New Testament, Jefferson did a cut-and-paste job on the Christian Bible, cutting out all the components he thought were irrational, including the crucifixion and the resurrection, but including the moral teachings of Jesus, which he thought most sublime and the essence of Christianity.

But where Jefferson got into the most trouble was in his attack on Christian ministers, whom he reviled as "priests" and whom he believed had corrupted religion and had used it as a mask for their own power grabbing and as a source of oppression. Jefferson hated religious ministers, and they hated him in return. The religious Right probably does not want to admit that the famous words that emblazon the Jefferson Memorial, "I have sworn upon the altar of God eternal hostility against every form of tyranny over the mind of man," were not directed at political tyrants, but at the Christian ministers of Philadelphia who condemned Jefferson from their pulpits when he ran against Adams for the presidency in 1800. Like other luminaries of the Enlightenment, Jefferson's analysis of tyranny was twofold. It combined the tyranny of kings and political potentates with the tyranny of religious ministers and priests. For his views, Jefferson was blasted as "a fanatical atheist" and, even worse, "a French infidel," neither of which was true. But in the spirit of deism, Jefferson's religious views veered toward tolerance and inclusion. He famously wrote in his *Notes on Virginia*, "It matters to me not whether my neighbor believes in twenty gods or in No God. It neither picks my pocket nor breaks my leg."

If time permitted, I would include a discussion of the beliefs of Madison, who was as responsible as Jefferson for the doctrine of the separation of church and state. Let it just be said that relatively little is known about Madison's private religious views. When president, he was wary of making religious-sounding proclamations, and there can be little doubt, though he spent his college years at Princeton, which was very much a center of orthodox Presbyterianism, that as an adult he affirmed a belief in the deistical view of God.

In summation, we can reach several conclusions about the religious views of the Founding Fathers and how they envisioned the relationship of church to state. Despite the omissions of the religious Right, there can be no doubt that there is a direct line between the rationalism of the Enlightenment and its liberalizing dynamics and the primary ideas that shaped the Declaration of Independence and the US Constitution, including the Bill of Rights. Though Christians by birth, and nominal Christians throughout their lives, Franklin, Washington, Adams, Jefferson, and Madison were influenced overall by deism, which cut away from their religious beliefs elements of irrationalism, dogmatism, and intolerance. This Enlightenment was given religious expression in the views of the founders and inspired their political ideals. From creating a just and humane government to the role of religion in general, Enlightenment thinking shaped the views of the founders.

Contrary to the fantasies of the religious Right, the aim of the founders was not to create a Christian republic. It was rather—and this is the most important point—to find a way to preserve religious freedom in a land that in the eighteenth century was already comprised of a growing number of different religious sects and fledgling denominations. Their ingenious solution to this problem was to separate the power of religion from the power of the state. The Founding Fathers lived close enough to the great religious wars of the sixteenth and seventeenth centuries to know profoundly and fearfully that when the absolutism of religion is harnessed to the arms of state, it creates a wicked brew, simply unprecedented in its capacity for tyranny and oppression. It is a lesson that we today seem to have ominously forgotten. The Christian Right in our times may hunger for the Puritan model and may wish to restore a Christian theocracy to America. But its proponents have forgotten that in 1776 the Founding Fathers explicitly rejected that model and put in its place a government based on the principle of religious freedom. It is that principle that is being sorely challenged, and that we must vigilantly and aggressively defend.

May 2006

The First Feminists

We who like the children of Israel have been wandering in the wilderness of prejudice and ridicule for forty years feel a peculiar tenderness for the young women on whose shoulders we are about to leave our burdens...The younger women are starting with greater advantages over us. They have the results of our experience; they have superior opportunities for education; they will find a more enlightened public sentiment for discussion; they will have more courage to take the rights which belong to them...Thus far women have been the mere echoes of men. Our laws and constitutions, our creeds and codes, and the customs of social life are all of masculine origin.

The true woman is as yet a dream of the future.

—Elizabeth Cady Stanton

One of the most interesting disputes in the history of philosophy concerns the nature of knowledge. Philosophers have identified two types of knowledge. Take a painting, for example. I can go to an art museum and contemplate the painting on the wall. I can observe its colors, forms, and themes. I can come away with an understanding of the painting in many different ways and dimensions. But I can never know the painting in the way in which the artist who created it can. The artist stands in a privileged and unique relationship to the painting by virtue of the fact that he or she created it. The relationship of the artist to his or her creation is an immediate and intimate relationship that, in a certain sense, stands inside the creation itself, rather than outside of it. This fact is even more obvious in the case of a novel. As a reader, I can come to know and understand the characters in a novel. But I can never know them with the directness of the novelist who made them up and out of whose imagination they were spun. I can only know them from the outside and imperfectly. They are objects for me. But the author knows them with immediacy and intimacy because they are nothing but his own thoughts thrust onto a piece of paper. Let me say, to correct this a bit, that the novelist does not know his creation perfectly, because he uses language and words that he did not himself invent. And furthermore, the characters of the novel may in part be projections of his unconscious mind, which he remains partially unaware of. Nevertheless, he knows the characters he creates with an interior knowledge and an intimacy that no one else can possibly share.

The same dichotomy of knowledge applies to the world of lived human experience as well. As an American I can study the history, culture, language, and habits of the people who inhabit France. But I can never know what it means to be a Frenchman in the way in which a Frenchman does. I can only know what it means by observation and external scrutiny. But the Frenchman knows what it means spontaneously and unavoidably through every act and fiber of his being. In this vein, a white person can never know what it means to be black. A Christian can never understand what it means to be a Jew. Nor can a man understand what it is to be a woman. Or vice versa, for that matter.

This differentiation between insiders' and outsiders' knowledge raises some interesting questions with regard to how we speak about the experience of others and the limits we appropriately have to place on that speech. It also raises sensitive issues when the political empowerment of the groups in question is not equal; when we have a dominant group and politically subordinate subgroups.

Let me pose the question with a concrete example. Within the context of an academic setting, is it possible to have a course on African American history taught by whites? Can a Christian teach a course in Jewish studies? And can a man legitimately talk about the present and historical condition of women? These are actually very complex questions that can only properly be answered within a sensitive appreciation for context in each case. My short answer to them is yes, but it will be a different rendition toward history than would be taught by a black, a Jew, or a woman, and it needs to be constrained by at least two considerations. First, outsiders need to be humbled in their approach by the dichotomy that I have just noted. A white can describe the fact of, let's say, antiblack discrimination. He might even know the historical facts better than a black person. But he can never know such discrimination as a felt experience. And so he needs to approach a discussion of those facts with an attitude that is always open to correction based on the testimony of insiders. Second, he needs, as a member of a dominant culture, to realize that any act of description is an act of definition. And, in the final analysis, the right of definition belongs to the members of the "in" group themselves. All this implies a stance of tentativeness, but I do not believe that it cautions total silence. Unless we envision a social condition in which blacks and whites, Jews and Christians, men and women live totally apart from one another, which, of course, is not possible, then observation and comment upon the other is simply inevitable. Also, if undertaken in the spirit that I've suggested, I think it is also desirable for us to know the thoughts of people other than ourselves if we are to move toward greater cooperation and equality.

I have tried to make a case for "outsider" knowledge so that I can approach the topic of the origins of the feminist movement. My purpose is simply to demonstrate how some of the social issues confronted by the first feminists remain as issues today, even as many political victories have been won. Indeed, a historical view of the condition of women, as it does with racial minorities, makes it clear that political entitlement and equality are not identical to social and economic equality. We are the heirs to a civilization that has been sexist from its very beginnings, and sexist it remains even as women have won tremendous achievements in political rights and entitlements in the past 150 years. A historical view helps to clarify this contradiction.

But I have a more immediate purpose. I'm also motivated by what I see, which I find disturbing. Working closely in student environments over the past several years, I don't often hear what I would consider the right values being espoused. There's a conservative backlash on campuses, as there is in the culture as a whole. This conservatism tends to legitimate traditional stereotyping with regard to sex roles. In this era of greater social tension and nastiness, indeed of interpersonal violence, women are particularly vulnerable as targets.

Stereotyping and violence feed off of each other, and the situation seems ominous indeed.

I have few illusions that real behaviors were much different twenty-five years ago. But at least the ideologies seemed to be moving in the right direction—which was a source of hope for feminists and progressives. But today, to be a feminist is to place oneself on the margin of respectability, and an ideology of greater egalitarianism between the sexes seems to be fading.

With that said, I would like to present a brief survey of the very beginnings of the feminist movement.

In the year 1762, the philosopher Jean-Jacques Rousseau published a classic volume on education entitled *Emile*. The book traces the education of its main character, the young Emile, from early childhood until the time when he is ready for marriage. It was this monumental work that helped gain for Rousseau a historical reputation as the father of progressive education and as a defender of the child.

In one of the chapters, Rousseau turns his attention briefly to the education and social role of women. Among his observations are the following:

> In the union of the sexes each contributes equally to the common aim, but not in the same way. From this diversity arises the first assignable difference in the moral relations of the two sexes. One ought to be active and strong, the other passive and weak. One must necessarily will and be able; it suffices that the other put up little resistance.

> Once this principle is established, it follows that woman is made specially to please man. If man ought to please her in turn, it is due to a less direct necessity. His merit is in his power; he pleases by the sole fact of his strength.

> If woman is made to please and to be subjugated, she ought to make herself agreeable to man instead of arousing him. Her own violence is in her charms. It is by these that she ought to constrain him to find his strength and make use of it.

Woman and man are made for one another, but their mutual dependence is not equal. Men depend on women because of their desires; women depend on men because of both their desires and their needs. We would survive more easily without them than they would without us. For them to have what is necessary to their station, they depend on us to give it to them, to want to give it to them, to esteem them worthy of it. They depend on our sentiments, on the value we set on their merit, on the importance we attach to their charms and their virtues. By the very law of nature_women are at the mercy of men's judgments, as much for their own sake as for that of their children. It is not enough that they be estimable; they must be esteemed. It is not enough for them to be pretty; they must please. It is not enough for them to be temperate; they must be recognized as such. Their honor is not only in their conduct but in their reputation.

The whole education of women ought to relate to men. To please men, to be useful to them, to make herself loved and honored by them, to raise them when young, to care for them when grown, to counsel them, to console them, to make their lives agreeable and sweet—these are the duties of women at all times and they ought to be taught from childhood. So long as one does not return to this principle, one will deviate from the goal, and all the precepts taught to women will be of no use for their happiness or ours.

The children of both sexes have many common entertainments, and that ought to be so. Is this not also the case when they are grown up? They also have particular tastes which distinguish them. Boys seek movement and noise: drums, boots, little carriages. Girls prefer what presents itself to sight and is useful for ornamentation: mirrors, jewels, dresses, particularly dolls. The doll is the special entertainment of this sex. This is evidently its taste, determined by its purpose. The physical part of the art of pleasing lies in adornment. This is the only part of that art that children can cultivate.

Observe a little girl spending the day around her doll, constantly changing its clothes, dressing and undressing it hundreds and hundreds of times, continuously seeking new combinations of ornaments—well or ill matched, it makes no difference. Her fingers lack adroitness, her taste is not yet formed, but already the inclination reveals itself. In this eternal occupation time flows without her thinking of it; the hours pass, and she knows nothing of it. She even forgets meals. She is hungrier for adornment than for food. But, you will say, she adorns her doll and not her person. Doubtless, she sees her doll and does not see herself. She can do nothing for herself. She is not yet formed; she has neither talent nor strength; she is still nothing. She is entirely in her doll, and she puts all her coquetry into it. She will not always leave it there. She awaits the moment when she will be her own doll.

...Almost all little girls learn to read and write with repugnance. But as for holding a needle, that they always learn gladly. They imagine themselves to be grown up and think with pleasure that these talents will one day be useful for adorning themselves.

There comes a docility which women need all their lives, since they never cease to be subjected either to a man or to the judgments of men and they are never permitted to put themselves above these judgments. The first and most important quality of a woman is gentleness. As she is made to obey a being who is so imperfect, often so full of vices, and always so full of defects as man, she ought to learn early to endure even injustice and to bear a husband's wrongs without complaining. It is not for his sake, it is for her own, that she ought to be gentle. The bitterness and the stubbornness of women never do anything but increase their ills and the bad behavior of their husbands. Men feel that it is not with these weapons that women ought to conquer them. Heaven did not make women ingratiating and persuasive in order that they become shrewish. It did not make them weak in order that they be imperious. It did not give them so gentle a voice in order that they utter insults. It did not give them such delicate features to be disfigured by anger. When they get upset, they forget themselves. They are often right to complain, but they are always wrong to scold. Each sex ought to keep to its own tone. A husband who is too gentle can make a woman impertinent; but unless a man is a monster, the gentleness of a woman brings him around and triumphs over him sooner or later.

The remarkable point to be made about Rousseau's observations is not that, by our standards, they are irredeemably sexist, but that he made them at all. To my knowledge, his was the first exposition by a major thinker of the role of women. What Rousseau has done is make explicit the implicit status of women as it had existed, virtually unmentioned, from time immemorial. What he asserted was the common and unchallenged assumption that women and men were divided by nature into two separate but unequal spheres, each with its distinctive virtues to cultivate. In Rousseau's mind, and virtually everyone else's who gave it a thought, women by nature were inferior, lacking in anything but the most rudimentary rational capacity, inherently subordinate, and fitted almost exclusively for nurturance and child rearing. For Rousseau, as for others, women suffered under dual and contradictory expectations: that they are morally stunted on the one hand, yet repositories of moral strength sufficient to raise and guide children and nurture families. As Rousseau makes clear, women's value is relative to male assessment. Whatever empowerment she has is through a perverse employment of her weakness as an expression of beauty to be used as a seductive tool to manipulate men for her own designs. She has no authentic strength of her own. What Rousseau had provided was a secular justification for the biblical notion of women as temptresses and moral predators.

Rousseau's observations are significant because they compel us to accept that any celebration of the Enlightenment must come to terms with a stubborn fact: its exponents excluded more than half the human race from their program. Such values as liberty, equality, indeed, fraternity, even universalism, were meant to apply to white European males only. Others simply did not rise high enough on the scale of rational capacity to count.

But Rousseau's assessment of women was significant for another reason still. It was significant because it received an answer, and that answer was the opening event of what was to evolve much later into the women's movement.

Exactly thirty years after Rousseau published his *Emile*, and at the height of the French Revolution, Mary Wollstonecraft wrote *A Vindication of the Rights of Woman*, a philosophical manifesto of great polemical power that aimed at steering the French Revolution in the direction of including women in its revolutionary program.

A Vindication of the Rights of Woman reflects the vehement independence of its author. Wollstonecraft came from an unhappy middle-class English family. She was self-taught, became a founder of schools, and wrote twelve books before her untimely death in childbirth at the age of thirty-eight. Her work in education put her in touch with a circle of rational dissenters that included Joseph Priestley, Thomas Paine, William Blake, and William Goodwin, the anarchist and atheist minister, whom she married a year before her death.

A Vindication of the Rights of Woman, although not all that easy to read, is extraordinarily modern in exposing the pretenses surrounding the psychosexual relations between men and women. If corrected for its florid language, one would think that it was written yesterday and not two hundred years ago.

As a philosopher of the Enlightenment, Wollstonecraft argued that the cultivation of reason was essential for the development of moral virtue. She then argued that reason is universal and so there cannot be separate virtues or spheres for women and men, as Rousseau had maintained.

She says, for example:

> Women are to be considered either as moral beings, or so weak that they must be entirely subjugated to the superior faculties of men.

Let us examine this question. Rousseau declares that a woman should never for a moment feel herself independent, that she should be governed by fear to exercise her natural cunning, and made a coquettish slave in order to render her a more alluring object of desire, a *sweeter* companion to man, whenever he chooses to relax himself. He carries the arguments, which he pretends to draw from the indications of nature, still further, and insinuates that truth and fortitude, the cornerstones of all human virtue, should be cultivated with certain restrictions, because, with respect to the female character, obedience is the grand lesson which ought to be impressed with unrelenting vigor. What nonsense: when will a great man arise with sufficient strength of mind to puff away the fumes which pride and sensuality have thus spread over the subject! If women are by nature inferior to men, their virtues must be the same in quality, if not in degree, or virtue is a relative idea; consequently, their conduct should be founded on the same principles, and have the same aim.

Connected with man as daughters, wives, and mothers, their moral character may be estimated by their manner of fulfilling those simple duties; but the end, the grand end, of their exertions should be to unfold their own faculties and acquire the dignity of conscious virtue.

I am aware that this argument would carry me further than it may be supposed I wish to go; but I follow truth, and, still adhering to my first position, I will allow that bodily strength seems to give man a natural superiority over woman; and this is the only solid basis on which the superiority of the sex can be built. But I still insist that not only the virtue, but the *knowledge* of the two sexes should be the same in nature, if not in degree, and that women, considered not only as moral, but rational creatures, ought to endeavour to acquire human virtues (or perfections) by the *same* means as men, instead of being educated like a fanciful kind of *half* being—one of Rousseau's wild chimeras.

Wollstonecraft was tremendously insightful, incisive, and radical in her analysis of how the status quo kept women as children, transformed them into nothing but coquettes and playthings to satisfy male interests, and evoked a superficial and phony gallantry in men. In the final analysis, it is a condition that not only debases women and violates the basic canons of reason, but also corrupts men and undermines the strength of the family. Passages such as the following are typical:

> Gentleness, docility, and a spaniel-like affection are, on this ground, consistently recommended as the cardinal virtues of the sex; and, disregarding the arbitrary economy of nature, one writer has declared that it is masculine for a woman to be melancholy. She was created to be the toy of man, his rattle, and it must jingle in his ears whenever, dismissing reason, he chooses to be amused.

And as for Rousseau's conclusions about little girls, their love of dolls, and their mode of play, she asserts the following:

> I have, probably, had an opportunity of observing more girls in their infancy than J. J. Rousseau—I can recollect my own feelings, and I have looked steadily around me: yet, so far from coinciding with him in opinion respecting the first dawn of the female character, I will venture to affirm that a girl whose spirits have not been damped by inactivity, or innocence tainted by false shame, will always be a romp, and the doll will never excite attention unless confinement allows her no alternative. Girls and boys, in short, would play harmlessly together if the distinction of sex was not inculcated long before nature makes any difference—I will go further, and affirm, as an indisputable fact, that most of the women, in the circle of my observation, who have acted like rational

creatures, or shown any vigour of intellect, have accidentally been allowed to run wild—as some of the elegant formers of the fair sex would insinuate.

Though Mary Wollstonecraft's assault was radical and uncompromisingly polemical, her actual proposal for change was relatively tame. In the final analysis, her plea was for more equal opportunity. There being no women's movement, her efforts could only be those of persuasion, and the objects of her persuasion could only be men. Strictly speaking, she did not even argue that women are men's equals, not because she was not confident that given the opportunity they would rise to that level, but because they had not been given the chance; there was, therefore, scant evidence to drawn upon.

As a consistent exponent of the Enlightenment, her program centered around equal opportunity in education for girls and boys and the subsequent entrée of women into the professions as equals. As an Enlightenment thinker, her tools were those of disinterested reason and the sturdy faith that the degraded status of women was a result of the social environment in which they were forced to be raised, and not because of any natural defect.

Though Mary Wollstonecraft had a few female precursors, and some women did achieve status as the owners and managers of intellectual salons where the elite gathered to spread the doctrine of the Enlightenment, she was essentially a lone voice in the wilderness, at least fifty years ahead of her time.

It was not in the stuffy class-bound societies of Europe that the idea of women's rights gained currency, but in the fertile fields and open stretches of the New World.

America held forth the promise to be different. The condition of women in colonial America and up until the 1840s was similar to that of Europe. Women had no political or civil rights. A married woman, especially, fell under the doctrine of *femme couvert*, which meant that she was a political nonentity, totally subordinate to her husband. In practical terms, this meant that women could not sign contracts, did not own the wages that they had earned, did not own their property even if they inherited it, and had no claims over their own children in the rare instances of divorce. Indeed, the very physical person of the woman was construed to be the property of her husband. This notion of "civil death" for women was reinforced by custom, by English common law, and also by religion. The church, in particular, reinforced the doctrine that men and women occupied by nature separate spheres, which stringently upheld a woman's oppressed status. Also limiting the empowerment of women was the customary sanction prohibiting women from traveling unescorted by men. Nor could women speak in public.

These conditions were taken for granted until there emerged agitation for change, at which point they had to be justified. The justification usually given, by enlightened and unenlightened alike, was woman's natural condition of dependence. No economic independence, no political rights. When John Adams asked the question "Whence arises the right of men to govern the women without their consent?" he found his answer in the notion of men's power to feed, clothe, and employ women, and therefore make political decisions on their behalf. This idea is important, because it meant that the movement for political rights, and in particular the right to vote, signaled the radical transformation of women's social and economic status. This would move them out of the sphere of the home, where they had been from time immemorial, and into the sphere of public life.

Certain conditions on the American scene permitted that slowly to happen.

First, America's frontier areas brought with them a rugged egalitarianism in the world of work. Economic necessity often forced women to work alongside of men in wilderness areas. Women were indispensable. And because life was perilous, many women found themselves widowed with small children to support, and thus were forced into carrying on their husbands' businesses. More important was the development of industrialization, particularly around textile mills in New England in the early decades of the nineteenth century. The need for labor brought women out of the home in large numbers for the first time. With the growth of industry and urbanization came the need for increased education, and it was here that women made their first independent initiatives on the American scene. Women such as Emma Willard and Frances Wright organized the first subsidized schools for women. Inspired by the writings of Mary Wollstonecraft, Wright, in particular, promoted radical equality in education, and became the first woman to give public lectures, which had great appeal to the working class, both men and women, at a time when speaking to mixed audiences was particularly verboten.

But the beginning of organization for political rights for women was propelled by women's involvement in the great movement for the abolition of slavery in the 1830s and 1840s. It was in the abolitionist movement that women found an ideological parallel for their own condition and developed the practical skills that enabled them to organize on their own behalf. This does not mean to imply that women discovered their oppression in the abolitionist movement, but that it gave them a vehicle by which they could turn the perception of their condition into a political movement.

Here the church was a two-edged sword. On the one hand, the early movement for abolition came out of the churches. Women, who were always active in religious life, formed antislavery groups within the churches. But once these groups became overtly political and started to organize, the heavy hand of the clergy came down hard, particularly on women, and the established churches dropped their commitment to abolition. The exception was the liberal churches—the Unitarians and particularly the Quakers—in which women had from early on a virtually equal role with men, including the right to speak before the congregations and to serve as "ministers." Consequently, it was no coincidence that many of the leaders of the abolitionist and early feminist movements were, in fact, Quakers.

It was not until William Lloyd Garrison attacked the Protestant clergy for their regressive stance on slavery that the abolitionist movement grew, and with it the feminist movement. Garrisonian abolition provided a vehicle by which women could escape the control of the clergy and begin to organize on behalf of abolition and, out of that initiative, for women's rights. It provided them with an opportunity to move beyond their "separate sphere" and into the maelstrom of public and political life. And so they did. Women began to organize their separate antislavery groups, to petition, to take an active and dangerous role in the Underground Railroad, and to hold antislavery rallies, which at times ended in physical violence.

Among the early feminists who were organizers of the abolitionist movement were Lucy Stone, Lucretia Mott, Frances Harper, Sojourner Truth, and Susan B. Anthony. The first to take up the cause of women's rights out of their commitment to abolition were Angelina and Sarah Grimke, two sisters from a slave-holding family in South Carolina who hated slavery. The Grimkes became fervent lecturers and organizers in the cause of abolition, and because they stepped far beyond the bounds of female propriety, they attracted the wrath of the clergy. It was in response to that assault on them as women that they began to organize for women's rights, and many were to follow. As one can imagine, the Grimkes were implored to drop the women's issue lest it undermine the cause of abolition. To which Angelina Grimke responded, "Why, my dear brothers, can you not see the deep-laid scheme of the clergy against us as lecturers?...If we surrender the right to *speak* in public this year, we must surrender the right to petition next year, and the right to *write* the year after, and so on. What *then* can *woman* do for the slave, when she herself is under the feet of man and shamed into *silence?*"

The cause of abolition also played a fateful role for the women's movement in the unfolding of a key historical event. In the summer of 1840, a World Antislavery Convention was held in London. Among those who attended were Lucretia Mott, the founder of the first Female Antislavery Society, for which she had become internationally known, and Elizabeth Cady Stanton, who was married to an abolitionist. Yet when the conference began, they were denied seating as delegates because they were women. The contradictions hit home.

Upon returning to America, Stanton and her family moved to the small community of Seneca Falls, New York. Faced with the intolerable drudgery of housework in an isolated community, she later wrote:

> I now fully understood the practical difficulties most women had to contend with in the isolated household, and the impossibility of woman's best development if in contact, the chief part of her life, with servants and children....Emerson says: "A healthy discontent is the first step to progress." The general discontent I felt with woman's portion as wife, mother, housekeeper, physician, and spiritual guide, the chaotic condition into which everything fell without her constant supervision, and the wearied, anxious look of the majority of women impressed me with the strong feeling that some active measures should be taken to remedy the wrongs of society in general and of women in particular. My experiences at the World Antislavery Convention, all I had read of the legal status of women, and the oppression I saw everywhere together swept across my soul, intensified now by many personal experiences.

It seemed as if all the elements had conspired to impel me to some onward step. I could not see what to do or where to begin—my only thought was a public meeting for protest and discussion.

It was out of that frustration that Stanton, Lucretia Mott, and three other women put out a call for a women's rights convention, which they published in the county newspaper on July 14, 1848. Within five days three hundred people arrived from a radius of fifty miles to sign a "Declaration of Sentiments and Resolutions." The declaration was deliberately preambled with a paraphrase from the Declaration of Independence to include women. It contained twelve resolutions calling for the complete equality of women and men with regard to social responsibilities and behaviors, with regard to access to the trades and professions, and in matters of religion. It was explicit in asserting that men held a tyranny over women. In its resolutions it incorporated all the major demands of the women's movement for the next one hundred years. All the resolutions passed unanimously with one exception, which passed only with a narrow margin, and that was the right of elective franchise. In 1848 a women's right to vote was still considered too radical and too daring to leave the framers and signers of the declaration secure in their demand. As hesitant as they were in making that demand, the Seneca Falls Convention marked the beginning of the organized women's movement in the United States and the last time the issue of female suffrage was ever again controversial within that movement.

The movement for women's rights lay dormant during the Civil War and received a cruel blow when the Fourteenth Amendment explicitly excluded women in its intent to enfranchise freed slaves. The support women gave to the abolitionists was not returned in kind. From then on the movement for women's suffrage became an independent grassroots movement, in time engaging the energies of hundreds of thousands of people, and the ceaseless commitments of such leaders as Elizabeth Cady Stanton and Susan B. Anthony.

It was a long seventy-two years from the Seneca Falls Declaration to the passage of the Nineteenth Amendment in 1920. In fact, only one of the signers of the Seneca Falls Declaration lived long enough to exercise the franchise to vote.

After the Civil War, the women's movement seized upon the right to vote as their guiding issue. They dedicated themselves to winning the right to vote not as a narrow institutional reform of American political life. Rather, they did so because they saw in suffrage the promise of transforming their lives and lifting the burdens of the social oppression. In hindsight we sadly know that it was a promise only partially kept.

July 2008

Emerson: The American Sage
At Two Hundred

In 1903, in Concord, Massachusetts, at a ceremony observing the one hundredth anniversary of the birth of Ralph Waldo Emerson, the famed American philosopher William James noted the following:

> The pathos of death is this, that when the days of one's life are ended, those days that were so crowded with business and felt so heavy in their passing, what remains of one in memory should usually be so slight a thing. The phantom of an attitude, the echo of a certain mode of thought, a few pages of print, some invention, or some victory we gained in a brief critical hour are all that can survive the best of us. It is as if the whole of a man's significance had now shrunk into the phantom of an attitude, into a mere musical note or phrase suggestive of his singularity—happy are those whose singularity gives a note so clear as to be victorious over the inevitable pity of such a diminution and abridgment.

Then speaking of Emerson, who had died scarcely twenty years earlier, James observed:

> The form that so lately moved upon these streets and country roads, or awaited in these fields and woods the

beloved Muse's visits, is now dust; but the soul's note, the
spiritual voice, rises strong and clear above the uproar of the
times, and seems securely destined to exert an ennobling influence over future generations.

Well, we are now at the year (2003) marking the two hundredth anniversary of the birth of Emerson, and we are part of the future generations of
which James spoke. Turning James's prophecy into a challenge, I ask whether
Emerson's voice is still heard today and whether it continues to exert an ennobling influence over our times, as it did over his own.

If truth be told, I think Emerson's voice is not heard today as loudly as it
was one hundred years ago. But it is not silent, nor, by any stretch, are Emerson's
words and deeds irrelevant to our self-understanding as Americans two hundred years after his birth. For Ethical Culturists, his relevance is incalculably
great, for Ethical Culture was inspired into existence by Emerson's thought,
and we continue to resonate with his spirit and remain guided by his vision.

In this chapter, I want to look at his contribution and its distinctiveness and
what endures in his message.

This is not easy to do, because Emerson was a complex thinker. If he has
been the bane of every high school English student, there is good warrant for
this. Emerson's thought is often enigmatic, his metaphors erudite, his rhetoric
highbrow, and his message elusive. Emerson speaks in aphorisms, not in tightly
drawn paragraphs. He is like an oracle who descends from the stratosphere
and encourages you to rise up to meet him halfway. To read Emerson is to be
provoked by his substance and his style, for he is surely a provocateur. His aph-
oristic pronouncements always imply more than they say, and he invites you,
the reader, to take his pithy wisdom and round out and complete his thoughts
with thoughts of your own. He often offends your values while he challenges
your mind and inspires your creativity. To read Emerson is to soar to new
heights and plunge into the depths, beyond which you sense even more wisdom resides, and to come away challenged, maybe even transformed. To read
Emerson is not to saunter with him, but to grapple with him in the service of
a kind of intellectualized therapy.

Who was Ralph Waldo Emerson, and what was his contribution? Emerson
was the unchallenged leader of what is often referred to as the American

Renaissance. He was at the center of a club of fascinating and creative individualists who flourished in the three decades before the Civil War. They were the movers and shakers of what history refers to as the transcendentalist movement. Among the major transcendentalists we find, in addition to Emerson, figures such as Orestes Brownson, George Ripley, Bronson Alcott, Margaret Fuller, Theodore Parker, and Henry David Thoreau. Out of transcendentalism from the mid-1830s to the Civil War grew the first rumblings of the abolitionist movement, feminism, utopianism, and literary romanticism. Not only were the transcendentalists religious radicals and social reformers, they were also master prose stylists, essayists, poets, correspondents, and obsessive diary keepers. They communed with nature as they did with one another, and with the times in which they lived. Here was a small band of individuals who knew each other, were ingeniously creative and energetic, and had a disproportionate influence in transforming the American landscape, artistically, religiously, and politically. Among their heirs were such luminaries as Louisa Mary Alcott, Walt Whitman, Emily Dickinson, Robert Frost, even Abraham Lincoln.

The transcendentalists all came out of Boston Unitarianism, and at least half of them were Unitarian ministers. The Unitarianism of the day was the liberal wing of Calvinist Christianity, which still echoed with the austerity of its Puritan heritage. Unitarianism then was not what it was to become one hundred years later, and what it is today. It was, in Emerson's time, heavily doctrinal, intellectually dry, rationalistic, and very proper.

Ralph Waldo Emerson was born on May 25, 1803, and for all but thirty-two years, his male ancestors on his father's side were Congregational ministers in Concord, Massachusetts, going back to 1635. Like several generations before him, Emerson went to Harvard in 1817, graduated in 1821 at the age of eighteen, studied for the ministry, and became a pastor at the Second Unitarian Church in Boston in 1829.

But in 1832, Emerson's growing religious doubts became a crisis. He felt that he could no longer in good conscience administer the central rite of Christian devotion, the ritual of Communion. When his congregation refused to go along with him in dropping the ritual, he quit. He left the ministry and pursued a religious path that took him outside of Christianity. He became a religious radical, a heretic, and abandoned the ministry to become an itinerant sage.

At the moment he refused to administer the rite of Communion, Emerson became Emerson. His reasons for leaving the ministry foreshadowed the central thrust of his developing world view and his contribution to American thought and values. He went public with a sermon, and among his reasons, he gave the following: "This mode of commemorating Christ is not suitable to me," he said. "Freedom is the essence of Christianity....Its institutions should be as flexible as the wants of man. The form out of which the life and suitableness have departed should be as worthless in its eyes as the dead leaves that are falling around us."

This seemingly simple protest that the religious rituals of Christianity were not suitable to him implies far more than it says, and, as noted, presages Emerson's subsequent philosophy, for in that protest Emerson is saying that he rejects second-hand religion. To engage in the rites of the Last Supper is to engage in an act of imitation. It is to do it because someone else did it before. It is to be obedient to the authority of another, and another time, rather than to one's own inner authority. Because it is religious experience second hand, and not one's own immediate and direct experience, it is drained of authenticity, and it is drained of life.

Let me put it this way. Emerson, like his fellow transcendentalists, was an exponent of what is known as the Romantic movement. What is Romanticism? One way of defining it is to note that for the Romantic, a person's feelings, emotions, and intuitions are an organ of knowledge. The Romantics believed that one's feelings were like a sixth sense that could, with near infallibility and with immediacy, know with certainty and conviction things that the mind, intellect, and reflection could never so securely grasp. With the intellect we can only know the surface of things. But with the heart, with the emotions, with intuition, we can immediately grip, they believed, Justice, Truth, and Beauty with a certainty that was self-evident. For the Romantic, you simply know in your heart Beauty and Truth when you see them. Cogitating over these things will never quite get you there.

Emerson articulated this Romantic principle with extraordinary eloquence and power. He argued for men and women to see their lives not through the lives of others, or in response to what others want them to be, but to have their own individual, authentic, firsthand experience of life. Moreover, he bade people to trust their inner selves, the voice from within, which he believed spoke with a type of universal truthfulness. In order to trust ourselves, Emerson believed, we need to put aside the mystique and the authority of other people, of social conformity, and of the past, with which we are so willing to endow those agencies external to us.

The opening lines of the initial essay of his book *Nature* make this program clear. He says,

> Our age is retrospective. It builds the sepulchers of the fathers. It writes biographies, histories, and criticism. The foregoing generations beheld God and nature face to face; we, through their eyes. Why should not we also enjoy an original relation to the universe? Why should not we have a poetry and philosophy of insight and not of tradition, and a religion by revelation to us, and not the history of theirs?...
>
> The sun shines today also. There is more wool and flax in the fields. There are new lands, new men, new thoughts. Let us demand our own works and laws and worship.

With these lines we can begin to put Emerson in his context and see why he is a preeminent bard of the American experience.

Emerson was born in 1803, the date when the Louisiana Purchase more than doubled the size of the United States. American horizons were boundless and the frontier limitless. We were a vast, open land that beckoned limitless opportunity. America represented a pristine place that had potentially thrown off the shackles of stuffy, aristocratic, class-bound, history-enslaved Europe. Moreover, there were the first glimmers of the Industrial Revolution in America—the steamboat, the telegraph, the emergence of factories. In America, one could make life anew.

Emerson's thought resonates with that newness. He wants to provoke Americans to take seriously their possibilities, their birthright for creativity, novelty, and spiritual invigoration. In his own terminology, Emerson divides the history of America into the party of the past and the party of hope. On one side, we have writers such as Hawthorne and Melville with their brooding pessimism, tragedy, and generally dark vision of the human condition. On the other side, we have people such as Whitman, and Emerson himself, who are the heralds of optimism and faith in the future.

What are the sources of the optimism and this hope? For Emerson, they reside in our capacity for self-reliance, which is also the title of one of his most famous essays.

Emerson presupposes an initial state of timid, unhappy conformism. The antidote is to go deeply into the self to the realm of what Emerson refers to as the "aboriginal self," the me at the bottom of the me, beyond the zones shaped by daily preoccupations, the expectations of others, and the pressures of conformity. When you have touched these depths, Emerson believes, you will be able to tap the font of your creative energy, your genuine selfhood. You will touch the wellsprings of authenticity, originality, creativity, and life.

Let me give you some powerful examples from Emerson himself, from his essay "Self-Reliance":

Whoever would be a man must be a noncomformist...

Nothing is at last sacred but the integrity of your own mind...

No law can be sacred to me but that of my nature. Good and bad are but names very readily transferable to this or that; the only right is what is after my own constitution; the only wrong what is against it...

I am ashamed to think how easily we capitulate to badges and names, to large societies and dead institutions. In every work of genius we recognize our own rejected thoughts; they come back to us with a certain alienated majesty.

Man is timid and apologetic; he is no longer upright; he dares not say "I think," "I am," but quotes some saint or sage. He is ashamed before the blade of grass or the blowing rose. These roses under my window make no reference to former roses or to better ones; they are for what they are; they exist with God today. There is no time to them. There is simply the rose; it is perfect in every moment of its existence. Before a leaf bud has burst, its whole life acts; in the full-blown flower there is no more; in the leafless root there is no less. Its nature is satisfied and it satisfies nature in all movements alike. But man postpones or remembers; he does not live in the present, but with reverted eye laments the past, or, heedless of the riches that surround him, stands on tiptoe to foresee the future. He cannot be happy and strong until he too lives with nature in the present, above time.

The other terror that scares us from self-trust is our consistency; a reverence for our past act or word because the eyes of others have no other data for computing our orbit than our past acts, and we are loath to disappoint them.

And then my favorite quote from Emerson:

A foolish consistency is the hobgoblin of little minds, adored by little statesmen and philosophers and divines. With consistency a great soul has simply nothing to do. He may well concern himself with his shadow on the wall. Speak what you will now in hard words and tomorrow speak what tomorrow thinks in hard words again, though it contradict everything you said today. "Ah, so you will be sure to be misunderstood." Is it so bad then to be misunderstood? Pythagoras was misunderstood, and Socrates, and Jesus, and Luther, and Copernicus, and Galileo, and Newton, and every pure and wise spirit that ever took flesh. To be great is to be misunderstood.

It is the assertion of this kind of militant individualism in the face of all forms of social pressure and conformity that made Emerson Friedrich Nietzsche's favorite American. For Nietzsche, the only constant in nature is "the will to power," the primordial thrust of the individual to perpetually over-come others and to perpetually overcome the self. In Emerson, he saw a part-way kindred spirit.

But what, we may ask, saves Emerson's individualism and self-reliance from quickly becoming nothing but egocentricity, narcissism, selfishness, and sheer idiosyncrasy? It is here that Emerson's thought turns metaphysical and religious.

There is a paradox in Emerson's thinking, which is one of the things that makes him difficult. He claims that the deeper you go into the individual self, the less individual you become.

Emerson, the Romantic, is a pantheist. He believes that the divine spirit, God, permeates everything and, as such, flows through us as well. But Emerson's God is austerely impersonal, both transcendent and immanent; a force or spirit that in a way is more real than the physical and material world we experience through our senses. When we bore into the deepest part of ourselves, our aboriginal selves, we tap the flow of the divine, which is the same impersonal force that flows through all of us, as it flows through all of nature. It is as if there is an impersonal divine mind of which our own indi-vidual minds partake. We are manifestations of that divine mind, as is every-thing else in nature. Emerson refers to this divine flux that passes through us as "the Oversoul." For Emerson, God is not "out there"; God is within each of us. "As a man's prayers are a disease of the will," says Emerson, "so are his creeds a disease of the intellect." "Obey thyself," he says. "That which shows God in me, fortifies me. That which shows God out of me makes me a wart and a wen." Sometimes Emerson goes as far as to imply that at the deepest level we are all the same. The deeper you go into your individuality, the less individual you become, but the more God-like you become. Hold this idea in your mind because I will get back to it when I talk about Emerson's relation-ship to Ethical Culture.

Emerson once summed up his own thinking by saying, "In all my lectures, I have taught one doctrine, the infinitude of the private man." That is, there is a direct line from the inner recesses of the individual, private self that leads all the way up to infinity, to God.

Needless to say, this kind of doctrine scandalized Emerson's respectable religious peers, because there is nothing Christian about it. In fact, Emerson was among the first Americans to discover Asian religions, and his religious thought is explicitly closer to Hinduism than it is to Christianity.

Back to "Self-Reliance." Emerson writes,

> What is the aboriginal Self, on which a universal self may be grounded?…The inquiry leads us to the source, at once the essence of genius, of virtue, and of life, which we call Spontaneity or Instinct. We denote this primary wisdom Intuition…In that deep force, the last fact behind which analysis cannot go, all things find their common origin…When we discern justice, when we discern truth, we do nothing ourselves but allow passage to its beams…Every man discriminates between the voluntary acts of his mind and his involuntary perceptions, and knows that to his involuntary perceptions a perfect faith is due…Wherever a mind is simple and receives divine wisdom, old things pass away— means, teachers, texts, temples fall; it lives now and absorbs past and future into the present hour.

And in a famous scenario in the essay "Nature," Emerson is walking in the forest and makes the following observation:

> In the woods is perpetual youth…There I feel nothing can befall me in life—no disgrace, no calamity, which nature cannot repair. Standing on the bare ground—my head bathed by the blithe air and uplifted into infinite space—all mean egotism vanishes. I become a transparent eyeball; I am nothing, I see all; the currents of the Universal Being circulate through me…The greatest delight which the fields and woods minister is the suggestion of the occult relation between man and the vegetable. I am not alone and unacknowledged. They nod to me, and I to them.

These metaphors were over the top even in Emerson's day, and the image of the "transparent eyeball" was the source of caricatures by contemporary cartoonists.

This unity of self with Universal Being is, of course, mysticism, and we can correctly conclude that Emerson was the first New Age guru, an early apostle of the Age of Aquarius, as well as a forerunner of humanistic psychology with its emphasis on self-actualization and peak experiences.

These few themes, needless to say, only begin to scratch the surface of Emerson's thought. But with this introduction, it is not hard to see why Felix Adler, the founder of Ethical Culture, was attracted to Emerson. In fact, in one of his essays, Emerson expresses his hope that in the future America will create a new religion of pure ethics. And we can rightly regard Ethical Culture as a fulfillment of Emerson's vision.

Adler liked Emerson's appeal to the new. He liked the fact that Emerson's commitment to the individual made him a philosopher of democracy. And his call to America to recognize its own greatness and originality appealed to Adler, the immigrant, who was striving to establish himself in his new land.

Adler was also strongly attracted to Emerson's religious radicalism. Both Adler and Emerson shared a conviction that the modern world and modern science had trumped a belief in a supernatural and personal God who is outside of us and who performs miracles.

Moreover, Emerson's transcendentalism and his conviction that man is not merely a material being, but that there is divine spirit that is part of us, and of which we partake, resonated with Adler. Most importantly, Adler was attracted to the fact that Emerson consecrates the human being; that he makes the person holy and sacred. This was the center of Adler's own philosophical quest—how to ground or justify the sacredness or worthiness of the person.

In 1875, when Adler was twenty-four and the Sage of Concord was seventy-two, they met. Adler was duly impressed. He later wrote, "Divinity as an object of extraneous worship for me had vanished. Emerson taught that immediate experience of the divine power in self may take the place of worship. His doctrine of self-reliance also was bracing to a youth just setting out to challenge prevailing opinions and to urge plans of transformation upon the community in which he worked."

For a while, Adler states, Emerson intoxicated him, and he walked with his head in the clouds, clouds with which Emerson enveloped him. But as he matured, Adler became critical of Emerson for reasons that we hinted at above. Recall that for Emerson, the more we dig into ourselves, the more we touch upon the spiritual substance within, which Emerson tells us is undifferentiated. The fact that at bottom we are all the same caused Adler to believe that there was something wanting in Emerson's ethics. For Adler, what makes us worthy is not our sameness with others, but, on the contrary, our distinctiveness, our uniqueness. If we were all replicas of each other, then we would be replaceable and expendable. It is our differences that make us unique and, therefore, ultimately worthy. In Adler's words, "According to Emerson, life is a universal masquerade, and the interest of the whole business of living consists in the ever renewed discovery that the face behind the masks is still the same. Difference is not cherished on its own account." He concludes his critique of Emerson by saying, "He is genuinely American—a rare blend of ancient mystic and modern Yankee, a valued poet, too, but as an ethical guide to be accepted only with large reservation."

These are technical but perhaps not unimportant differences. Of more importance is the question of the lasting significance of Emerson to us today. What does he leave us of lasting value?

Emerson's influence since he hit his prime before the Civil War has ranged broadly across the American landscape. His influence has been felt in philosophy, literature, religion, psychology, and in the field of progressive social action. Mathew Arnold thought Emerson was the most important prose writer of the nineteenth century. John Dewey wrote that Emerson was the only American thinker worthy of being ranked with Plato.

Speaking for myself, in a broad sense, I owe my job to Emerson, for Emerson was America's first important public intellectual. Emerson was not a technical philosopher. He was not a novelist nor a playwright. He gave lectures and wrote essays, thousands of lectures and hundreds of well-crafted essays. He referred to himself as a poet, but history has defined him primarily as a seer and a sage, and he has become a public icon. He was a founder of what was known as the lyceum movement, a movement of loosely connected forums in cities and towns devoted to lectures, debates, and entertainment. In the latter decades of the nineteenth century, Ethical Culture replicated this model when Felix Adler rented Carnegie Hall to address crowds of thousands on the issues of the day. Our platform and the Ethical Society continue in the tradition Emerson made popular.

Emerson also transformed religion, creating what the Yale critic Harold Bloom has called the "American religion." Emerson allows you to be religious and spiritual and believe in a transcendent reality without believing in the supernatural. His religious views imply a type of aesthetic that merges religion with literature and poetry. In the words of the historian of religion Sydney Ahlstrom, "Emerson was a new kind of romantic pagan, one who throws from the temple not only the money changers, but the priests as well, and with them their beliefs, creeds, and rituals."

Emerson provides an antidote to tragedy, and he is the philosopher of optimism and hope. In great measure, his philosophy of self-reliance was a response to tragedy of his own. Emerson's father died when Waldo was only eight. His first wife, Ellen, died just a year and a half after they were married. As a young man, Emerson lost two of his brothers, and then his own beloved son, Waldo, died before he was seven years old. To read Emerson then and now is to find anchorages in a changing and often tragic world in which one can face a new day inspired by hope and confidence in one's own powers.

But we cannot lose sight of Emerson's inspiration as a social reformer. He lacked the grit of his colleague, Henry David Thoreau, and he was not as radical as Theodore Parker, who was perhaps the greatest intellectual, activist preacher America has ever had. Yet Emerson was deeply committed to redressing the injustices of his day.

His philosophy of the divinity of each person stood against the oppression and degradation of the individual and served as a basis for justice, democracy, and freedom. Anticipating Thoreau's civil disobedience, Emerson proclaimed, "Every actual State is corrupt. Good men must not obey the laws too well."

Though he came to it later than some of his fellow transcendentalists, in part because his individualism made him skeptical of all organizations, Emerson became an outspoken and courageous defender of the abolitionist cause, which, of course, was the most pressing moral and political issue of the day. He spoke on platforms with the great Frederick Douglass and by the late 1850s threw himself totally into the cause of the abolition of slavery. He forcefully opposed the Fugitive Slave Law, which he called a "filthy enactment," and he lauded John Brown, who led the raid on Harper's Ferry, as a true hero.

In Emerson's individualism some have seen a defense of free-market capitalism, even admiration for the successful businessman who asserts his powers within the dynamics of the market. And there is no doubt some truth to this. What is also true is that Emerson hated the vulgarities of the excesses of the marketplace. He characterizes the emerging capitalist economy as a "system of selfishness...of distrust, of concealment, of superior keenness, not of giving, but of taking advantage." He goes so far as to claim, "There is nothing more important than to resist the dangers of commerce." Moreover, it was Emerson who warned us that "things are in the saddle and they ride mankind."

To my mind, Emerson's most lasting legacy is this: In his tremendous erudition, scholarship, and eloquence, he reminds us of the dignity and nobility of culture. In his ability to make nature sacred and to sanctify the mundane, he brings to our world elegance and beauty. In his abiding regard for the individual, he urges us to believe in ourselves and to bring our creative potentials to the light of day. In his faith in the genius that resides in each of us, he endows us with the courage to be nonconformists in the face of everything that deadens the human spirit.

We live in a time of mass conformity, driven by the vicissitudes of the market. We live in a time ruled by technology and the demands of the machine. It's an era when democracy is in danger, and the individual feels less empowered in the face of government. It is an era when old-time authoritarian religion has made an ominous comeback and people have given themselves over to powers not of themselves. It is a time that Emerson would recognize, and that he would not have liked.

If we can wrest from Ralph Waldo Emerson's words even a little bit of hope, optimism, and faith in ourselves, we will have proven his relevance to our time, as he so powerfully did to his own.

May 2003

John Dewey And Us

To be a liberal or a progressive in these times is to be swamped in rough seas, clinging to a lifeboat that is sinking fast. The tides of political reaction have all but drowned the once mighty forces of progressivism in America, while liberals hold their breath, hoping the storm will, in time, be stilled and then move on.

Before our very eyes, and with lightning speed, the New Deal, together with the humane and decent values it embodied, is being run in reverse. The noble and civilized idea that all of us, through the instruments of government, are responsible for the poor, the sick, and the undereducated is being replaced by the idolization of the free market and the glorification of selfishness. For all practical purposes, the social safety net is being reconstructed. It is being destroyed. It is a triumphant maneuver, as immoral as it is reckless.

Congress is playing a dangerous game. We, the hurting and vulnerable middle class, are being told the cause of our plight is those unfortunates and social parasites who demand more of our tax dollar while giving nothing in return. We are told that our attention and anger, born of insecurity, should be turned on the least among us.

We need to be very cautious. What we are witnessing is a war against the poor—scapegoating that has as its aim the further enrichment of the wealthy at the expense of the rest of us. Make no mistake: despite problems caused by the global economy, America remains awash in capital. The strategy is to concentrate that capital among those at the top while we all look the other way. In a masterful maneuver of political leadership, the hurricanes of reaction, from Ronald Reagan to Newt Gingrich, have condemned those at the bottom while silencing, marginalizing, and anathematizing liberalism's good name. It's a sad and, for many, a demoralizing era.

It is also confusing. In the light of that confusion, many once-proud liberals have been cowed into silence. Others have defected from the liberal camp and become neoconservatives. Still others have given up on politics and retreated to their own private gardens. And many, feeling the political and philosophical foundations crumbling under their feet, have sought a new sense of meaning and security through a pursuit of God and religion.

America, to be sure, has always been a conservative society. But weaving their way through conservatism there have always been golden threads of idealism and progressivism, which we in the Ethical Culture movement have identified with the best in America. Pulling against the conservative tide has been the vision that American society can redeem, renew, and reinvent itself, inspired by the ideals of justice, equality, and freedom. Unlike Europe, the progressive spirit of America has been not revolutionary, but reformist. Its spirit was kindled in the abolitionist movement, the union movement, the movement for women's suffrage, the New Deal, and lastly in the civil rights movement. But in the past three decades, that visionary, progressive sensibility with its great moral sweep has been replaced by the narrower politics of special interests and individual greed.

It is this predicament, felt most painfully by liberals—scattered and with their backs against the wall—that has caused them to seek new foundations and new sources of inspiration. It is this need that has led in intellectual circles to a resurgence of interest in the thought of American philosopher John Dewey.

We in the Ethical movement should have particular interest in what Dewey has to say, for Dewey was very much a humanist. Moreover, as I will show, Dewey had a very strong influence on our movement, both directly and indirectly. In fact, it would be correct to conclude that the philosophy of most Ethical Culturists today is implicitly Deweyan; certainly closer to Dewey than it is to our founder, Felix Adler. The importance of Dewey's thoughts and our closeness to them suggest that Ethical Culture is on the right track and that what we are doing is more significant than we in the movement and those outside it give us credit for.

It is not that Dewey, who died in 1952, provides programmatic answers to the problems we confront today. Rather, Dewey's approach to problems of politics, society, education, and religion offer compelling ways for us to think about ourselves in our relationship to society. Without absolutes, without God and irrationality, Dewey's philosophy nevertheless points optimistically to a better future and inspires self-confidence and hope.

John Dewey was the greatest American philosopher of the twentieth century, perhaps in all American history. But what made Dewey distinctive was his direct influence beyond the academy.

Dewey lived a very long and awesomely productive life. Born in the small but emerging industrial city of Burlington, Vermont, in 1859, Dewey died in New York in 1952—thinking, writing, and working until almost his last day. Hence, Dewey was born before the Civil War, lived through the height of the Industrial Revolution, witnessed the tumultuous changes of an increasingly urbanized America, and died after World War II.

Dewey's philosophical output was enormous. He worked philosophically and at great length on problems of ethics, art, psychology, sociology, logic, religion, politics, and the area for which he is best known and was most influential—education. Dewey's influence on American culture has been far reaching and deeply resonant for reasons I will shortly explain. But it is all the more extraordinary because Dewey, consistent with his roots in Vermont, was a shy, modest, and taciturn man all his life. Moreover, his writing style is difficult and dry, long on detail but with few illustrations and metaphors to engage the reader. More significantly, Dewey was not an exciting speaker. Yet when Dewey spoke publicly, as he often did, working people, activists as well as academics, came out in large numbers to learn what the great mind was thinking. Henry Steele Commager once said of him, "So faithfully did Dewey live up to his own philosophical creed that he has become the guide, the mentor, and (the) conscience of the American people; it is scarcely an exaggeration to say that for a generation no issue was clarified until Dewey had spoken."

What Commager meant by Dewey's "creed" was his philosophical conviction that the importance of ideas, the very process of thinking, is tied directly to action. Ideas, for Dewey, are not sterile abstractions to be revered, refined, and worshipped. Rather, ideas are intertwined with and lead back to the gritty, inelegant, and often grimy world of experience and action.

Though moving into the "real" world is too often sneered at by academics today, Dewey was an intellectual activist, a true man of the people. Dewey believed ideas needed be applied in a reformist spirit to educate children, and in the struggle to organize labor, and in the struggle for justice wherever there was injustice.

In the 1890s Dewey met Jane Addams, who had established Hull House as a settlement for immigrants in the middle of Chicago slums. It was Addams who took Dewey on tours of Chicago's red-light districts and meat-packing plants and exposed him to the corruption and destitution of big-city life and politics. At Hull House he witnessed democracy in action, where good works were done not *for* the poor, or *to* the poor, but where an environment was created in which the poor could govern themselves and use the condition of self-governance as a vehicle toward self-development and self-fulfillment. That very idea—that democracy isn't merely a political platform, but a far-reaching process that molds and creates character and in which personal fulfillment is achieved—became a cornerstone of Dewey's philosophy. It was also at Hull House that Dewey established his "laboratory school" as his first experimental effort at progressive education, for which he became famous.

Dewey served as the chairman of the Philosophy Department at the University of Chicago from 1894 to 1904. Prior to that he did his undergraduate work at the then tiny University of Vermont, and he taught high school for three years in Oil City, Pennsylvania. He received his Ph.D. from Johns Hopkins and taught briefly at the Universities of Minnesota and Michigan before going to Chicago. Dewey left Chicago for New York in 1904 to take up an appointment in Columbia's Philosophy Department. It was at Columbia that Dewey came into his prime as the leading luminary of that department in its golden age.

It was also the period in Dewey's life when he became internationally famous. That he could think and write as much as he did was quite extraordinary given the number of causes to which he devoted himself—not merely as a figurehead, but also as a grassroots worker and organizer.

Dewey traveled to Asia and lived and lectured for two years in China (1919–1921), gaining an outstanding reputation as a visiting sage. He lectured in Japan also, where it is said that his theories of cooperative education had more lasting influence than in this country. Back in New York, during the years before the Depression, Dewey wrote tirelessly about the need for public ownership and public control of the economy and the need for a third party, which would be socialist in fact, but not in name. Dewey was a tireless supporter of the trade union movement and wanted to see labor democratized so that assembly-line workers would share in decision making as well as profits.

Closest to his activist's interests was the unionization and professionalization of teachers. Dewey saw teaching as a noble profession that played a key role in creating a better, more democratic and humane society. For more than thirty years he was in the vanguard of winning greater independence and political and economic power for teachers. Dewey was a left-of-center Social Democrat who acted against conservative and authoritarian school boards on the capitalistic Right as he attempted to prevent takeovers of teachers' union by Communists on the Left.

Dewey defended academic freedom and argued against loyalty oaths for teachers. He walked picket lines on behalf of the American Federation of Teachers and participated in endless committee meetings defending everyone and everything, from the innocence of Sacco and Vanzetti, to Odell Waller, a Southern black sharecropper who had been framed for murder, to the need for art education in public schools.

Dewey was a stalwart liberal who exemplified Voltaire's dictum that "I disapprove of what you say, but I will defend to the death your right to say it." With this in mind, perhaps the most colorful events in Dewey's activist career occurred in 1937 and 1940 when he was well into retirement and about eighty years old.

Although not a Marxist and contemptuous of Soviet communism, Dewey nevertheless volunteered to travel to Mexico City to chair a commission investigating the guilt or innocence of Leon Trotsky. Trotsky, as almost Lenin's entire inner circle, had been condemned in Stalinist show trials for having allegedly betrayed the Bolshevik Revolution. Dewey believed that Trotsky was a brilliant, though absolutist, fanatic. Nevertheless, he had been wronged, and since most of the members of the commission were themselves Trotsky sympathizers, Dewey felt that his leadership of the commission would aid its impartiality. And so he went to Mexico City in 1937, took a deposition from Trotsky, won his respect, and found him innocent. Trotsky was, of course, murdered by one of Stalin's henchmen in 1940.

In that year, Bertrand Russell, a don at Oxford, had been denied a teaching position at City College. A complaint had been lodged against Russell by a parent with the backing of conservative religious groups, and it was upheld by the courts. The complaint alleged that Russell's teaching of logic to the complainant's daughter had been "lecherous, salacious, libidinous, lustful, venerous, erotomaniac, aphrodisiac—and also unscholarly."

Russell was indeed an advocate of free love, but Dewey saw this as a critical battle in the struggle against the forces of dogmatism, reaction, and intolerance, and came to Russell's defense. Dewey gave Russell a place to stay in his apartment, helped edit a series of essays in Russell's defense, and found a position for him to lecture at the Barnes Foundation in Philadelphia. This was a pretty noble act for Dewey to undertake, because Russell was a philosophical adversary who had often maliciously and rudely criticized Dewey's work on logic.

But what was Dewey's contribution as a philosopher and thinker that is relevant to us today? I can, of course, only touch upon some prevailing themes.

To begin, if you are looking for a glitzy, enchanting, rapturous, sexy philosophy of life that will grab you while answering all of life's problem and riddles, you won't find it in John Dewey. For Dewey there are no answers for us to discover. There is no cosmic assignment revealed to us that will instruct us as to what to do. There is no easy way out of the human predicament. Dewey rejected absolutes. He was neither a revolutionary nor a utopian. He would have detested the culture of narcissism and rejected New Age, self-help psychobabble and those varieties of teaching that provide formulaic and somewhat ecstatic answers to life's difficult problems.

So what were the centerpieces of Dewey's philosophy? Speaking philosophically, Dewey's overreaching project was to break down the dualities that most plague the thinking and behavior of both philosophers and nonphilosophers alike. Dewey's grand intellectual effort was to show the harmony and continuum between ideas and action, thinking and doing, science and religion, science and art, means and ends, facts and values, ideals and reality, and, most all for our interests, the interrelatedness of the individual and the community. Classical philosophy usually emphasized the separateness of these categories. Dewey, inspired in his youth by the philosophy of Hegel, sought to show their similarities and connections with each other.

But unlike Hegel, Dewey was a naturalist. What this means is that our science, our art, our ethics, even religion, do not come from outside the natural world; they are not supernatural. Rather, Dewey believed that human experience is the sole authority for what we can know. He was confident in our ability to rely on our own resources, the resources of emotion, observation, thought, and intelligence, in order to gain a secure understanding of ourselves and the world we inhabit. In this sense, Dewey was certainly a thoroughgoing humanist.

What it also meant was that Dewey distrusted not only supernaturalism, but rarefied, abstract reasoning as a way to get at knowledge. The only way we can acquire knowledge and gain some leverage on our condition is by experiencing the world and seeing where that experience leads us with regard to human satisfaction and happiness. Thinking about reality is not enough, Dewey declared. Thought alone is too sterile and leaves our lives meaningless. Rather, we must take our ideas as if they were hypotheses, insert them into the world, and test them against experience to see if they work for us.

As you might guess, Dewey was exceedingly impressed with the scientific method. But what is important about Dewey is that he believed that in our daily lives, we are all scientists of a sort. He believed that in our normal course of behavior we act like scientists, even when we are not conscious of doing so.

A central idea of Dewey's is that life confronts us on all levels, on the level of conscious thought and on the level of our biological functioning, with problems. Life is inherently problematic, and the process of living is the process of continuous problem solving.

Life is in continual flux, Dewey believed. As we move through life and interact with our environment, we bump up against problems and frustrations. As thinking beings, we bring our intelligence to bear in order to resolve these problems and relieve our frustrations. When we do so, we change not only our environment, but ourselves as well, and situate ourselves to confront new frustrations and resolve new problems. To the extent that this process gives us more control over ourselves and our environment, more ability to rethink our problems, and the potentiality for fruitful changes along the same lines, we may talk about "progress," though Dewey preferred the word "growth."

Central to Dewey's philosophy was what he called "creative intelligence." Again, the life of the mind is not sterile. Rather, he believed that in the act of solving problems, we can and must use our capacities for insight, observation, judgment, reason, and reflection, and also emotion, to analyze problems, test hypotheses, set goals, develop plans and methods by which to carry them out, and thus ensure that the result be as satisfactory as possible. When our ideas work in this way, when they test out in experience, we can claim that we have acquired knowledge. In fact, Dewey said this is the only knowledge that we can ever claim. To be sure, this knowledge is not Truth with a capital *T*. Dewey preferred to call it "warranted assertability." But it is significantly stable to give us a sense of confidence in ourselves and in our relationship to our world. Because of its radically experiential character, Dewey referred to his philosophy at various times as "pragmatism," "instrumentalism," and "experimentalism."

It is easy to see how these ideas can be applied to education and the development of children. Dewey hated rote learning in which unquestioned truths were handed down to children to be passively absorbed. While he did not romanticize children, he did believe that they are naturally curious and have an innate desire to explore their world. In a way that synthesized thinking and action, Dewey affirmed "learning by doing." He wanted schools to be living laboratories in which educational environments would as much as possible mirror the outside world, and thus enable children to learn by becoming problem solvers.

Dewey's conservative critics falsely accused him of being child centered, as if to imply that he felt teachers should play no active role in the classroom and that children would learn of their own accord if only left to their own natural devices—sort of like the assumptions employed by free schools of the 1960s. But this was not Dewey's view. He held to the firm belief that children are shaped by the creative efforts of their teachers, and that there was much content to be conveyed in order to enable schoolchildren to become active participants in a democratic society.

For Dewey, education and democracy are deeply interrelated. For most people, when thinking of democracy what comes to mind is pulling a lever in a voting booth once every four years, if that much. For Dewey that was democracy in its minimal, political form. What he meant was something much more enriching and engaging. For Dewey, democracy is not merely a political form; it is a social, moral, and psychological phenomenon. It is a far-reaching way of life that molds character, and through which we develop our purposes and find our sense of meaning. For Dewey, democracy is a moral ideal. It is through our active and democratic participation with others that we realize our individual potentials as we strive to perfect society. In short, through democratic participation, through the open flow of ideas, through working with others to solve common problems, we become ourselves.

Such ideas imply that human beings are inherently social and communal. There is no individual divorced from society. Again, the dualism that pits the individual against society is a false one. Our identities are deeply embedded in social relations with others—those who share our society and those who come after us. While we grow as individuals, we do so only through our active engagement with others, both in creative conflict and cooperatively; through living, learning, and acting democratically.

This, to my mind, is Dewey's most important message for today. We live in an era of hyperindividualism; a time when people feel the pain of isolation, of being lost without a sense of meaning; of being spiritually cut off from wider associations, allegiances, and purposes.

Dewey is what we today call a "communitarian." He tells us that our sense of meaning and purpose is not found in being a coach potato or amassing greater wealth or indulging the life of consumers. Our lives are molded through the active dedication and commitment to the welfare and improvement of the community. It is the dynamic immersion in a committed social life that evokes our intelligence and our other potentials, and through this process we find our place in the world. To be a communitarian in Dewey's philosophy is not to be a collectivist; it is not to lose the self in the life of the group. It is rather to become oneself through interactions in the life of the community. We may conclude that when the Ethical Culture Society functions well, it fulfills the Deweyan social ideal.

Dewey had a lot to say about religion, but in a modern idiom that should resonate clearly with us. As mentioned, Dewey was not a supernaturalist, and he did not accept the creeds and rituals of his Congregationalist background. Yet it is Steven Rockefeller's thesis that Dewey's entire philosophy sustained a religious outlook, even as he did away with religion. For Dewey, as for many of us, one could be religious, even as one did not adhere to specific beliefs, traditions, and practices of a particular religion.

Dewey devoted one book, which he called *A Common Faith*, extensively to religion. In the book, he denies that being religious requires adherence to any specific belief. Rather "the religious" is an experience or attitude of connection with the objects of our devotion, and especially with our ideals. Ideals for Dewey are unseen powers that move and inspire us to greater heights. But for Dewey, naturalist that he is, our ideals are not created by God, nor are they merely fantasies or wish fulfillments. In true Deweyan fashion, he says, "The aims and ideals that move us are generated through imagination, but they are not made of imaginary stuff. They are made out of the hard stuff of the world of physical and social experience."

What Dewey means is that we live and interact in the real world. Through the use of our imagination we rearrange that world and mentally project a state of affairs that would be better and more perfect. We then relate to those ideals in a way that inspires us to move toward them and so beyond ourselves. That experience of being connected to something beyond our current condition, be it a vision of a just society or greater beauty or the ideal of perfect peace, is what Dewey calls "the religious experience."

As I think I have implied, there is a sturdy optimism running through Dewey's thought. He believed in progress; not revolutionary progress, but progress that comes in slow, incremental steps. Moreover, Dewey believed that human beings, through hard experience, through the strength of the communal bond, through trial and error, and through the use of our creative intelligence, have the resources to create a better society.

Dewey had a confidence in what we might call the "viability of our everyday life." He did not share the sense of meaninglessness of our experience in the world without God that many of the existentialists, such as Sartre, were proclaiming. Nor did he feel the need for any cosmic support or custodian to guarantee the meaning and success of the human enterprise.

Late in Dewey's career, the great Protestant theologian Reinhold Niebuhr, who shared many of Dewey's liberal views, nevertheless criticized Dewey's philosophy as being naïve. For Niebuhr, Dewey was shallow for not recognizing man's sinful nature and the depth of evil that exists in the world.

But Dewey held to the view that the world was self-sufficient; that it posed no cosmic problem, other than that of emancipating ourselves from the habit of thinking that it did. This theological battle, of course, still rages, more so, perhaps, than in Dewey's time. But in my view, Dewey's thought is a source we humanists can turn to for support and inspiration; a place we can return to renew our humanistic faith.

I would like to close by reading the last paragraph of Dewey's *A Common Faith*, which sums up the human project as he understands it:

> The ideal ends to which we attach our faith are not shadowy or wavering. They assume concrete form in our understanding of our relations to one another and the values contained in these relations. We who now live are parts of a humanity that has interacted with nature. The things in civilization we most prize are not of ourselves. They exist by grace of the doings and sufferings of the continuous human community in which we are a link. Ours is the responsibility of conserving, transmitting, rectifying, and expanding the heritage of values we have received that those who come after us may receive it more solid and secure, more widely accessible, and more generously shared than we have received it. Here are all the elements of a religious faith that should not be confined to sect, class, or race. Such a faith has always been implicitly the common faith of mankind. It remains to make it explicit and militant.

November 1995

Three Moral Heroes Who Were
Also Ethical Culturists

In 2002, a thirty-two-year-old Irish-born American journalist won the Pulitzer Prize for a monumental book documenting the history of genocide in the twentieth century. Samantha Power's *A Problem from Hell* narrates in elegant prose the litany of mass atrocities from the Armenian genocide to the slaughter in Kosovo, bookending the Holocaust, the killing fields of Cambodia, the massacre of the Kurds by Saddam Hussein, the murder of eight hundred thousand Tutsis in Rwanda, and the ethnic cleansing and mass murder that was the war in Bosnia. No rendition of mass atrocities, whether in print or cinema, can hold an audience unless it focuses on specific individuals, which Samantha Power does, while never sacrificing the documentation of the larger tragedies nor providing a hint of sentimentalism.

 ˙ Among the themes threaded throughout the book is Power's depiction, in each of the genocides, of the heroic deeds of a single individual who was witness to mass death and felt morally compelled to warn the world of the horrors that were going on around him or her. And in each of those cases, the witness then brought his or her astounding stories to officials in the American government. The response of the United States was to rationalize, temporize, and do nothing while masses of humanity were slaughtered time and time again. Though as a sober historian, Samantha Power seldom moralizes, there is a powerful moral message that comes through, namely that our country, the world's greatest power, has a moral responsibility to intervene when genocide is about to occur or is ongoing. I should say, parenthetically, that Samantha

Power has had the opportunity to put her moral principles into action. She went from being a writer to being a director of the Carr Center for Human Rights at the Kennedy School of Government at Harvard. She got to know Barack Obama, became a member of Obama's National Security Council and today is the American ambassador to the United Nations. Though it did not get any appreciable press, I know for a certainty that Samantha Power and a few others close to the president developed and promoted America's recent policy of intervention in Libya, which arguably helped save the lives of untold thousands from the vengeance of a madman.

The initial chapter of *A Problem from Hell* deals appropriately with the Armenian genocide that the Ottoman Turks perpetrated against their Armenian Christian minority. There had been precedents, in that in the 1890s, a Turkish sultan had killed two hundred thousand Armenians.

Power's identified witness to the Armenian genocide was the American ambassador to Constantinople, Henry Morgenthau Sr. Morgenthau was the progenitor of a distinguished American family in that his son, Henry Morgenthau Jr., became the secretary of the Treasury under Franklin Roosevelt and was a major formulator of the New Deal, and his grandson, Robert Morgenthau, recently retired after thirty-five years as Manhattan's district attorney. Barbara Tuchman, a prominent historian, is his granddaughter.

Henry Morgenthau Sr. was born into a prosperous Reform Jewish family in Germany in 1856 and immigrated to the United States with his parents and ten siblings when he was ten. It is not incidental to our story that Morgenthau had a background not dissimilar from that of Felix Adler, Ethical Culture's founder. Morgenthau graduated from City College and got a law degree from Columbia University. As a major supporter of the Democratic Party, he came to the notice of President Woodrow Wilson, who appointed Morgenthau ambassador to the Ottoman Empire in 1913. His responsibilities as ambassador were extensive. They included looking after Americans, including missionary groups, American corporations and ships, and the Jewish minority in Turkey, as well as diplomatic duties of Britain, France, and Russia, which, as belligerents during World War I, withdrew their ambassadors from the Ottoman Empire. From a moral perspective, it is noteworthy that Morgenthau took an active interest in protesting what was then called the "white-slave trade," which today we refer to as "international sex trafficking."

In 1915, as World War I was raging, Morgenthau began to receive fragmentary reports from American consuls posted around the Ottoman Empire and from missionaries about atrocities committed against Armenians. At first, as Power relates, he could not distinguish the killings from the usual collateral damage of war. But by July of that year, the desperate reports from an increasing number of Armenians, many of whom wept before him in his office, caused him to realize that what was taking place was not the usual fallout of warfare. Though the word *genocide* would not be coined for another twenty years, Morgenthau correctly identified what was happening to the Armenians as "race murder."

Morgenthau did whatever he could to save the Armenians, but two major factors constrained him. The first was that Wilson wanted to keep America out of World War I and steadfastly maintain a position of neutrality. Picking a fight with the Ottoman Empire was not a good way to do this. The second relates to the way in which the international community has organized itself for the past five hundred years, namely, around the doctrine of national sovereignty. Each nation-state is sovereign to treat its own citizens as it sees fit, and it is presumed to not be the business of other nations how it does so. The doctrine of sovereignty has broken down somewhat since the Nuremburg trials and the growth of the human rights movement worldwide, but it is very much how international relations are governed, and even more so in 1915 during the slaughter of the Armenians. So it is no surprise that when Morgenthau sent cables back to Washington, pleading with his superiors in the State Department to do something to intervene with the Turks to get them stop the massacres, the US government would reply by doing nothing. As Power notes, he found this commitment to noninterference to be maddening. But Morgenthau took whatever measures were left to him within these huge limitations. For example, he met in his office Mehmed Talaat, the Turkish minister of the interior and a foremost architect of the genocide. Samantha Power recounts that when Morgenthau would confront Talaat with eyewitness accounts of the slaughter, Talaat snapped back by saying, "Why are you so interested in the Armenians anyway? You are a Jew, these people are Christian…What have you to complain of? Why can't you let us do with these Christians as we please?" Morgenthau responded that he was not appealing as a Jew but as the American ambassador and not in the name of a race or religion, but merely as a human being. On other occasions, Talaat even boasted of killing the Armenians rather than try-ing to hide it.

With direct intervention with the Ottoman interior minister leading nowhere and the American government being unresponsive to his pleas, Morgenthau worked around the government. An old friend was Adolph Ochs, the publisher of the *New York Times*, who saw that the *Times* published in 1915 145 stories on the massacre of the Armenians. By year's end headlines would read, "A Million Armenians Killed or Exiled," with content stating that what was transpiring was "nothing more or less than the annihilation of a whole people."

Morgenthau got help from religious organizations that raised money for relief. Congregationalist, Baptist, and Roman Catholic churches made dona-tions. The Rockefeller Foundation gave $290,000. A Committee on Armenian Atrocities raised $100,000 and held public rallies denouncing the massacres. In 1915, Morgenthau offered to raise $1 million to help transport the Armenians who survived the slaughter to the United States. He urged the Western states to raise money to equip a ship to transport Armenian refugees to the United States and care for them. The Turks originally agreed to the plan, but then reneged and blocked the exit of the refugees, and Morgenthau's plan, as Power notes, went nowhere.

After twenty-six months in Constantinople, Morgenthau left in early 1916. As Samantha Power notes, "He could no longer stand his impotence." And as Morgenthau himself said, "My failure to stop the destruction of the Armenians had made Turkey for me a place of horror—I had reached the end of my resources."

By the close of World War I, it is estimated that 1.5 million Armenians were slaughtered in massacres and on forced marches. The world did almost nothing to stop it, and it has done little to stop subsequent mass atrocities that have killed tens of millions of innocents. In the midst of that horror, the conscience and the voice of Henry Morgenthau Sr. stand out almost alone in the service of doing what was right, even when others did not care to notice or to act.

I tell this story because Henry Morgenthau found a home in the Ethical Society. He was one of the coterie of young men who surrounded Felix Adler and helped found the New York Society for Ethical Culture in 1876. He participated in assisting Adler in constructing model tenements on the Lower East Side, and he helped in establishing the Ethical Culture Schools. And when it came time for the New York Society to build its magisterial meeting house on Central Park West, it was Henry Morgenthau who helped purchase the land on which it was built.

Henry Morgenthau Sr. was a dedicated member of Ethical Culture for several decades and by his own testimony was deeply and personally devoted to its ideals. In my opinion, it should be a source of great pride and inspiration for us that his values are our values.

Born three years after Henry Morgenthau and into a very different social milieu, Florence Kelley's theater of action was very much at the center of Ethical Culture's early social reform efforts. The mainstay of her activism was in militating against the worst excesses of the Industrial Revolution and winning protections for its most vulnerable victims, namely, women and children.

Florence Kelley was the daughter of a congressman and the only daughter of five daughters to survive childhood. She came from a Quaker background. She was also among the first generation of American women to attend college. She studied at Cornell University and then in Zurich, Switzerland. While in Europe, she befriended socialists, corresponded with Friedrich Engels, and translated one of his books into English. After returning to the United States in 1891, she settled in Chicago and lived at Hull House, the famous settlement house founded by Jane Addams. In Chicago, she got a powerful sense of the conditions of factory labor. Perhaps her most important contribution to social justice was developing specific strategies to combat discrete evils. In ways that have a resonance in today's antiglobalization campaigns, she organized consumer boycotts of clothing produced in sweatshops. She had made mandatory the labeling of clothes to verify that they were legally produced, and, to combat the exploitation of child labor, she fought for the requirement that states register births and that employers, not desperately poor parents, document the age of people applying for work. She also agitated for mandatory school attendance to keep children out of factories.

Kelley toured factories and tenements in Chicago and found children as young as three years old working there. As a result of her pioneering work in documenting the abuses of factory labor, Illinois passed the first factory law, prohibiting the employment of children under fourteen. Kelley was appointed by Illinois's progressive governor, John Altgeld, to be the state's first factory inspector to ensure that companies complied with the new laws. It was a very unusual position for a woman to hold in the nineteenth century. In 1899, Florence Kelley moved to New York and took up residence at the Henry Street settlement, founded by Lillian Wald. Upon her arrival she helped found the National Consumers League, a radical pressure group that was primarily committed to establishing a minimum wage and limitations on the working hours of women and children.

In addition to organizing, protesting, and public speaking, one of Kelley's major contributions to the struggle for justice was to inform new law and judicial decisions through the careful garnering of empirical data. Among her victories was the Supreme Court's decision in a case know as *Muller v. Oregon*, which established the legality of the ten-hour workday. What was precedent setting about this case was that Kelley worked long and hard with Louis Brandeis, a brother-in-law of Felix Adler and a future Supreme Court justice, in marshaling reams of scientific and social data regarding the harmful effects of long working days on women's health. What was known as the "Brandeis Brief" became a model for the foundation of creating new law and deciding judicial cases by resting on social science data. It was an approach that was employed perhaps most famously in *Brown v. Board of Education*, but also in innumerable court cases since.

In addition to her commitment to labor rights, Florence Kelley was active in the cause of women's suffrage, was a founder of the National Association for the Advancement of Colored People, and was a colleague of W. E. B. DuBois, the great African American luminary and intellectual of the period. Kelley was also a good friend of Josephine Goldmark, who was the sister of Felix Adler's wife, Helen Goldmark. Her life is memorialized in her biography, *Impatient Crusader: Florence Kelley's Life Story*, written by Josephine Goldmark. In 2010 the *Nation* magazine named Florence Kelley as one of the fifty most influential progressives of the twentieth century. Florence Kelley, to our collective ethical credit, also found kindred spirits and a spiritual home in the Ethical Culture Society.

My final moral hero brings us back to the cultural environment that nurtured Henry Morgenthau and Felix Adler. Franz Boas was the founder of modern anthropology. He was also a lifelong foe, both in his pioneering academic work and in his life outside the academy, of racism and ethnocentrism.

Boas was born in 1858 to a freethinking German Jewish family. In the 1880s, he took a course in anthropology, traveled to Baffin Island in Canada to do field work among the indigenous groups that lived there, and decided to devote his life to anthropology. He moved to New York in 1884, returned to Germany, and in 1886 decided to immigrate to the United States, and he remained here until his death in 1942.

In 1896, Boas got a position at the Museum of Natural History and at Columbia University, where he would later found the Anthropology Department. He continued to do field work, mostly in the Pacific Northwest with native Canadians. Though he was not politically active during this period of his life, what he did academically was to revolutionize the field of anthropology in a way that bore extraordinary consequences both politically and in the way in which we view humanity. What he did in the anthropological field was totally in accord with his deeply held conviction that science needed to be employed to improve the human condition and that anthropology was an important tool with which to fight for the rights of the oppressed and the mistreated.

Anthropology as an academic discipline came into being and found a place in the universities after the middle of the nineteenth century in England and the United States. Classical anthropology was built on the premise of what was called evolutionism, laced with a heavy dose of social Darwinism. In other words, it was assumed, as virtually a given, that the various cultures around the world evolved through stages, from the most primitive to the most advanced and civilized. We could thereby compare cultures to each other and draw conclusions about which were backward and which were advanced, which were morally superior and which inferior. Needless to say, white, European culture was construed to be the most advanced and civilized; the cultures of the Pacific islands, Africa, and indigenous cultures, the most backward and primitive. In the field of physical anthropology, the nineteenth century was obsessed with phrenology, that is, the comparative study of the size and shape of the skulls of people from different groups and sexes, in order to draw conclusions about their relative intelligence. Such were the deliverances of what was accepted to be normative science.

It should be no surprise that such scientific presumptions nicely comported with such politically realities as imperialism, racial segregation, Jim Crow laws, and anti-immigrant crusades—both comported with those viciously prejudicial political realities and validated them.

It was this notion of evolutionism, with its conclusions about superior and inferior racial and ethnic groups, that Boas radically attacked. He held to the view, which ultimately transformed anthropology, that the notion of the evolution of cultures is false, and with it that the establishment of racial and cultural hierarchies is wrongheaded. Boas argued that it is a mistake to compare one culture with another. Each culture, he maintained, stands on its own and needs to be assessed by its own internal criteria. Moreover, he argued that there was no difference between the mental capacities of so-called advanced cultures and so-called primitive people. All people, he argued, maintain a common humanity. There is no difference between "our minds" and "theirs," he maintained. He argued "achievements in race do not warrant us that one race is more highly gifted than another." He also asserted what now has become common knowledge: that each race contains so much variation within it that the average differences between it and others are much less than each contains within itself, and that racial prejudice, he maintained, is the most formidable obstacle to a clear understanding of these problems. When it came to the concept of race, Boas's research led him to deny the usefulness of the concept, to stress that each person needs to be assessed as an individual and not as a member of a race, and that socioeconomic conditions greatly affected the well-being and achievement of various populations. Among other things, Franz Boas's research called into question seventy years of "scientific" racial determinism, which was the intellectual justification for segregation. Quite astoundingly, I believe, in the late nineteenth century, Franz Boas was advocating intermarriage between blacks and whites.

Perhaps many will notice in Boas's anthropology what has come to be known as cultural relativism, which was a basis both then and now for undergirding the value of tolerance and is a precursor of what we refer to as multiculturalism. In my own field of human rights, the presumptions of cultural relativism have emerged to challenge the very concept of the universality of human rights, and therefore have proven to be problematic. In its most radical form, it is contended by some that cultures are so different from one another that cross-cultural understanding and dialogue are impossible. Hence the criticizing of a cultural practice from outside that tradition is impossible, and because it is impossible, it is unwarranted. If culture A promotes the equality of women and the practices of culture B promote the subordination of women, then culture A has no legitimacy to criticize culture B in doing so, since that is simply the way different cultures behave, and when it comes to values, it is "culture all the way down," so to speak. Even in its less radical form, cultural relativism becomes a knotty problem. It supports, no doubt, the value of tolerance, but creates a lot of debate and confusion when we try to draw a consensus between cultures with regard to behaviors that ought not be tolerated by anyone.

However, it is extremely important to note that while Franz Boas believed that one should not assume that one's culture, be it German, American, Western, or whatever, is superior to others, he did not feel that one should suspend judgment on matters of ultimate values. He was a cultural relativist, to be sure, but he was not an ethical relativist. He believed that there are fundamental truths that are common to all humankind, even as they may find different expressions in different cultures. Such norms as equal rights, equal opportunity, freedom of expression, the pursuit of truth, were universal values that needed to be defended and preserved. In this sense, I believe, he was very much in line with Ethical Culture.

One final observation about Boas on the academic side. At time when only a few women went to college, Franz Boas's most accomplished students and primary disciples were women—researchers and writers who became the pillars of anthropology in the twentieth century. The most notable were Ruth Benedict, Margaret Meade, and Zora Neale Hurston, a folklorist and novelist who was the first African American to attend Barnard College. It was these illustrious women who carried forward Boas's work with a deep appreciation for other cultures and their distinctive contributions.

While Boas was not a barricades activist, he did take his commitments outside of academia. Early in the twentieth century, Boas became aligned with black causes. He worked together with such luminaries as Alain Locke, Booker T. Washington, and especially W. E. B. DuBois. He assisted African Americans in finding jobs, gaining foundation support, and supporting studies in African American history and culture. At DuBois's invitation, he lectured at the all-black Atlanta University in 1906, urging a pride in the accomplishment of the peoples of West Africa. As a result of his relation with DuBois, Boas became deeply involved with the NAACP. He wrote for years on racial issues for the

NAACP magazine, which Dubois edited. He later on fought against the poll tax, which made it difficult or impossible for blacks to vote in the South, and lent his name and gave money to the defense of the Scottsboro boys.

When anti-immigrant and nativist backlashes emerged in the early decades of the twentieth century, Boas wrote and spoke out often condemning the bigotry. Indeed, he was committed to antiracism throughout his life.

Boas was reflexively an antimilitarist and spoke out and wrote continuously, urging the United States not to enter into World War I. He vociferously defended colleagues who were accused of disloyalty for opposing the war and who lost their jobs because of it. He spoke out against imperialism and colonialism and such American ventures in Latin America, and he early on condemned Nazism and fascism when they arose in Europe in the 1930s.

Herbert Lewis, a retired anthropologist at the University of Wisconsin, said of Franz Boas, "He was as far sighted and clear eyed as anyone in his time, an opponent of racism, ethnocentrism, chauvinism, imperialism, war, and censorship...Franz Boas both professed and acted upon the highest and finest ideals of his (and our) culture and time. These are: concern for the dominated and oppressed; respect for 'others' as individuals as well as for other cultures; tolerance and humane dealing; and respect for the eternal quest for knowledge about ourselves and the world."

Franz Boas found a hospitable environment in which to nurture his ideals at the New York Ethical Society as a member and associate for thirty years. In 1911, Felix Adler organized the first International Congress on Race Relations, which was held in London. Adler and DuBois were the American representatives to that congress, which attracted delegates from five continents. But the inspiration for it was the pathbreaking work and influence of Franz Boas.

What Henry Morgenthau, Florence Kelley, and Franz Boas had in common as members of Ethical Culture was, no doubt, the substance of the ideals for which Ethical Culture stands, though they expressed those ideals in very different ways and through different avenues: Morgenthau standing against genocide, Kelley for those crushed by the forces of inequality and poverty, and Boas against the legacies of racism and imperialism. They three were all critics of the environments in which they found themselves, and in their critiques, one can almost hear the strong voice of moral conscience calling them to action. Though one can never know the mind of another, especially those of the past, the sense I get is that not only were their consciences strong, but they held their moral values with a sense of conviction. We today, perhaps, live in more complex and confusing times, when it may be more difficult to be firm in our convictions. Felix Adler stated Ethical Culture is to inspire us with "the knowledge, love, and practice of the right." But in our times, what is right is perhaps more ambiguous, a mature moral conviction harder to hold on to.

That's why, I think, we need to derive inspiration from the lives of illustrious men and women. Adler, believed that a good way to grow morally is to study biography, and I think he was right. In that regard, the lives of morally outstanding men and women are certainly of historical interest, but it is by no means dead history. We can use those lives and deeds to inspire us in the challenges that we confront.

They confronted their challenges, and we confront ours. These are times that call for such inspiration. We live in an era when our political lives are in the grip of huge and powerful corporations; wherein market interests and not human interests and needs hold sway, and big money buys out politicians, turning us into an oligarchy that leaves our democracy hollow. We live in an era when the division between classes has never been greater; in which financial institutions have acted criminally with obscene impunity at the top, while law-abiding and economically oppressed citizens bail them out. We live in a time when government is being gutted, from education to environmental protection to scientific research to basic humanitarian services; those things that made us a civilized and hopeful nation.

Ours is a time that calls for idealism, for smart organizing, and for militant struggle in order to bring our society back to where it ought to be. I think we can learn from the examples of these illustrious Ethical Culturists, who believed in the power of standing for the right thing and acting on it. These people were our people. We can do no better than to appreciate their unwavering faith in their ideals and in themselves, and make it our own.

December 2011

Interpretations of Ethical Culture

What Humanists Believe

Life does not stand still for long. All of life is a cycle of motion and rest. We grow, we push ahead, we exert ourselves, we rest, and then we move forward again.

For humanists, such as we are, the purpose of life is to live—to live fully, to live comprehensively, to live strenuously, to bathe ourselves in the riches of experience. But motion that is unguided is erratic, chaotic, unsatisfying, and sheer restlessness.

It is a cliché that life is a journey. But as much as we are inspired by the wanderlust of life's journey, at some point we need to return home again. We need to come home so that we reflect upon where we have been, renew our energies, and chart our future as much as it is in our power to do so. Life presses us onward toward the expansion of our energies and the assertion of our wills. But as much as we are driven to roam through life, we also need fixed points, anchorages, and safe harbors within which we can restore ourselves and take a moment to reflect and get our lives in order.

This brings me to the Ethical Culture Society, its philosophy, and the role that it plays in our lives. I believe it is an important role.

We live in demanding and tension-producing times. We are experiencing a dangerous moment in American society and on the world scene. There is a sense of menace resonating through our lives. Seldom have we felt that large political and world events affect us so intimately, as if to get under our skin and upset us in our day-to-day activity. The terrorist assault of 9/11, which in moments killed almost three thousand of our neighbors, has transformed the tenor of our lives every day. We live in the aftershocks of terrorism, and we are continuously reminded of it, and of violence on a massive scale, be it "orange" alerts, extremist conspiracies, and wars that, through their destabilizing effects, may serve as a matrix of more terror and more violence. War is convulsive, and once set in motion it leads to consequences that are uncontainable and unforeseeable. We sense, perhaps correctly, that the ill-conceived and ill-fated war in Iraq will render us less safe rather than more.

Never in my own lifetime has the future seemed so uncertain. Never has it seemed so anarchic. The menace of the Cold War, with the threat of nuclear annihilation, was in a sense greater. But at least the feeling of menace was contained. One feels now that the forces that confront us and will inhabit our future are more unpredictable, more diffuse, and threaten to metastasize beyond our effort to restrain or control them.

For those of us who are progressives, the domestic situation can hardly bring us comfort. The Bush administration in Washington was bent on spreading its ideology over American society as it was committed to blanketing the globe with its military power. Unprecedented tax cuts, which are a gift to the rich and the superrich, and the gaping deficits that they have created will ensure that social spending for those in need will grow scarcer and scarcer. Indeed it seems to have been the intention of the administration to return American society to the 19th century, when government provided virtually no services at all and those in need were left to survive on handouts from churches and other private agencies. Unemployment was higher than it had been in decades. So meager has been the commitment to the common good that even Bush's proclaimed "compassionate" conservatism had proven to be a campaign gimmick and a fraud. Every promise to support education, AmeriCorps, drugs plans for seniors, and fighting AIDS in Africa had been followed by a refusal to allocate funds to support those very promises.

And we who cherish our freedom and are rightfully skeptical of the power of government had to have been very wary of that ultraconservative administration that was far too eager to use the mask of security to severely compromise our civil liberties. Never since the McCarthy era had our constitutional liberties been so threatened as they were.

Working fist in glove with Far Right politics, and fuelling it, are the dark religious forces of a vast evangelical and fundamentalist subculture in America. We are involved in a type of culture war, pitting the forces of authoritarian religion against the values of modernism, secularism, liberalism, rationalism, and, if you will, humanism—what we would equate with the elements of the free and enlightened mind.

The 2003 standoff involving Justice Moore, chief justice of the Alabama Supreme Court, over the placement of his boulder-size monument of the Ten Commandments in the courthouse on one level seems silly. But on another, it's representative of this very culture war in America, one side of which tires of the secular character of American government and, by extension, the diverse society we have become. Judge Moore claims that the Ten Commandments are the basis of American law. Never mind that the US Constitution is a totally godless document and never mentions the Deity nor the Ten Commandments. Never mind that the Founding Fathers of the Republic in their concept of law were far more influenced by the ancient pagans, such as Cicero and Seneca, than they were by the Bible. And never mind that of the Ten Commandments, only two commandments—those prohibiting murder and theft—involve activities that have anything to do with law in this country. A point here is that to certain crusading religious minds, facts and history and reason matter very little. All such values, which we hold dear, are trumped by the righteousness of the cause of the faithful. In great measure this is what we are up against in the current moment.

Perhaps if there were a concerted, courageous leadership in the opposition party, we could feel less isolated. Perhaps if the ultraconservative ideology that rules Washington were confronted by an articulated, progressive ideology that carried an inspiring moral message, spoke to the needs of people on the grass roots, was truly democratic, and had integrity and gravity to it, those who are alienated from the current administration would feel more hopeful. But such does not seem to be the case.

It is within this context, and amid the tensions of our times, that the value of Ethical Culture becomes that much more important. The questions I pose are: What is Ethical Culture's value? Whom are we for? What beliefs do we, as humanists, hold that bring us together? For our beliefs are assuredly distinctive, and becoming more so within the context of the present moment.

We should never underestimate the importance of our community. As human beings we are social beings. We need others in order to play out our lives and become who we are. A person alone withers and dies. It is in our active life with other human beings that we potentially flourish.

By coming together in a community, we derive strength from each other. We break down the barriers of isolation, which instill insecurity and weakness. We fortify our values, recommit ourselves to our beliefs, and restore the sense of confidence we need to meet the challenges of life and the demands society places on us, including the extraordinary demands we confront at this political moment.

I think of the Ethical Society as a refuge for like-minded people; for people who share a common outlook, a common world view, and a common appreciation for what matters most in life. We are an island of respite in a frenzied world. We are a home in which we can recharge our energies in order to move on to meet the challenges of life.

Members of this society will sometimes say to me that being part of this community allows them to be honest with themselves and with others and speak their minds truthfully in ways in which they cannot when they are in the workplace. Members will sometimes tell me that the Ethical Society provides them with an outlet to do social justice work, some for the first time in their lives. Sometimes parents tell me of the importance of our Sunday school in supporting their efforts to raise moral children. Sometimes members tell me that the opinions and values they hold, which make them feel alien in most environments, find acceptance in this community, and thereby enable them to feel comfortable here as they seldom do elsewhere. Some talk of the connections they make with other people, the abiding friendships that in some cases last a life-time. Some tell me that Ethical Culture is a place where they can reflect on, refine, and reconfirm their own philosophies of life, and find the inspiration to live better, more ethically sensitive lives—and of course, this is Ethical Culture's highest calling.

This is no small thing. As social beings we need others to help us clarify our belief systems and sustain our convictions. We all need a sense of meaning in life. We cannot live without it. We need beliefs and something to believe in that gives us a sense of purpose, a sense of our place in the universe, and sustains us with hope as we relentlessly move into an unknown and risky future. If we wish, we can refer to these needs as relating to the spiritual side of our natures. It is the role of religious societies to provide this, as it is of Ethical Culture.

The pursuit of this spiritual quest, of the search for meaning, for a guiding and workable philosophy of life, is a social activity also. No person works out his or her relationship to life and the universe totally alone. We borrow from the thought and experience of others. We learn from others. And, as mentioned, we need others to help us sustain our convictions and beliefs.

If a purpose of our Ethical Culture community is to help us reinforce our beliefs, what in fact are the beliefs that bring and bind us together? What is it that Ethical Culturists as humanists believe?

To begin, the belief system of Ethical Culturists is paradoxical. It is paradoxical in the sense that Ethical Culture affirms freedom of individual thought and conscience. We have no overarching doctrines or dogmatic beliefs that one must hold in order to be an Ethical Culturist. Rather we encourage freedom of belief, and the diversity of belief that inevitably follows from encouraging that individual freedom.

But at the same time, in order to come together under the same roof, there needs to be a broad range of accepted beliefs that we hold in common, or else we could not come together at all.

Ethical Culture, and humanism more broadly, is a particular, identifiable world view, a life stance, and an orientation; it is a particular slant on life and our place in the universe that is distinctive and, in many ways, makes us different from others, even as we affirm our connection with the entire human family, of which we are a part.

What are some of Ethical Culture's and humanism's beliefs, intuitions, and assumptions?

First of all, humanists honor the importance of ideas. They appreciate the value of ideas in guiding life and molding our characters. Another way of saying this is that a central assumption around which we gather is that integrity, including intellectual integrity, counts for a great deal in life. We operate on the presumption that there is nothing virtuous, admirable, or dignified in professing what we do not believe.

This central conviction, which I hear repeated in so many ways by people here, significantly sets us apart from many people these days.

People are returning to the churches and the synagogues in large numbers. I have no doubt that many are led by sincere beliefs in what the traditional religions profess. But I know that many are not. They are willing to recite prayer, espouse doctrines, and engage in rituals in which they do not believe. They either bracket the contradiction or, in the privacy of their minds, struggle to give the God language a metaphorical meaning it was never meant to have. Such folks are flocking and flocking back to the traditional houses of worship for reasons of nostalgia, to seek out a warm sense of community with others in an alienating world, or because religion and spirituality have attained a certain cache and attractiveness, and they are following the crowd. There is nothing terrible about these socially driven motivations, and they may even be good. My point is that many (again, not all) such folks are willing to subordinate intellectual consistency, intellectual integrity, for the sake of these experiences. People who come to Ethical Culture are not.

Perhaps they would agree with me that religion speaks to what Paul Tillich called one's "ultimate concerns." And when it comes to what one considers one's ultimate concerns and ultimate truths, intellectual integrity should count here more than anywhere else in life. If one has to fudge what one considers one's religious truths, then I would argue that one's religious convictions are contradicted and a sham. If one cannot be honest in one's religious views, where should one be honest?

This is not to say that Ethical Culturists are across the board more honest than others. As mortal creatures we are all self-deluding to varying degrees. All I am saying is that when it comes to this important component in the realm of beliefs, we are not willing to profess what we do not believe. Perhaps, in the face of the blandishments, benefits, and comforts of the traditional religions, most people are willing to pay the price of subordinating intellectual consistency. They see it as no big deal. For whatever reasons, perhaps reasons of temperament most all, we do. This fact both distinguishes us from many others in society as a whole and may account in great measure for our small size.

Second, Ethical Culturists are committed to ethical ideals and living out their ethical values *as life's highest aspiration.* Ethical Culture exists "to create ethical personality," said Felix Adler, who founded our movement 127 years ago. We live to make of ourselves morally better people. When it comes to the ends and purposes of life, nothing is more important than this. While we seek to survive and be materially comfortable, while we seek success in our work and strive to acquire competence, and perhaps secure a reputation for ourselves among our peers and in the world, all these things are subordinate to the claim that life makes on us to be better, more ethically refined and involved human beings

What does this mean in more specific ways?

Ethical Culture sketches a path and an approach. It says that action, experience, and engagement are the way. One does not become more ethical by thinking or dreaming about it. "If you wish to become courageous," said Aristotle, "you must do courageous things." We would agree. Likewise if you wish to become more compassionate, kind, and loving, you must do more compassionate, kind, loving things. *Engagement* is the word.

What kind of engagement? It was the spiritual premise of Dr. Adler, in a way, that preceded what we would call today system theory, the idea that all human beings are organically related to one another. While we are all distinctive and different, we are, at the same time, all connected in a vast family, in a vast systemic organism, so that what I do to others affects them and reciprocally changes me in the process.

Ethical Culture is primarily outer directed. It says, "If I wish to grow, the best way is to enable others to grow. If I wish to be a beloved person, I need to strive to be a person who extends love to others. If I wish to realize my own sense of worthiness, I need to treat others with worth." I cannot passively wait for these values to come to me. I need to put them into action myself in order to realize them for myself.

What distinguishes this humanist life stance is that one does not behave ethically because one will receive a reward in this life, or the next that is bestowed after the fact by a God in heaven. It recognizes that that our field of engagement is with other human beings. It sublimely recognizes, as Buddhists do, that blessedness is not deferred to a life after death, but blessedness can be now and can be experienced in this moment by how we relate ourselves to others, when we truly help them, when we recognize the precious, irreplaceable core of their humanity and strive to elicit what is best in them. The ethical moment reveals itself to us, as Adler put, "when we enter into the life of others and enable them to think well of themselves." The humanist sensibility is to see our own face mirrored in the face of the other. It is to be moved to a feeling of empathy when we realize that we, members of the human family, spring from a common ancestry and are bound to one another by a common destiny.

What humanists see as their commitments in the world of interpersonal relations, they extend outward to the broader sphere of social and political realities. To be a humanist is to long for a more ethical world; a world founded on the ideals of justice, equality, dignity, and respect for all. The humanist is therefore dedicated not only to human beings, but to humankind. To be a humanist is to be, in one aspect of one's being, critical of the status quo, of the way things are, in the service of the way things might be. It is to see oneself as a shaper of one's community and one's world. To be a humanist is to believe that the destiny of humankind is not preordained. It is rather to believe that the future of humanity is an open future and not a closed future. If one is a traditional religionist, and certainly a fundamentalist, one believes in a closed future. The future is foretold in the scriptures and will assuredly come to pass by act of divine will. If one is a humanist, one believes in an open future that human agency, intelligence, and good will can increasingly bend in the direction of justice and goodness.

Humanism is often criticized as being too rationalistic, sterile, and sort of crusty and humorless. I have never seen it this way, for the field of humanism is as wide and deep as human experience.

While Ethical Culturists put ethical experience at the center, humanism more broadly advocates the good life for all. It says that the best life is the life that enables human flourishing, the unfolding and development of our talents, abilities, and potentials to their highest degree. The humanist is dedicated to developing not only our ethics, but our minds, our imaginations, our bodies, our emotions, our capacity for pleasure, for sociality, for sex, for laughter, for art, for music, for whatever makes an enriched, cultured life that partakes of the greatest creations of men and women. The fulfilled life is an essential aspiration of the humanist ideal and world view.

But humanism also recognizes that within the envelope of human experience is our falling short of the ideal. A more sober and sophisticated humanism recognizes that there is tragedy that courses though the human experience. It recognizes that much of the greatness of life is not found in the manifest victories that we win, but in our capacities to cope and find a sense of renewal when adversity, loss, and tragedy threaten to overwhelm us.

And, finally, humanism is sometimes criticized for being too humanocentric, for concentrating too much on the human world to the neglect of nature and the wider universe.

Though humanism focuses on human concerns, ethical relations, and human flourishing, I don't think it need end there, nor should it. We know, of course, that we are natural beings, children of nature, and we are dependent at every moment on the viability of the natural world. This undeniable realization should lead us to be stewards of the earth and to feel a kinship with living things. It should lead us to feel a sense of piety and humility before the grander universe, which, by an accident of nature, has given us birth and has endowed us with consciousness to reflect on its grandeur.

Humanism has sometimes been accused of arrogance for placing humankind too much at the center of things, in contrast to the theistic religions, which humble humankind before the majesty of their Creator.

This accusation, I believe, is misplaced. Rather than leading to arrogance, a reflective humanism is deeply appreciative of human limitations. It recognizes that we are finite before an infinite universe. It recognizes that the cumulative knowledge of humankind is like a pebble on a beach, before which there extends a vast ocean of our ignorance. It recognizes that nature is infinitely powerful and, with regard to our ultimate fate, will have the last word.

It is this fact of our finitude before an infinite universe that can give rise to feeling of wonder, of awe, of our sense of connectedness and participation in the fabric of nature and being. It can be a source of our most sublime reflections and spiritual intuitions. It comprises the apprehensions that can lift us beyond the petty preoccupation of daily life and endow us with moments of heightened awareness and appreciation for the gift of life.

All these elements—the importance of ideas and intellectual integrity, the appreciation for the worthiness of ourselves and others and the pursuit of ethical ideals, the struggle for a just world, the striving to maximize our potentials, an appreciation of our dependence on and integrality with nature, and our sense of spiritual uplift in the contemplation of our finitude before an infinite universe—all these are elements of the humanist world view, which is a distinctive world view.

Humanism is not for everyone. The attraction of myth and ritual, the need for cosmic guarantees, the desire to worship a transcendental being beyond nature, and the yearning for future rewards seem to grip the allegiance of masses of mankind. For most of humanity these allegiances trump the critical faculties of reason, the findings of science, the sublime satisfaction of doing what is right and good for the sake of right and good alone. The power of these attractors is great. But, I believe, so is the power of skepticism, and history has yet to throw the last stone.

We who are humanists and Ethical Culturists are dedicated to a great and noble cause. We stand for those values identified with the modern and enlightened outlook. We are committed to those values necessary for the civilized survival and flourishing of humankind. And these values are severely challenged in our times by the forces of authoritarianism, unreason, religious fundamentalism, and extremism.

So much more important, therefore, is our community of like-minded souls. For it is here that we can rededicate ourselves to our ideals, borrow strength from one another, reconfirm our beliefs, and within these walls find a home where we can bring to light what is best in others, and thereby nurture it in ourselves.

September 2003

Why The Ethical Movement Is So Small And What We Can Do About It

One day in the year 1820, in the farm country of western New York, an angel visited a fifteen-year-old boy. The angel led him to a place in which was hidden a cache of plates made of gold. On these golden plates were inscriptions written in a cryptic language reminiscent of ancient Egyptian hieroglyphics. With the angel's assistance, the boy was able to translate this strange writing, and in 1830 he published a five-hundred-page book resembling in style the King James Version of the Bible.

This unusual book told of the wandering, battles, and vicissitudes of America's pre-Columbian inhabitants. It told first of all of the Jaredites, who left the Middle East at the time of the Tower of Babel and sailed to America in marvelous barges. The Jaredites, however, destroyed themselves through continuous warfare with one another. Next, the book told of the Lamanites, who were the ancestors of the American Indians. These Lamanites waged destructive war on the good sons of Nephi until only two people, a father and a son, survived. These two buried the chronicles of their people in the year AD 384 so that in time the Lord would ensure that they would be found and their spiritual descendants would revive the race and fulfill God's plan by establishing a New Zion in a new land.

The young man began to preach his new gospel and to win and baptize converts. He proclaimed new revelations and the ability to heal and gave warnings about the impending millennium. Five months after the establishment of his new sect in America, he declared that a New Jerusalem would be founded "on the borders by the Lamanites," and his band of faithful followers headed westward across a still-virgin land.

They went first to Ohio, then Missouri, and back to Illinois, inspiring the hatred and wrath of their neighbors wherever they settled, in part because they kept themselves separate and engaged in strange practices. They were accused of corruption and lawlessness, and met their accusers with promises of great vengeance. Finally, on June 27, 1844, the founder of this new sect was taken from his jail cell in Carthage, Illinois, and lynched by a mob in broad daylight. He had become a martyr, and with his martyrdom his movement grew.

Authority for the church was passed on to a new leader, who declared himself the senior member of the twelve apostles, modeled on Christ's disciples. After a trek of three years, this band settled on the desolate banks of the Great Salt Lake in what was to become the state of Utah. Within the next two decades eighty thousand followed westward, and it is estimated that some six thousand died along the way.

As the years passed, the impoverished communitarianism of the founders was taken over by creeping capitalism, and the small sect became virtually a new people. And through hard work and a sense of their divine mission, they prospered and grew.

Among the characteristics of this new church and virtually new nation was a hierarchical structure that vested religious authority in a high priesthood led by a president who could receive new revelations; a strong commitment to the integrity and purity of the family; a set of dietary taboos; a strong sense of ingroupness that differentiates members from others; and the demand that members give great devotion, time, and money to the mission of the church. Among the beliefs of the church, as we have seen, are those that combine an enthusiasm for the manifest destiny of America with a rootedness in biblical times. In fact, one of the more interesting of their beliefs is that Christ, after his ascension to heaven, came to the New World and preached to the Indians. They believe literally in heaven and hell. And their missionary zeal is strengthened, moreover, by a belief in retroactive baptism, so if one's ancestors can be located and named, they can gain entrance to heaven even though they lived before the church was founded.

This combination of belief, historical experience, and social organization has resulted in the Mormon Church growing in a period of less than 160 years into a wealthy and powerful religious movement claiming more than four million adherents, many now far beyond America's borders.

Compare the scenario above with the following one. Scarcely fifty-six years after Joseph Smith had his vision, another young man, only three hundred miles away, was busy creating another distinctly American religion. Being of a rational and scientific temperament, he held forth the notion that religious belief must be brought up to date with the times. He believed that modern scholarship had shown that literal belief in the traditional creeds was outdated and ought not to hold sway over the minds and thoughts of modern man and woman. Neither affirmation of dogma nor ritual practice but moral striving is the centerpiece, the gemstone, of religion. Rather than external authority serving to direct one to religious truth, this new prophet held that one's free, unfettered, and, moreover, *individual* conscience must be the ultimate authority. Authority that comes from within and is not imposed from without is the only type that upholds and promotes the dignity and worthiness of human beings. Rather than establish differentiating boundaries between true believers and those outside the faith, he declared that all people can aspire toward moral betterment, and their creedal commitments are really very much of secondary concern. Consequently, in the spirit of modernity and individual freedom, he downplayed the need for cult and ritual.

Today, after almost 112 years, the Ethical movement, which Felix Adler, a brilliant professor of philosophy, outstanding biblical and linguistic scholar, and accomplished social reformer, created, claims barely four thousand members.

The contrast between the tangible and worldly success of these two American religious movements begun almost in the same time and in the same place could not be more striking.

The question that begs to be answered is, why?

How is it, we might ask, that a faith such as Mormonism, which has at its heart beliefs that seem so irrational and so profoundly to defy common sense, flourishes, while Ethical Culture, which upholds a belief as basic and intuitively self-evident as that all people wish to be treated with respect and that we need so treat them, appeals to so few? Rather than put itself at variance with science and with the world, Ethical Culture accepts and applauds the scientific world view, the fruits of what some of the planet's greatest minds have espoused, and what is essentially the world view of our great academic and cultural institutions.

Although they were not members, we can with considerable justification claim such worthies as Spinoza, Jefferson, Emerson, Einstein, Julian Huxley, Eleanor Roosevelt, and Bertrand Russell as kindred spirits. Perhaps they would serve as our first candidates for retroactive baptism.

Again, how is it that our movement, which espouses beliefs that seem and in my opinion are so eminently correct and so intuitively self-evident—and heaven knows, in a world as dehumanizing as ours, so critically important—how is it that we appeal only to a fringe of the population, however talented and however much they love this movement and devote themselves to it?

I will attempt one possible answer to this enigma.

We ask the question, how is it that a religiophilosophical group such as Ethical Culture, which has at its heart such a reasonable set of beliefs centered on the dignity of the person and the need to create a decent world in which humanity will flourish, does not have a mass appeal? The answer to this question, which many in our movement have asked many times, is that the question itself is misplaced and is based on a false assumption. It is, in fact, the wrong question to ask. What the question overlooks is the basic fact that matters of belief have very little to do with religious affiliation and religious identity. They are eminently secondary concerns.

In my opinion, matters of belief are merely one factor among many that influence a person's religious affiliation, and often a minor one at that.

So, for example, if you stop someone in the street and ask him, "What is your religion?" and he responds by saying, "I am a Southern Baptist," the chances are that he did not at some point in his life place the tenets of Southern Baptism before himself, lay beside them the precepts of Methodism, New England Congregationalism, Roman Catholicism, Shintoism, etc., and then say to himself, "The tenets of Southern Baptism are truer or more reasonable; I'll go with that." This weighing of belief, I contend, seldom happens. The chances are overwhelming that he professes the faith of the Southern Baptist denomination simply because that was the faith of his parents and he was born into it. I suspect that the accident of birth has far more to do with religious affiliation and identity than belief in all but an exceptionally few individuals. I would guess that the affiliation lingers on in some vestigial sense even after active faith or religious practice is gone. Many of us in Ethical Culture may have arrived here primarily because of matters of belief, myself included. But admittedly very few people feel compelled to act that way.

Good enough, you might say. Few people will move from one creed to another on the grounds that one better meets the test of reasonableness than the other. But then why is it that more people don't become atheists, agnostics, freethinkers, or nonbelievers of some sort, or even Ethical Culturists?

This is really the key question, and answering it gets down to the real nitty-gritty of what I want to share with you this morning.

Let me try to get to my point by comparing two theories of religion. The first says that the most important way to understand religion is to look at its beliefs, that is, what it consciously stands for. The second attempts to understand religion not by looking at its beliefs, but rather at how religion actually functions in the real lives of its members; in other words, what it really does for people, both consciously and unconsciously. Let's call this "the functionalist theory of religion."

Looking at the beliefs a religion espouses, the rationalist concludes that religion is fundamentally a vast system of errors. The rationalist concludes that by ascribing matters of birth and death and natural phenomena and the like to God or the gods, the religious believer is essentially making a mistake. According to this rationalist theory, religion is essentially a product of ignorance and superstition, which will fade away as scientific and rational explanations about man and the universe show themselves to be more adequate than the answers provided by religion to the same questions. In this sense, religion is not something that is a permanent feature of the human condition, but something that will pass away as our knowledge of the physical and social sciences increases.

The Enlightenment for the most part regarded religion as little more than superstition, and so did many thinkers of the nineteenth century.

As compelling as the rationalist explanation might be, and I think that it is up to a point, I don't feel that it is the most adequate explanation, nor do I believe that it exhausts an explanation of religion, which is really a most complex and far-reaching human phenomenon.

More and more, I find the functionalist theory more adequate. What this theory suggests is that if we really wish to understand religion, we have to look not so much at belief, but we need to explore what deep anthropological, psychological, and social role religion plays in the lives of human beings. In other worlds, religion remains a powerful influence in many people's lives not because its central tenets are deemed to be true or reasonable, but rather because religious association and practice fulfill a deep and potent need in the psyche of human beings. In fact, it is the very nonrationality, or even irrationality, of religious belief that adds to the compelling strength of religious identification. This is a point I will get to later on.

Perhaps the most influential exponent of the functionalist theory of religion was the brilliant French sociologist Emile Durkheim. What Durkheim found from his massive study of the primitive tribes of Australia, *The Elementary Forms of the Religious Life*, was that belief is almost incidental to religion. What he concluded was that there was something going on unconsciously in the lives of believers, and that religious belief and religious ritual were ways of expressing it. What Durkheim espoused was the notion that religion is essentially an expression of the power of the community, although this, its true nature, is something hidden from the believer.

In short, religious symbols and religious rituals, according to Durkheim, are really unconscious projections of the community. And the strength of religious symbols and rituals is derived from the invisible power of the community and the social bond. So, for example, if one feels dependent before one's all-powerful God, it is really a hidden expression of one's dependence upon society, which is all powerful in relationship to the individual, who is powerless alone.

For Durkheim, the sociologist, man is intrinsically a social being, and religion is *par excellence* the celebration of man's social nature and his dependence on the communal bond, which is the wellspring of his potency and his life. To participate in religious activity is primarily to celebrate and strengthen the deep-seated social ties with all other fellow believers. It is to feel at one with them. And by feeling at one with our fellows, we enhance our sense of well-being and increase our own sense of power.

This is abstract, so let me give a few examples of what I mean.

The ritual of the Eucharist is central to Christian religious practice. From a functionalist point of view, engagement in the ritual has little to do with the literal truth of the transubstantiation of the wafer and wine into the body and blood of Christ. Those who partake in the rite have little interest in performing a chemical analysis of the materials involved before and after. What the ritual does, however, is strengthen the social bond horizontally, so to speak, between all who are in the family of Christians. It does so among those alive today as well as back into history with all Christians for the past two millennia and forward into the future until the end of time.

An example in Judaism is the reconstructionist movement developed by Mordecai Kaplan. Kaplan attempted to modernize Judaism and transformatively identify peoplehood with religion. He placed new wine in old bottles, so that when a Jew recites the *Sh'ma*, the central creed of Judaism, he or she is not making a theological pronouncement as much as expressing the thrill of being a Jew. In Durkheimian terms, Kaplan explicitly attempted to demystify the mystifying elements inherent in faith. The result has been that Reconstructionism is today almost as small as Ethical Culture.

Although it may be a hard pill for rationalists, who feel that dignity is compromised by being unreasonable, to swallow, human beings are guided by needs other than and beyond the need to be rational. In addition to our very basic need for social solidarity and being rooted in community, as Durkheim emphasized, human beings have a need to be inspired by myth, story, drama, and narrative. We live to a great extent by metaphor, by symbol, by story, and by images.

Anyone who loves or is moved by poetry, theater, art, music, literature, or the movies knows this very well. Language itself is symbol and metaphor and appeals to this deep need in us for the imaginative and the grand. And there is simply no human activity that gives expression to this indwelling, semiconscious, but pervasive need more compellingly or powerfully than does religion.

The exodus from slavery in Egypt, the revelation at Sinai, and the passion, martyrdom, and resurrection of Jesus are very powerful human images, and partaking in rituals that connect one with these stories taps a deep-rooted aspect in vast numbers of people and in ways in which appeals to reason seldom can. As a humanist and rationalist, on the literal level I think the cognitive claims made by the religions are false, and I do not believe in them. But on the metaphorical level, I am willing to grant that they do speak a type of truth about human nature and man's existential needs, and therefore can't be totally dismissed or disregarded. I am here and not there because I am the type of person who values the truth claims of religion very highly. But without drawing moral judgments, I have to conclude that most people simply are not temperamentally put together as I am. In fact, I would submit that if archeological evidence could show, with as reasonable certainty as these things can, that the revelation at Sinai never took place, or that Jesus never lived, or even that Joseph Smith plagiarized the entire Book of Mormon, then it would make hardly any difference at all to the faith convictions of contemporary believers. This is why I personally find the efforts of some humanists to debunk religion very often superficial and off the mark.

Where does this analysis leave us, and what does it mean for Ethical Culture?

In the first place, in my opinion, it suggests that Ethical Culture will probably never be a mass movement. Why so?

The explanation for this, in my view, is that by claiming to be a rational movement, which means that our beliefs must somehow meet the test of reasonableness, we undercut and erode at our very heart that element of the mysterious, of the nonrational, and even of the mystifying that speaks to a deep-rooted need felt by many and that is met successfully by the powerful imaginary and emotional consolations the traditional faiths supply. By trying to make religion rational and unmysterious, we move that very component that gives religion its drawing power. What this means, in my opinion, is that Ethical Culture will continue to attract that segment of the population for whom its rational appeal outweighs the immense mythic, historical, symbolic, and communal appeals of the traditional faith communities—and, within this group, only those who feel strongly enough about the issue to overcome the inertia that keeps them within the faith communities of their origin and so are willing to cross over denominational lines. Those who care enough about this kind of rational consistency in their religious lives, I contend, are a very small segment of the population.

To put it another way, if Ethical Culture wished to become a mass movement, sociology and psychology tell us that it really wouldn't be so mysterious. Here is what we would do:

First, adapt a set of doctrines that are arcane, mystifying, and counterrational, the more irrational and extreme the better.

Second, develop a mythology that traces the lineage of all such believers back to Adam. The more rooted in the hidden recesses of antiquity, the more justified your claim.

Third, divide the world into good guys and bad guys and take extreme, black-and-white positions on moral issues.

Fourth, claim that all true believers in the Ethical faith are especially blessed and everyone else is sinful and damned. Be vitriolic about it and make sure that you antagonize those whom you condemn in such a way that they despise and persecute you so that you can feel morally superior and thus strengthen the commitment of the faithful.

With regard to practice:

Develop your own distinctive jargon to be used only by insiders.

Adopt dietary and dress restrictions that help to differentiate Ethicals from all others.

Develop a clear code of sexual behavior. What it is isn't as important as just having one.

Adopt your own calendar with its own holidays and days of mourning based on your mythology.

Establish group rituals particularly of a repetitive nature, such as chanting. Relate the ritual in an integrated way to some wished-for psychological reward or benefit.

And lastly, marshal all the financial resources of the Ethical movement and hire the sexiest, most attractive, intelligent, charismatic, authoritarian megalomaniac you can find and promote him as a strict expounder of the doctrine and leader of the faith.

Follow this formula, and I guarantee that Ethical Culture within five years would become a mass movement.

The problem with this solution, as you can guess, is that the movement we would thereby create would be far from recognizable as the one we identify as Ethical Culture and in which we would feel comfortable. The fundamental rational core and the focus on individual autonomy and dignity would be long gone.

No, I don't think, for these very basic reasons, that we could ever be a mass movement. But I do think that we can be, indeed ought to be, much bigger than we are. A movement of fifty thousand or even five hundred thousand, I don't believe should be impossible for us in this modern age and in this large pluralistic society. How do we begin to do this?

The theoretical task is to learn from the sociological dynamics of the traditional faiths and apply them, but in such a way that the bedrock rationality and traditional outer directedness of the Ethical movement are upheld and not violated.

What I am framing is a narrow window to pass through, but I do think that we could do a better and more creative and energetic job than we have so far. Let me give a preliminary list of suggestions:

With regard to belief, I personally would have little objection if we made the notion of the dignity of the human person an explicit first principle or article of faith in Ethical Culture.

The idea of the intrinsic dignity of the person is an inspiring and glorious idea from which many others grow, such as justice, equality, decency, and mutual support. I think our task must be to raise the profile of this ideal within our societies and far beyond, for in addition to its focal sociological value, it is an idea, in this dehumanizing world, that is increasingly crucial. In my own association of professional Ethical leaders, I am working to encourage a greater unified consensus with regard to the identification of this ideal as the absolutely central and guiding idea of Ethical Culture. In short, we need to make it much more explicit and uniformly promoted.

With regard to the need for myth and narrative, we cannot claim the special inspiration of the Bible, nor can we create significant myths willy-nilly, but there is much we can do. As I see it, the central story line of Ethical Culture is the adventure of the free mind and the expression of conscience throughout human history. What we need to do is take biography more seriously. Without unwarranted distortions, we need to study the lives of men and women who were champions of conscience. We need to organize and study through continuous and systematic courses those people who were the heroes of humanist thought and action. In other words, we need to work harder so that we can find our place within that narrative. In briefest terms, we need to take biography and texts, particularly relevant historical texts, far more seriously as part of our group life.

Next, I think we have to much more aggressively appeal to people on the basis of their real needs, and in a way that we relate to our central value of human dignity. If we relate exclusively to people's intellectual interests, but do not address their underlying pains, anxieties, and sense of isolation, we simply will not grow. We need to do so within the context of a supportive and nurturing community. In short, we need to build a much stronger program around human needs, be they related to family, interpersonal, professional, or recreational needs. For example, we might consider making ongoing programs dealing with family development the centerpiece of the Ethical Society. Organize them so that several days out of the week there would be well-run participatory programs on effective parenting, the moral development of children, couples' relations, etc., augmented by workshops, weekend retreats, summer outings, and so forth. In other words, as a part of our group life, we need to provide continuous opportunities for people to share with one another their experiences and insights around issues of great personal concern and value, and to do so under the philosophical framework of reverence for human worth and in the spirit of mutual search and support. A crucial by-product of such activity is that it will serve to bind people close together as a group and a living community.

Next, we need to develop a stronger ceremonial life, a ceremonial life that will touch participants on a level that is deeper and nonrational, and that will help to bind us more tightly together into a community. We cannot, in my opinion, create such ceremony out of thin air, nor can we entertain the mysterious and mystifying, but we can create those forms that will better lend expression to the communal celebration of cherished human values. We already have ceremony in our weekly platform meetings, in our marriage, in memorial and naming ceremonies, and in our festivals. We need to elevate these more, especially the festivals. A Day of Remembrance when we recall the contributions of our members who have died is a way of rooting ourselves in our own history and celebrating the lives and human gifts of members who have made the Ethical Society what it is. Again, it is a way of establishing narrative and ceremony in a form that is celebrative and thoroughly humanistic and binds our contemporary members to the past.

And lastly, each member needs to reflect on his or her motivation for affirming Ethical Culture and then work on developing a sense of mission about it. We need to take ourselves and our purpose more seriously. One consequence of taking our purpose more seriously would be that the sense of organization would be more "professional" and much tighter. In my view, we are not simply a social or educational organization, by any means. Rather we are the guardians of an ideal and vision that are crucial to the meaningful survival of the human race. We live in a dehumanizing world in which bureaucratization, commercialism, selfishness, institutional injustice, ideological, ethnic, and religious strife, and just plain bigness bulldoze and crush the human spirit and human dignity at every turn.

In such a world we have an imperative and inspiring message to proclaim—and that is that the human dimension must be preserved in each and every circumstance of life.

If we are clearer about our message and proclaim it without defensiveness in word and deed, and do so with a sense of sophistication and organization; if we provide a strong program that addresses people's real interests and needs; if we enrich our sense of nurturing community and build into it celebration, story, art, poetry, and music, unified under a common understanding of our Ethical mission—if we do all these things, people will come to us and say, "These are people of substance and integrity who stand for something, and I wish to stand with them."

July 1987

A Religious View Of Life

In a platform address given long ago, the founder of our movement, Dr. Felix Adler, made a fateful remark that has characterized Ethical Culture from its earliest days. He described the Ethical movement by saying that it "is religious to those who are religiously minded and to those who interpret its work religiously, and it is simply ethical to those who are not so minded." I say that this was a fateful observation because it reflected an ambiguity at the heart of our identity, which, I trust, many within Ethical Culture perceive as a burden and which many outside our movement perceive as a source of vagueness and perhaps institutional sloppiness.

But Adler's remark was neither off the cuff nor out of context. It was a direct consequence of what he meant Ethical Culture to be. The very foundation of Ethical Culture, its defining characteristic, was intended to be a shared commitment to moral striving, to recognizing the supreme importance of attempting to live out a life inspired and guided by moral values.

Adler realized that temperamentally some people are compelled to interpret their moral values in such a way that they have what we might call "a cosmic reach." They might believe that the desire to do good, or the moral nature of human beings, is somehow reflected in the way in which reality, broadly speaking, is put together. Or they might be sustained by a sense of trust that their moral efforts are not ephemeral gestures, but are supported somehow by forces and processes greater than themselves that give them a deeper meaning; that there are, as Matthew Arnold put it, "forces not ourselves which make for righteousness." Or perhaps they sense that their lives are part of an unfolding structure or plan embedded in the very nature of things, and by their moral efforts they are working to complete that plan.

On the other hand, there are people who in their thoughts and feelings temperamentally have no such cosmic reach. They see morality exclusively in human, practical, and utilitarian terms. They might argue that morality is supremely valuable because it serves human survival and happiness, or is necessary for a well-ordered society, or is part of what it means to be a psychologically fulfilled person. For such people, ethics in its origins and purposes is played out exclusively within the useful and the more or less tangible, and not against the background of a broader cosmic tapestry. We might say that such people have a completely secular view of life.

Because Adler put ethics, and not metaphysically derived creeds, at the center of Ethical Culture, it is clear that he wanted to include people of both types: those who are religiously minded and those who are not so minded. A shared commitment to ethics was to be the common ground for action, creating a community in which there was to be a diversity of creeds, but a unanimity of deeds.

Behind Ethical Culture is the assumption that the modern world makes it difficult to believe in the creeds of the historical religions. Our modern period is, rather, characterized by individual freedom of belief, and the persistence of traditional creeds imposes an element of intellectual authoritarianism that runs against the prevailing currents of our time.

Adler affirmed that in a democratic age and in a free land in which diversity flourishes, people inevitably will believe or not believe as they will. But what they can hold in common is a supreme desire to act rightly and work to create a more just, more humane society.

Adler also clarified two other points. First, that he personally interpreted ethics religiously, that is, against a broader cosmic background. He had worked out for himself an elaborate metaphysical scheme that he referred to as the "infinite ethical manifold." In briefest terms, Adler believed that modern science rendered the notion of a personal and patriarchal, monotheistic God no longer credible. In his view, it bore the stamp of an earlier period. Instead, he posited the notion of an impersonal "godhead," which, in an ideal realm, depicted the perfect society in which all members were necessary to complete the idea of the whole and were interrelated, yet retained their independent integrity.

The one would be no more important than the many; the many no more important than the one. For Adler, this conceptual scheme, like Plato's forms, really exists and frames the way in which reality is at bottom constituted. He asserted that it was not a metaphor nor a symbolic projection of how we might wish things to be. Our goal is to make this ideal of the perfect moral society actual here on earth. The second point he averred was that members of Ethical Culture did not have to see things his way. He made it clear that in Ethical Culture one could adopt a different metaphysical scheme, or none at all, as long as one was pledged to the supreme importance of moral values.

I share with Felix Adler the religious temperament, though I do not accept his particular religious metaphysics. What I wish to do is to present a religious view of life, contrasting it with the secular, while noting that what I have to say is very much my own personal view. In the spirit of Ethical Culture, it need not be yours.

I should mention that religion is an activity that very much allows for this personal interpretation. While all words are conventional, *religion* is a term that is more malleable than most. This is so because religion pertains not only to a set of practices and beliefs that are objectively observable to all, but also to very subtle and subjective feelings and interpretations about life, the world, and human experience. While we immediately think of religion in terms of the great systems of Christianity, Judaism, Islam, etc., it is also correct to think of religion in very personal terms fashioned out of our unique experiences.

I should start out by saying that I am not religious in the sense that I believe in a realm of disembodied spirits that stands outside the realm of nature. I do not believe in a personal God who is made of incorporeal spirit, who created the world, and who enters into history. I am not a theist. Nor do I share with Felix Adler the belief that behind this world there is a realm of ideals that is more real than this world of sense. I do believe, however, that our senses *are* limited and that there is a dimension of reality that our senses cannot know because we are constrained to apprehend the world only from our limited perspective. I do believe that an awareness of our own limitations and the humility that flows from it can inspire us with religious feelings. But I do not believe that we can say with certainty anything positive about what reality is like beyond the use of our senses. Unlike Felix Adler, I am not an idealist in this literal sense.

And unlike the theist of traditional faith, I do not believe that knowledge of another realm has been specially revealed to us: no Revealer, no revelation.

Having stripped away the negatives, what am I left with? I am left with the natural world, human beings, the interactions of human beings with the world, and the meaning we impress upon the world out of our interactions with it. For me, what I understand to be religious ultimately finds its reference point within the world of nature and human experience, and not outside of it.

For me, religion centers around the meaning we attribute to and derive from the world and our experience. It has to do with a way of valuing, perceiving, and appreciating the world. To see the world in strictly secular terms is another and contrasting way of perceiving it, and I would like to try to highlight the difference.

Human beings are meaning- and symbol-creating animals. We live to a great extent in the imaginary projections that we impose upon the reality around us. Wordsworth has a beautiful line in which he says, "All the mighty world of eye and ear, both what they half create/And what perceive." I believe this is true. I believe the mind is not merely the passive recipient of stimuli passing through our senses, but is an active force in giving shape and meaning to what we call reality. Take the following example. Imagine you see a man running quickly down the street and you know nothing else about him. Depending on the context of his activity, he could either be fleeing from someone who wants to harm him; himself pursuing someone whom he wishes to harm; running for a bus; hurrying home to tell his wife about his promotion; or getting in some exercise after work. As you watch this man running, your emotional state—whether it be fear, joy, anger, admiration, or amusement—is going to be dependent on the meaning you give to this very basic activity. Until you know the story behind the activity, the meaning of this episode is the meaning you project onto it. To move from the microcosmic to the macrocosmic, we might say that human life and the universe at large are like this man running without a context in an event to which we can never learn the background story. We can never see the universe at large against a broader context, if broader context there be. Consequently, when it comes to life and existence as a whole, our imaginations are relatively free to impose meaning upon them, perhaps picking up whatever little clues we can from internal evidence and fashioning the significance of it all to our liking.

The religious view of life is one such framework of meaning we can impose upon the world, and it can arouse within us particular responses and particular emotions.

We live in our projections and in our enchantments. I look at the starry heavens on a clear and cloudless night and I am engaged and charmed. The nighttime sky captures my attention and I am moved with a sense of wonder, beauty, and awe. You look at the same sky and you are not interested or engaged or moved. Your response is a humdrum, "So what?" The same sky has different meanings depending on who's looking at it.

Why this object should engage my interest while the same object does nothing for you is itself an interesting question. My hunch is that it often has nothing to do with utility. A painting in a museum has no utilitarian value. You may be drawn to it and find it exquisitely beautiful while I am bored to tears. The causes for the disparity of interests do not lie in our rational selves, I believe, but in the fact that beneath our conscious, reasonable minds, we house a repository of symbols. I find this painting or that landscape or that person beautiful; I am charmed and drawn to them because being in their presence touches and arouses my psyche on the level of the symbolic. What I experience through my senses resonates with something deep within me where rational thought and argument cannot reach.

Religious appreciation partakes also of the symbolic, the parts of our beings that produce and respond to symbols.

So where does this lead in more specific terms? Again, let me begin with a negative contrast. I have long been dissatisfied with a strictly secular view of life because it seems too readily to reduce the world and human experience to their material, practical, and utilitarian components. It seems to rob life of the possibility of deeper meaning and a greater richness. In short, life, like the painting in the museum, has a far greater meaning than the use to which we can put it. And in a subtle way, I would argue that it has a meaning that reaches deeper than even the happiness that we can extract from it. To my understanding, a completely secular interpretation of life is overly concerned with analyzing, manipulating, and employing the world for the sake of human ends, usually the end of human happiness. In this sense, the world around us, and in its most extreme form even the social world of other people, has value only to the extent that it fulfills our needs, wishes, and designs. This view suffers from a certain dryness, one dimensionality, and superficiality. It can often fail to see the forest for the trees. To use a technical term, it suffers from the limitations of *reductionism*. In other words, life and the world are reduced to their component parts, but a sense of the world with an integrity of its own in its wholeness is lost or underappreciated. I can say that a forest is *nothing but* a summation of all its individual trees. But in so doing I would be missing something, namely that a forest is an organic whole in its own right, with its own integrity, beauty, and systemic character. I can say that a violin concert is nothing but the movement of a horse's hair over the gut of a cat. Indeed, I could analyze it scientifically according to the laws of physics and acoustics necessary to produce the requisite sounds. If I were sufficiently adept, I could probably provide a total explanation of the concerto in conceptual and scientific terms. But such an explanation could never possess nor convey the meaning that the music itself does. Likewise, I can at least in principle provide a total analysis of a human being in theoretical and scientific terms, describing him or her as a summation of all the chemical, biological, and psychological processes contained therein. But a human being is more than the summation of his or her parts so analyzed and described. A human being is rather a *unique pattern of meaning* that we call a "person." Like the forest and the violin concerto, a person is something greater than, indeed other than, the summation of his or her parts. We can see the world and the things and processes in it either from the perspective of reductionism or the perspective of holism. The former lends itself more readily to utilization; the latter to a stance of appreciation. I can pluck the flower and relate to it as an object of scientific scrutiny. Or I can behold it in its entirety, not to be analyzed, employed for my benefit, or understood, but simply to be appreciated on its own terms, so to speak. Such consciousness, which takes profound notice of the existence of things, devoid of their use, consumption, or value relative to my interests, is the first step along the way to a religious view of life. In a more technical way, we can say that it appreciates the ennobling importance of a search for absolutes, even as it recognizes the dangers of claiming to possess the absolute. It is the consciousness that intuits that in the profoundest sense there is something unsatisfying, confining, and shallow in a life stance in which it is supposed that everything exists for oneself or humankind in general; wherein the world becomes an extension of human wants and needs, and the only mode of relating to the world is from the perspective of how it fulfills those wants and needs.

Bertrand Russell, atheist that he was, implied this when he noted, "The greatest use of a life is to spend it for something that outlasts us." In other words, we touch the further reaches of life's meaning by directing ourselves to those things that transcend our immediate interests and that are not measurable on the scale of a cost/benefit calculus.

Much of the language of humanism speaks of the end of life being self-fulfillment or self-realization. Humanist that I am, this formulation has always seemed a bit disquieting to me unless it is meant to include an appreciation of those things that are *not* directly tied to the fulfillment of our interests.

You might be asking, what difference can this make in a more tangible sense? Let me try to give a few examples.

To take a religious view of things is to see them over the long range, and not solely in terms of immediate gratification. Take marriage, for example. We can say that marriage exists for the mutual fulfillment of both partners. But we can define *fulfillment* in either a crass or sublime way. If we are crass, then we might conclude that as soon as the fulfillment stops, we split. In the sixties it was *au courant* for couples to vow to remain together as long as it was "groovy." That always seemed to me more than a little shallow and to miss the point of marriage, especially in a society that allows couples to live together unmarried. A more sublime view partakes of the understanding that marriage inevitably has its ups and downs, its periods of heightened joy, but also periods of sadness, tension, and strife. Its meaning comes not from a ceaseless surge of unmitigated happiness, but from a sharing of lives together for better and for worse. Its meaning comes from an appreciation of the entire package in all its triumphs and struggles and in the knowledge we gain of ourselves and each other over the course of a lifetime. Needless to say, this view has its limits, and I certainly believe in divorce in cases of insurmountable incompatibility. My point is simply that marriage involves not only a commitment to happiness, but in some sense a commitment to the very *idea* of marriage itself, which transcends the immediate fulfillment of both partners. It is an idea that does not fall from "above," but emerges out of the concrete nature of what marriage is and can be.

Moving to a very different arena, consider our relationship to the natural environment and to nonhuman species. We can, again, look at the natural environment and our place in it from two different perspectives. We can say that we will measure the value of the various species only to the extent that their continued existence supports human interests and fulfills human need as far as we can know and predict such things. In other words, we can conclude that the natural world is a hierarchy with ourselves on top and with the rest of nature under our dominion to be exploited for our interests. Consequently, if plant or animal species are considered useless, there is no reason why we should feel restrained in destroying them if we so desire. On the other hand, we can respect their existence, and temper our arrogance with a more sublime realization that we have our place in the scheme of things and they have theirs. We can transform our relationship from one of use to one of appreciation. A religious view of nature so construed commends us to shift from a position of exploitation to one of ecological integration and stewardship. Again, I am not an absolutist. The assumption that nature is benign is a romantic fallacy, and we need to protect our own species from those living forces that threaten us.

What I am calling a religious view of nature, let's call it a "spiritual ecology," imbues nature with a different meaning, evokes different feelings from us as we reflect upon it, and counsels a transformed behavior from us as we interact within it.

My last example is perhaps the most crucial and comes closest to the heart of Ethical Culture as a religious view of life. We live in an advanced, capitalist, postindustrialist society, which biases how we value human beings as producers within a market-driven economy. Whom the advertising media focus on is perhaps a good barometer of which human types this culture esteems most highly and around whom its normative ideals, values, and aspirations are generated. But how do we assess those not within this gilded, neo-Grecian ideal of the young, the rich, the unblemished, and, we might add, the white and male? How do we assess and esteem those on the margins? The elderly, the dimwitted, the poor, the ugly, the ethnically *outré*, the sick, the outcast, the antisocial, the chronically obnoxious, the handicapped, the retarded, the severely retarded—those who on the equation of a cost/benefit calculus drain society and ostensibly add little to it?

The time will come in the not very distant future when we will, through early fetal detection and genetic engineering, be able to create a world in which retarded people, for example, need not be born. Implicit in such a modern eugenics program is a profound judgment about the relative value of human lives, how we value them, and who does the valuing. Do we want to live in a world in which there are no retarded people? Or might we argue that the existence of those whose lives are not productive, or even happy, according to some ideal standard of what we imagine, makes some claim on the rest of us? I recall that in the days of the Roman Empire, 25 percent of all female children were put to death at birth. Sons added to the wealth and prestige of families in a way in which daughters did not. Such are profound questions that go to the very heart of how we esteem human life. The utilitarian approach to society, if brought to its logical extreme, declares that those who are not useful need not exist. But is this the only way to assess the meaning of human life? Is this the sole perspective? Is this what we want?

I recoil at the absolutists who declare on unbending principle that human life *qua* life is the standard we must adopt. Life has to be preserved at all cost, regardless of the will of the subject in question, no matter how much pain and agony he or she might be suffering, no matter how meaningless such sufferers profess their own lives to be. The position of such absolutists, which is totally reckless of the consequences, especially for the person himself, is itself without compassion, heartless and cruel and ultimately inhuman.

But I must confess that I am equally uncomfortable with the position of what we might call the "absolute relativist," for whom the quality of life is the only standard. Implicit in this notion is the estimation that human life has no intrinsic or prior value. It ultimately reduces the value of a human life to its utility. Useful, productive, happy lives are assessed as more valuable than those that do not pass these tests. To assess the value of human lives solely on the basis of their usefulness to others, and even to oneself (and this is very tricky!), is to commit the ultimate act of reductionism. It is to dehumanize the human. We assess the value of a table, a car, and stereo sets by their consequences for us, by their usefulness, and by the extent to which they make our lives more comfortable and happy. But are these the only criteria by which we measure the value of human beings? Or is there a dimension of estimation that remains after we have peeled away all the questions of whether they, *or we*, are productive and contented? Is the life of a person whom fate has slated to be burdened by trag-edy, misfortune, and misery less valuable than those who live cheerier and more fulfilled lives? Who is qualified to make such a judgment? Do we dare to let go of a notion of transcendent human value lest we assess human beings as we assess tables, cars, and stereo sets? In my view, the answer to these fundamental and vital questions must be framed between the poles of relativism and the absolute. To lose sight of either pole is to slide into the abyss of inhumanity one way or the other.

The religious view of life declares what it cannot prove: that there is a sacred dimension within the human that proclaims that every life is worthy regardless of whether the person in question is rich or poor, beautiful or ugly, fulfilled or unfulfilled, or whether his behavior is pleasing or displeasing to the rest of us. To relegate any of these criteria to the standard of what makes human life valuable is to relativize, cheapen, and, to my mind, ultimately contra-dict the deeper meaning of the human experience. It is to transform the human being into a thing, a tool to satisfy the interests of whichever sector of society is doing the evaluating. To use the biblical metaphor, it is to commit a grievous act of idolatry.

The religious view of life resists the reduction of the human person into an ensemble of its parts and its usefulness; it stands against the forces of dehu-manization, whatever they may be. It declares itself to the rest of the world: "I have value in and of myself, even if all the forces around me conspire to tell me that I do not. My ultimate worth as a human being is not predicated on fulfilling anyone's interests, or any interests whatsoever. My sheer existence as a human being bespeaks its own worthiness."

Before I close, I must address all too briefly one issue that is of the utmost importance and relevance.

The traditionally religious person who believes firmly in the existence of a moral and personal God will look at my project of religious humanism, and if he or she is of a generous and liberal spirit might say, "Your ideas are noble and morally tend in the right direction. But they suffer from one fatal flaw, one crucial error, which undermines your approach.

"Because you disavow belief in a personal, transcendent God who, by his power and his divine plan for us, has made us in his own image and so is the cause of our transcendent worth, you have destroyed the very basis of that worth, of that human dimension you counsel us to esteem. There cannot be any worth without a worth giver."

Furthermore, my theistic critic would argue that by disavowing God as the source of religious value, and by keeping my project exclusively within the human dimension, my imputation of religious meaning onto the world and onto human experience is precisely that—an imputation, an attribution of special value and meaning to those things to which I simply choose to confer a privileged meaning and status. In the final analysis, my critic would contend that I am doing nothing other than what I assert the relativists are doing— simply expressing one human interest over another. "I say human beings are infinitely valuable, you say they are not, and who is to adjudicate the difference? Without an appeal to an absolute divine standard expressing God's moral will, all you are left with are competing human wills and human power struggles. If you do not invoke a divine standard that comes from outside the human realm, it is simply your wish against another's."

This is a criticism that should not be too easily dismissed. My response is basically to say, "You are correct, but don't be too complacent or righteous in your criticism of my humanism. I would contend that if you subject your own position to rigorous scrutiny, your position and mine are ultimately not as far apart as you think. In the modern period, people are going to believe or disbelieve in God as they will. It is a claim that is far from self-evident, as are all religious claims. The history of religious warfare is tragic testimony to that fact. The existence of God is something that one believes on faith or not. Consequently, to accept that the human being is created in God's image, you first have to persuade me through the use of reason, education, or whatever tools are at your disposal that there is such a God. You start with the existence of God to ground and validate your claims about the sacredness of the human being. I start directly with the human being. But in either case, we are left with the task of persuading our audiences to a position and an apprehension about life and its meaning that are not self-evidently true. Your task and mine are not so different, it is just that we start our efforts of persuasion at different points along the way."

"So," I say to my liberal theistic friend, "let us make an agreement, or, as you might say, a covenant. Since we are both passionately concerned about the moral status of contemporary society, since we are both committed to upholding the sacredness of the person against the forces of dehumanization, let us cool the acrimony between humanism and religion. True, when you see God standing behind the events of this world, I contend you are making a mistake. And, when I proclaim my agnosticism, you assert that I too am in error. On that important point, we part company. But once having clarified our differences, let us come together to affirm that point on which we share agreement. Let us work together to create a world in which the dignity of men and woman will flourish, and in which forces of poverty and war, oppression and injustice, will not have the last word."

November 1990

Ethical Culture Is Not Atheism.
But What Is It?

I t is my opinion, and I believe a well-grounded one, that Ethical Culture strives to shape a world view that is a broad and far-reaching perspective on life and reality. In that sense, Ethical Culture is not politics, but presents values and beliefs that underlie our politics, and all else that gives our lives direction and purpose.

Rather than talk about Ethical Culture in a vacuum, I thought it would be constructive to look at it in comparison with another perspective that has gotten a lot of publicity recently, namely, atheism. It is my contention that Ethical Culture as a world view has some important things in common with atheism, but they are not the same thing and shouldn't be identified with each other.

Atheism has come into its own in American life in the last several years. Perhaps in light of the extremism of the Christian Right and its intolerant politics, which has become very powerful, as well as terrorism perpetrated in the name of Islam, atheism has asserted itself in *reaction* to religion. The past decade has witnessed a spate of books promoting atheism by such writers as Sam Harris, Richard Dawkins, Christopher Hitchens, and others. These books, as well as dynamic social forces, have played a role in increasing tremendously the number of Americans who now claim to have "no religion." This cohort of the population now exceeds 16 percent, which is larger than the African American minority, or, if looked at religiously, is by far larger than the number of Jews, Muslims, Hindus, and Buddhists put together. A major sector of this cohort is younger people, the so-called millennial generation, who, when they look at religion, especially fundamentalist Christianity and its obsessions with abortion and homosexuality and its contempt for those who don't share its beliefs, conclude that if this what religion is, they don't want to have any part of it.

But it would be a mistake to draw the conclusion that those people professing "no religion" are themselves atheists. They are primarily people who are turned off to organized religion as promoted in churches. But such "nones," as they are called, may cultivate their own sense of spirituality and a rapport with what they construe to be divine. Studies have shown that the total number of atheists and agnostics in America does not exceed 5 percent of the population. Nevertheless, atheism has gained a certain legitimacy that it previously has not had, and this, to my way of thinking, being an atheist myself, is a very good thing. Atheism, if not thoroughly despised, has certainly been historically marginalized in American life. Atheism in a certain sense has come out of the closet, and in a moment of enthusiasm has spawned a growing number of atheist and secular organizations. The media thrive on contention and combat. And because by its nature it sees itself in a combative relationship with religion, atheism and atheist groups have been able to attract a lot of press by tweaking religion and its sanctimonious respectability, much of which it does not deserve.

As an important aside, let me say that this current excitement about atheism might encourage us in Ethical Culture to unreflectively jump on board and see ourselves as part of this atheist and secular movement. I do indeed think that Ethical Culture should join in coalition with some of these secular groups who, in their political mission, share interests that overlap with our own—as we should consider joining in coalition with any group with whom we have common cause. But my fear, as someone who has loved and been devoted to Ethical Culture for forty-four years, is that we should become identified with such atheist and secular groups, and that we set ourselves up to be swallowed by them. We should not allow this, because as my thesis puts forward, Ethical Culture is not atheism, and an assumption that it is, either by its members or in the public eye, is to give up what is distinctive about Ethical Culture at its core. It is to abandon its *raison d'etre* and lose something that is distinctively precious.

Back to atheism for a moment. From time immemorial, to be an atheist has been an object of contempt. In the biblical book of Psalms, it is written, "Only the fool says in his heart 'there is no God.' "Socrates was put to death for the crime of atheism. And John Locke, the great English philosopher who wrote a letter on religious toleration and helped inspired our founders to separate church from state, nevertheless had no place in his commonwealth for atheists.

• It is an interesting question as to why atheism and atheists have been the target of so much vituperation and contempt throughout the ages. There have been many reasons, one perhaps being that in a world in which almost everyone was a believer, to be an atheist was to be an outlier, someone who was perversely different from others and, because he or she was different, a nuisance and even a threat.

But the more compelling explanation has to do with morality. Since ancient times, and even still, I would assume a majority of the population believes that the capacity to be moral is predicated on a belief in God. In the most brute version of this belief, it was assumed by the aristocracy that if the peasants, who were uneducated, impulse driven, and not quite civilized, were to be held in check, that is, be decent, moral and well behaved, an effective mechanism for keeping them that way was to get them to believe that their good behavior would be rewarded by heaven and their immoral behavior would condemn them to eternal damnation. God and fear of God were required to keep people on the straight and narrow. Religion was employed for the purpose of social control.

A more sophisticated position that grounds morality in God belief is to assert that morality needs to issue from a source that is outside of human interests. Morality needs to be something that human beings have neither made nor which they can unmake, for if morality is merely a human creation, who is to say that what is assumed to be moral doesn't merely reflect the interests of those who hold power in society? Hence morality needs to be inscribed in an unchanging cosmic order lest it rest on the shifting sands of human whim and changing power configurations. We need a moral standard that transcends human interests, is absolute, does not change, and is eternal. In other words, that source is God, and those who cannot accept God therefore cannot be moral. John Locke, whom I mentioned awhile back, who advocated for religious tolerance and could not countenance atheists as citizens, did so on the grounds that atheists could not take oaths and therefore could not be trusted as loyal members of society.

This equation of God belief and morality is a testament to the pervasiveness of religion and its hold over the human mind. I say this because the assumption that one needs to believe in God in order to be moral is simply false to the facts. There is no empirical evidence that people who believe in God are any more ethical than people who do not. And they never have been. And so we can conclude that this assumption falls into the category of a prejudice, a prejudice that is thousands of years old and as deep as the ocean, but a prejudice nevertheless.

I am an atheist because I am one of those people who is committed to the notion that one's beliefs should be based on evidence as much as possible, and I simply see no evidence of a divine custodian. I see no evidence of divine agency in the natural world, and I see no evidence of it in the realm of morality either. Why a God who is both absolutely good and totally powerful would permit a young child to die painfully and slowly from a dreaded disease is something that the theologians have never been able to compellingly answer in all my study of religion, in my humble opinion.

That belief in God can bring good effects, I have no doubt. The lives and careers of Mohandas Gandhi and Martin Luther King are testaments to the power of religious belief. And it is because of religion's capacity to foster good and noble deeds that I retain a qualified respect for it, especially in its prophetic role. But to my mind, the great and admirable accomplishments of a Gandhi, King, Dorothy Day, and countless others says more about the power of belief than it does about the real existence of a being who putatively stands behind that belief. They are not the same thing.

But let me return to my main topic. Atheism has also played a positive role in human history, but in my view it is a negative philosophy without any content of its own. When I speak of atheism's positive role, I am thinking of the part it played during the Enlightenment, for example. The Enlightenment thinkers, especially in France, were keen to an unholy alliance between the corrupt aristocracy, the nobility, and the church. The church and religion played powerful roles in enabling and justifying the oppression of the masses, and their priests benefitted from this oppression. The attack on religion in the name of rationalism, science, and, at times, atheism was used as an instrument by which to unmask the deceptive and corrupt and oppressive role of the church in the service of bringing about liberty and eventually democratic forms of government.

Throughout history and to its disgrace, religion has all too often been a conservative force that has favored the status quo and has entered into alliances with the powers of state that have served the interests of oppression rather than freedom. This is true whether we are talking about the Vatican through much of its history, the Orthodox Church in czarist Russia, the church in Franco's Spain or in support of Argentinean generals in the late 1970s, and numerous other examples. By contrast, atheism has aligned itself often, but not always—Stalinism being a major counterexample—with the forces that have also been on the side of political and intellectual freedom. In its critical role, atheism has often been a powerful and productive idea.

But my concern is that once atheism has played that role of bringing down the negative and excessive aspects of religion, what are we left with? What are we left with as a life philosophy? I would argue we are left with a void, in that atheism is essentially negative and not positive.

Felix Adler, the founder of Ethical Culture, was also sensitive to the insufficiency of atheism. It is an interesting fact that when Felix Adler founded Ethical Culture, he did so out of a critical stance toward the historical religions. He felt that Christianity and Judaism, even liberally interpreted, still retained elements of authoritarianism as well as beliefs that were unsuited to the modern, scientific age. And yet, at the same time, he declared, "I never was an atheist." And he also stated that his intellectual struggles were to find "a way out of agnosticism," as he put it.

In fact, by starting Ethical Culture, Adler undoubtedly believed he was doing something religious. But for him, and for me, Ethical Culture does not start with the issue of whether there is a God or no God. Nor is that its primary preoccupation. Its frame of reference is different.

Ethical Culture starts with and is built upon what I like to refer to as an abiding intuition, an intuition as to what human beings and human relations are about at their deepest and most important level. When I say that Ethical Culture starts with an intuition, I am implying that it rests more upon a primal emotion and insight than it does upon an idea or a principle.

I live in a world of other human beings, some known to me, the vast majority unknown to me. The questions Ethical Culture asks are: How am I to look upon my fellow human beings? What should my approach to them be? How should I value them?

When Adler founded Ethical Culture, the world he lived in was one in which the rich were growing richer at the expense of the faceless masses. It was the Industrial Age. It was a world in which people were crammed into overflowing tenements that were disease ridden, and men, women, and children were crushed in the maw of faceless and dangerous factories, almost chained to their machines for endless hours of work to churn out profits for their industrial masters. The question back then was: How do we treat people as more than cogs and tools in a world in which their humanity is unrecognized and bled out of them? And it is, friends, certainly a question we can ask today.

The operative term here and for Ethical Culture is *humanity*.

We can look at the world and the human beings in it in a twofold way. When it comes to the world of things, whether it be the buildings we live and work in, our tools and appliances, or myriad other things around us, these things exist to satisfy our needs and wants—some very basic needs, others more sublime ones, such as our aesthetic needs. But in the end, we use and exploit them for the sake of our satisfaction. We are their masters.

But human beings are different. We can look at them as we do the inanimate things around us—as instruments and tools to satisfy our own interests, needs, and lusts. In the most basic sense we can treat people as mere objects, as things that fit into our own needs and purposes.

Someone might ask, do we really do this? And my answer is, of course we do. We do it all the time and in a multitude of different ways. And that is the problem. That is our great humanistic problem. It has always been our problem, and with seven billion people walking the face of the earth, the problem is potentially greater now than it has ever been. And this is the problem that Ethical Culture at its very core resists, and it is its central mission to resolve.

And what is that problem? It is the nullification, the obliteration, the annihilation, and the wanton suppression of the humanity of human beings. When does this happen? It happens most graphically and, I would argue, most inexplicably when tens of thousands, hundreds of thousands, and millions of men, women, and children are slaughtered in a mass phenomenon that has come to be known as genocide, slaughtered for the sake of the power of a few or sacrificed in the name of an ideology. It happens in warfare generally when human beings become nothing other than "collateral damage." It happens when members of minority groups are the victims of bigotry and are degraded and humiliated.

But it happens in other ways that are hidden from us, and I contend that their hiddenness enables them to flourish. It happens when uncountable workers in a globalized world labor in drudgery to bring favorable returns on a balance sheet. Each thing we enjoy, whether a pair of shoes or a bar of chocolate, contains hidden social and human processes behind it, processes that are out of sight and almost always out of mind. And it happens right here when thirteen million Americans suffer from job loss and the indignities of chronic unemployment.

In a more general sense, human beings are robbed of their humanity whenever they are turned into statistics. Social science, of course, does this, and I admit that it is inevitable. Researchers have found that a person can only get to know distinctively and personally at one time no more than about 150 other people. Beyond that, human beings begin to shade into an impersonal mass, into an ethnic group, a race, a tribe, a nationality, or a class. They become a stereotype, a generality, and their individual humanity is lost in the process.

But it is the purpose, again, of Ethical Culture to not allow this process, as inevitable as it is, to go down too easily.

At the center of Ethical Culture is what I would call "a feeling for humanity." And this feeling for humanity, this feeling of the humanity of the other, starts with what I believe is the capacity for empathy. And it is the supreme purpose of Ethical Culture, which exists to cultivate ethics, to cultivate this capacity for empathy. People are born, I believe, with certain temperaments. But our emotions, like our intellect, are not fixed, not incorrigible. Our emotions, I believe, can be widened and expanded; in other words, they can grow based on how we set our goals and by trying to become the kinds of people we want to be. We can broaden and sensitize our emotions through practice.

What is empathy? It is the ability, through the use of our projective imagination, to say to oneself, "What would it be like to be that other person? What would it be like to be like her, with her dreams and aspirations, insecurities and fears? What would the world feel like to be her and what would it be like to see the world as she does—subjectively, from the inside out? What would it be like to take her standpoint?" Needless to say we can never fully achieve this identification with another self. We are separate people. But I believe that we are not totally separate. As members of the same human species, our human-ity, mine and hers, does overlap. And even if I cannot totally identify with the other, I would argue that the very effort to do so stretches our capacity for empathy, putting us into contact with the humanity of the other and, in that process, humanizing ourselves as well. This is Ethical Culture's central task, its propelling mission: to rescue the human from the forces of dehumanization.

It is sometimes said that Ethical Culture, in contrast to the historical reli-gions, which have well-honed rituals elaborated over the centuries, lacks meth-ods by which to put its values into practice. For the most part this is true. But let me suggest a very simple meditation that I engage in from time to time, which helps me become a better Ethical Culturist. When at times I read a statistic, such as the number of Americans unemployed, it become useful to push my mental content aside and try to imagine what it must feel like for an individual person to lose his or her job. Ask: How would I feel if I were to lose my job? What would it do to my dignity and self-esteem? How would it affect my relations to my spouse and children? What would be my worst fear? On the positive side, I might reflect on how being unemployed rallied my spirits to overcome adversity, or to expand an appreciation for the love and support that my family and friends have given to me. In other words, through acts of empathy and through attempting to identify with the other, we can try to get beyond a world that dehumanizes human beings by brutally oppressing them or turning them into statistics.

Clearly, we can engage in these acts of empathy most easily with those with whom we actively share our lives, those with whom we are most intimate, our family members, and a few chosen friends. But we can't love everyone or actively extend our compassion and empathy to all humankind. But I think, nevertheless, it behooves us to take the emotions we experience in the intimate precincts of our lives and use these emotions as examples of how we might value people who are strangers to us. If I love my daughter, it behooves me to imagine that there are other fathers elsewhere who also love their daughters as I love mine, and through that act of identification of our shared humanity, I expand my own orbit of empathy and caring.

In a certain sense one might conclude that all this is a bit self-evident and too commonplace to harp on. Would that it were! If people did not find it so quick and easy to forget and not care about the humanity of others, as they care about their own, the great injustices that have marred the career of humankind would be greatly mitigated, I contend.

This sensitivity to the humanity that lies within the other is the heart of Ethical Culture and gives rise to its guiding principles and its practice. Everything spins out from that center. It suggests how we should strive to relate to those who are part of our intimate lives, how we should strive to relate to strangers, and it lays down the values that should form our politics and how we direct our lives, both as individuals and socially. Everything emanates from and is directed toward this ideal of preserving the humanity of human beings. It is the lodestar, the criterion that needs to govern our choices, large and small. When it comes to politics, we need to ask ourselves: Does this policy or political position in its very ultimate purpose serve to enhance the dignity of human beings, or does it oppress that dignity for the sake of the power, profit, or aggrandizement of a few? Does it lead down the line to the enhancement of the well-being and the dignity of human beings? Does it promote justice or injustice? Is it fair or unfair? These must be the criteria toward which politics ultimately leads, and if not, it needs to be radically reformed to make it so.

To return to my contrast, Ethical Culture overlaps with atheism in that it proclaims that it does not need God in order for Ethical Culture to execute its program. Empathy can grow deeper with the reinforcement that it is part of a cosmic purpose, or without it, as I fervently believe it can. But, as I have tried to suggest, Ethical Culture does not start or end with atheism, nor has that ever been its center of gravity. If it were, why would those inspired by Ethical Culture throughout its history create settlement houses and schools to educate the young, enable immigrants, workers, and refugees to improve their lives, battle the evil of child labor, and invest itself in a multitude of other humanitarian causes? These are our proudest achievements, and none of them has anything to do with atheism.

In closing, let me say that beyond the practical effects of attempting to humanize an inhuman condition, the effort to do so can also serve for us individually as the basis for our own world views. To borrow from an unusual source, we are all better off if we live "a purpose-driven life"; if we dedicate ourselves to something larger than ourselves that outlasts us. And so I would say, let us collectively, in the Ethical Culture Society, in our own hearts and minds, and in what we do with our individual lives, allow ourselves to be inspired by the overarching aspiration to make this world a better, more decent, and more caring place. Above all things, as we take our journey through life, let us dedicate ourselves to humanity.

June 2012

Four Types Of Religious Humanism

The religious character of Ethical Culture seems endlessly debatable. Is Ethical Culture a religion? Or is it a secular philosophy of life? Despite the fact that Ethical Culture is now in its 128th year, the question is still not resolved. Though many, and I would guess most, Ethical Culturists would identify Ethical Culture as their religion, at the same time, I know that a significant minority would not. For people in the latter category, religion comes with a lot of baggage in the form of creeds, rituals, and a very flawed history that they don't want to identify with. For many people attracted to movements like ours, religion is a repository of all things evil. Mention the word "religion" and what comes to mind are authoritarianism and self-righteousness, self-interested clerics who sustain their power by duping and exploiting the masses with superstition, obscurantism and dark mysteries to which only they have privileged access, strange and irrational cultic practices, not to mention xenophobia, crusades, inquisitions, pogroms, and holy wars. For such people religion is a virtual allergy, and there is much in religion's malignant underside to verify that they have a point.

On a more intellectual and technical plane, those who do not interpret Ethical Culture as religious will argue that as they see it, religion requires a belief in God. Since Ethical Culture is not focused on God belief and does not require it, it is, therefore, an unwarranted stretch to refer to it as a religion.

On the other side of the equation, there are people for whom religion carries no such baggage, or the baggage is not so heavy that the positive aspects of religion don't outweigh it. They see religion as a conveyor, though not necessarily a consistent conveyor, of very positive values such as brotherhood, compassion, justice, love, and the worthiness of human beings. If religion has been the focal point for great evil, then friends of religion can point to illustrious figures such as Mohandas Gandhi, Martin Luther King, or the Dalai Lama, whose worthy and humanitarian achievements cannot be divorced from their deep immersion in their religious faiths.

Those in the pro-religion camp might also argue that a totally secular outlook on life fails to satisfy a need that they feel very deeply. They may sense that behind the workaday world, behind the physical universe, there is, if not a personal God, a greater, more encompassing reality, and it is this reality that religion addresses. For example, they may feel that there is an intelligence that pervades nature. Or, if they are ethically inclined, they may feel that there is a moral law, a cosmic order of right and wrong, that is embedded in the fabric of reality. Perhaps they feel that justice will prevail in the end and that we are the instruments of its ultimate triumph. Perhaps many people with a sense of the religious resist the idea of an absurd universe, and they feel that there is a purpose coursing through nature and for which humankind exists, and toward which the human future is slowly but inexorably bending. Perhaps there are those people who feel that this material world is not all and that behind it lies a unifying principle that supports all things and that serves to bind everything together. And perhaps many sense that because we are finite, so there exists an Infinite, of which our lives are particular and transient expressions. Perhaps many intuit, as William James did, that there is something "more" to the universe than what we through our limited faculties and our limited senses can know and experience. After all, they might argue, our senses are like antennae tuned to only limited frequencies. Outside their range, perhaps there are many more frequencies, whose wavelengths we simply are unattuned to, but that we dimly sense are there.

Even without positing a father figure God, a divine custodian who created and judges us, those who have these sensibilities rightly refer to them as "religious." They constitute what William James, again, referred to as a person's "overbeliefs." For such folks, if Ethical Culture seems to have this broader reach, if it inspires them to this heightened sensitivity, especially as it pertains to a perceived moral order, then Ethical Culture can rightly be understood as their religion.

In certain more prosaic ways, Ethical Culture is undeniably a religion. For one, it is recognized by the government as such, with the result that its buildings are tax-exempt as religious facilities. In 1946, the Washington Ethical Society went to court to plead tax exemption as a religious organization. Deeming itself incompetent on theological matters, the federal court agreed that the Ethical Society is a religion on sociological grounds. The court noted that we meet as a congregation on a specific day for specific purposes that functionally resemble worship in the traditional churches. We provide moral instruction for our children. We carry on charitable work in the community as churches do. In other words, if it looks, walks, and quacks like a duck, it's a duck. And the court was right. In a functional sense, Ethical Culture is a religion, even though we don't affirm a belief in a Supreme Being.

When it comes to the deeper questions of belief, the ambivalence as to whether we are a religion or not was placed at the heart of Ethical Culture at the very beginning by Dr. Felix Adler, who created the Ethical movement. He declared very explicitly, "Ethical Culture is religious to those who are religiously minded, and merely ethical to those who are not so minded," implying that religion is virtually a matter of temperament. What Adler intended to do was to make ethics the cornerstone of his movement, and he realized emphatically that you could be ethical whether you construed your ethics religiously or in a secular way. What this implied is that ethical commitment is primary in Ethical Culture; the beliefs you employ to arrive at your ethics are secondary and open to the free conscience of all who subscribe to it. Ethical Culture invites all to join, whether you believe in a Higher Power or do not. "Deed before creed" became the working motto of the Ethical Culture movement.

While Ethical Culture welcomed both those who were "religiously minded" and those who were not religiously minded, Adler did not hide the fact that he himself was emphatically religiously minded. Though it sets many of us apart from our founder, Adler did believe in a nonmaterial, spiritual reality beyond the realm of our senses and outside of space and time. He believed that our ethical experience hinted at something transcendental in the universe that, though impersonal, was eternal and perfect and to which the ethical progress of humankind was tending.

Adler was among those religious thinkers of the late nineteenth century who found the conclusions of Darwinism to be upsetting as they related to the status of human beings. Although he thought natural selection was a reasonable theory to account for the physical evolution of the human species, he fretted over the implications that the human being could be understood as nothing but the movement of molecules and a complex of chemical reactions. If that were the case, what distinguished the human being from any other material thing? What protection does the person have from mere use or exploitation by others if there is nothing in the person that makes him or her worthy, sacred, or holy? So Adler sought to find a cosmic reality, impersonal though it was, that ensured that the human being somehow counted in the universe at large. Indeed, such impersonal cosmic entities flourished in the post-Darwinian period. Emerson had his "Oversoul." Herbert Spencer spoke of the "Unknowable," while Matthew Arnold posited "a power not ourselves that makes for righteousness."

Adler's religious theorizing was highly creative and brilliant, and it was very abstract. With his death in the 1930s, the religious aura of Ethical Culture began to fade, and our movement entered what we might refer to as its humanist stage. An influx of immigrants bringing with them unionism, socialism, and Marxism entered Ethical Culture and assuredly moved it in a more secular direction. By the 1960s, in the heyday of the humanistic psychology movement, the leaders of Ethical Culture drafted a paper that identified Ethical Culture as a humanist movement, a term that Adler shunned for its emphasis on human ends devoid of the spiritualizing dynamics inspired by transcendental ideals.

Felix Adler was a religious thinker, and although he denied the existence of a personal God, revelation, and miracles, his language, his metaphors, his imagery were saturated with a religious vocabulary. After his death, as Ethical Culture became more secular, Adler's transcendentalism was replaced implicitly with the scaffolding of philosophical naturalism, more closely related to the thought of the great humanist philosopher John Dewey.

Naturalism has many technical meanings, but in simplest terms it signifies a belief that nature is all there is and that there is no reality outside of nature. For a naturalist, there are no gods except as metaphors; there is no immortality, because the mind or the soul is linked to the natural functions of the brain, and when the brain decomposes, mental or nonphysical activity also ceases. For the naturalist, ideas are natural and have real influence on us, but they are ultimately derivative from the natural and social realities in which we operate.

The emergence of naturalism in our movement, indeed, the monumental phenomenon of the secularization of modern life and the triumph of the scientific and rational culture in which we live, raises a challenging question for us and for others. And that question is: Can you have religion or spirituality without belief in transcendental, spiritual beings? Or, otherwise put, does it make any sense to talk about a naturalistic religion or a humanistic religion that is ultimately grounded in nature?

If you believe that religion requires a belief in real spiritual beings, then by definition your answer must be no. But words and concepts change their meaning with the passage of time. Certainly in contemporary usage, religion has come to mean devotion to principles or ideas or realities that produce experiences and have consequences similar to those that traditional believers claim in their relationship to supernatural realities and to spiritual beings. I am quiet convinced, for example, that when young seekers return to the church or synagogue stating that they are looking for a religious or spiritual experience, what they most often mean is not rapport with an otherworldly God, but rather the uplifting and comforting experience of sharing a sense of community with fellow congregants—in other words, a totally this-worldly and naturalistic experience.

And so to the question, is a humanistic religious experience possible, my answer is yes. In fact, what I would like to do is to present four ways in which it is possible. In my description of four types of religious experience, I don't intend to explain anything strange or particular esoteric. In this community there are a great many art lovers. No one here would deny that when moved by beautiful art or music, they have had what we might call distinctive aesthetic experiences. When I talk about religious experience I am not talking about anything more unusual or, I think, accessible than that.

As I have explained in previous addresses, mystical experience is character-ized by transcendence of the ego, in which the felt boundaries between the self and the other disappear and there is a sense, usually ecstatic and compelling, of union with the object of the mystical experience.

Mystical experience is the most intense form of religious experience, but there are other forms of religious experience in which a sense of oneself remains preserved and is not totally absorbed.

As I understand it, such experiences involve a felt sense of connection between the person and some greater, more encompassing, enveloping reality of which he or she is a part. *Felt connection* is the operative term. It is virtually a cliché to say that we are a part of nature. Or, we are part of the human family or the human tapestry. To actually experience and feel these connections is what, in my assessment, makes for religious experience.

So what are the four types of religious humanism?

The first type, which is the most common, is what is frequently called "nature mysticism." It is the classic sunset experience. It is the sublime realization that we are children of nature, made of the same stuff as the stars, the stones, the trees, and the earth. We are the products of nature, of the same primordial evolutionary forces that have molded all life, indeed all of inanimate matter, and to nature we return. The religious mystic looks over the natural landscape, contemplates the immensity of the oceans, gazes at the stars, and says to herself, "I am that, and that is me." The felt connection between self and the enveloping natural world brings heightened feelings of wonder, of awe, of a paradoxical sense of comfort that comes from a realization of one's smallness, and perhaps, in special moments, feelings of sublime peace and the sense that it is a blessing to be given the gift of life and to be able to contemplate it all.

It is in search of such experience that people, I among them, feel a sense of spiritual uplift when hiking on the wooded trail, or paddling a canoe down a quiet stream, or seeking out magisterial vistas from mountain promontories. It is why people head to the woods seeking spiritual renewal, which the contrivances of urban landscapes could never deliver. For Emerson it was in the woods that "all mean egoism vanishes." And for Wordsworth, the greatest of the poets of nature mysticism, nature was "the anchor of my purest thoughts, the nurse, the guide, the guardian of my heart and soul, of all my moral being."

In nature mysticism we find a communion between the human being and the enveloping natural world that is infinite in space and time. Without reference to gods, miracles, or otherworldliness, it provides an experience of uplift and renewal—an abiding appreciation of the specialness of life and how good it is to be here.

The second type of religious humanism is what I call "reverent agnosticism." This metaphor, rendered by Isaac Newton, illustrates reverent agnosticism: looking at his extraordinary achievements in creating modern physics, Newton said, "I do not know what I may appear to the world; but to myself I seem to have been only like a little boy playing on the seashore and diverting myself in now and then finding a smoother pebble or a prettier shell than ordinary, whilst the great ocean of truth lay all undiscovered before me."

This is the human condition before the unknown. From the perspective of the agnostic, the cumulative knowledge of mankind is merely the tiniest speck amid an ocean of ignorance. Not only do we confront truths that are unknown and to be discovered, as Newton put it, but we also confront *unknowables*. It does not take much philosophical reflection to arrive at the realization that we can know the world only from our narrow perspective. Our knowledge is limited by our senses and the range of our marvelous, but finite minds. Outside the range of our mind and senses, we may conclude that there exists a much broader reality that is simply beyond the range of our faculties to know, just as x-rays are beyond the range of our sight. It is as if our minds are like searchlights reaching out in the darkness. The beam of our light extends only so far. But we know by deduction that there is reality beyond the point our beams of light can ever reach. Or, to invoke a final metaphor, it is as if we all live out our lives in a room that is completely sealed—in our case, sealed by the limitation of our faculties. Because we know that we are inside, we intuit that there is an outside, but we can never know what reality is like outside those boundaries.

This ignorance before a vast unknown is the stance of the agnostic. It calls us to recognize our limitations, and thereby engenders a sense of humility before an infinite universe.

In the discourse of religious polemics, agnostics are often condemned by traditional believers for being arrogant. By not acknowledging the existence and the rule of God, so the argument goes, agnostics are replacing God with man, and thereby making the idolatrous, arrogant, and dangerous mistake of identifying man with God. Man needs God, so it goes, to keep him humble, and thereby chastening his propensity for unbridled power, dominance, and cruelty.

In my view, the traditional believer has it all wrong. For it is the traditional believer who says he knows God exists and what God wants from us and thereby claims to know what he cannot know. That, to my mind, is the arrogant position. The agnostic's position, by contrast, is one of modesty and humility, because he recognizes the limits of the human capacity for knowledge.

This sense of limitation before an infinite universe generates not only a sense of humility, but, as with the nature mystic, a sense of wonder, indeed reverence, for the very fact of existence, and gratitude for even our limited ability to discern a parcel of the tapestry of reality, however small.

The third type of religious humanism moves us closer to the human realm and was outlined by John Dewey. I refer to it as Deweyan idealism. In contrast to Felix Adler, Dewey did not believe that ideals are inscribed in the universe. Rather he believed that human beings create ideals out of their imaginations, but, as he put it, they are not made out of imaginary stuff. Our ideals arise out of our frustration as problem-solving animals. We experience a frustration, such as being earthbound, and through our imagination we formulate an ideal response, such as a rocket ship. That ideal then becomes a motive force in inspiring us forward to creatively resolve the problems and place us in a more effective, fruitful relationship with our world. Take any problem and any ideal that comes out of it, let it inspire you toward more effective integration with your environment, and Dewey frames that relationship with the ideal as religious.

What Dewey did was to remove the religious from religion. Religion pertains to the institutions, the creeds, the rituals, the accoutrements we usually associate with tradition religion. To Dewey we can have a religious (today people would say a "spiritual") relationship with any ideals that inspire and move us toward greater creativity, satisfaction, and integration with our world. It is to be found in our vocations, in art, in science, in music.

Dewey might as well have been speaking of Ethical Culture when he wrote, "We who now live are parts of a humanity that extends into the remote past, a humanity that has interacted with nature. The things in civilization we most prize are not of ourselves. They exist by the grace of the doings and sufferings of the entire human community, in which we are a link. Ours is the responsibility of conserving, transmitting, rectifying, and expanding the heritage of values we have received that those who come after us may receive it more solid and secure, more widely accessible, and more generously shared than we have received it. Here are all the elements for a religious faith that shall not be confined to sect, class, or race. Such a faith has always been implicitly the common faith of mankind. It remains to make it explicit and militant."

My final variant of religious humanism I refer to with the inelegant term "noninstrumentalist holism." What I mean by this is a subtle appreciation for the invisible values that we derive from the tangible things of this world. To be spiritually or religiously sensitive is to be focused on the ultimate values for which things exist, and not on the things themselves.

To be spiritually or religiously sensitive is to be aware of the ultimate purposes or ends for which instrumentalities exist. When we perceive the beauty behind the painting or within the music, we have touched the spiritual. When we intuit the complexity and design of nature, we have touched the spiritual. When we perceive something as mundane as law and government, but see them as practical mechanisms that reflect the values of justice, equality, freedom, and cooperation, then we have gleaned the spiritual dimension that stands behind these instrumentalities. Likewise when we discern timeless human truths in a novel or poetry. To perceive the timeless ends behind the things of this world is to touch the spiritual or the religious and so endow our lives with a sense of edification that enriches us in ways that matter most.

This concept of "noninstrumentalist holism" can be applied most importantly to our relations to other people.

When we first encounter another person, the first thing we see is a form, and then a face. We then experience their gestures and hear their words. Only then do we develop a more holistic sense of who the person is. Sometimes we like what we see. Sometimes we are unmoved. At other times what we experience is repulsive. But if we are willing to make the extra effort, if we are willing to apply ourselves a little harder, as with applying ourselves to any task, what we often discover is that the person is more complex than he or she appears on the surface.

Every life from the inside out is a story. If we simply skim the text, we miss the story underneath. But if we apply ourselves a little harder, a coherent story may emerge. Each person's story is a composite of joys and tragedies, of struggles and triumphs, of dreams and frustrations. And each person in his or her triumphs and struggles is unique and precious to him- or herself. As I would not find a distinctive work of art something to discard or hold cheaply, so I need to honor the indwelling humanity of the person, however flawed that person may be on the surface. Just as the beauty of the painting transcends the value of the canvas, so the worth of the person transcends the creature of flesh and blood whom I encounter before me.

It seems to me that every human encounter presents me with a choice. I can choose in instrumentalist ways to ignore the humanity of the other and abuse him or her. Or, I can choose to treat people as ends in themselves through common courtesy and decency, through being honest with them and defending their interests and rights. Whether dealing with a serving person in a restaurant, a homeless person on the street, a child, an employee, a friend, or a stranger, I can choose to value him or her cheaply or strive to appreciate him or her in his or her humanity, in his or her wholeness, and with an intuitive sense of the other person as a subjectivity in his or her own terms.

This noninstrumentalist appreciation of human beings is the consciousness that gives rise to ethics. But the appreciation alone of this indwelling, priceless dignity of the person is not the culmination of a spiritual-ethical view. The fully ethical condition emerges when my own humanity touches and actively builds connections with the other. It arises when I experience the joy of the human bond, when we sing together and celebrate together, and when we work together under the inspiration of justice to serve the good of humanity. It emerges even more when I enter into the life of the person who is down and enable him or her to think well of him- or herself, as Felix Adler once wrote. It emerges when I express myself to another with support, empathy, and caring.

It emerges also in a grander sense when I understand myself to be part of the unfolding tapestry of the human experience, and then dedicate myself to the realization of what is best in me and all others with whom I share a common destiny.

Ethics so understood is the vibrant connection. It is the lived relationship. It is what elevates us beyond the banal, the self-interested, the mundane. It is the warp and woof of our highest purposes.

In closing, I have few doubts that the God believer will look at my sketch of religious humanism and judge it wanting. He or she will say that to be truly meaningful, religious experience must provide a sturdy cosmic connection. It must guarantee that the universe take note of our existence and log it down for all eternity.

By this eternal standard, my humanistic religious experience is too transient, too wispy, too much a product of human psychology to be meaningful.

To which the humanist can only respond, "Perhaps this emergence out of human psychology is all that religious experience ever means or ever has truly meant."

February 2004

Need Humanism Be Reasonable?

I want to dedicate these remarks to the life and memory of my esteemed colleague Dr. Matthew Ies Spetter, who died in December 2012 at the age of ninety-one.

Dr. Spetter's formative experiences were shaped by the Second World War. "Ies," as we used to call him, was born in the Netherlands and during World War II was a liaison officer between sections of the Dutch and French undergrounds in Nazi-occupied Europe. He was caught by the Nazis, condemned to death, and held captive at the Buchenwald and Auschwitz death camps. He escaped the gas chambers as a result of a clerical error and, once freed, served as a witness at the Nuremburg Trials before coming to the United States.

In the United States, he discovered the Ethical movement and worked as a leader intern in Brooklyn with the then leader, Henry Neuman. He then served for several decades as the leader of the Riverdale Yonkers Society for Ethical Culture, where he became best known to us, and finished his career as a part-time leader of the New York Society.

Ies received his PhD from the New School, trained as a psychotherapist, and practiced psychotherapy during his long career. In 1960, he founded the Riverdale Mental Health Clinic, which still serves the community. He long taught ethics at the Ethical Culture Schools, chaired the Ethics Department, and taught peace studies at Manhattan College. He, needless to say, lectured often and wrote several books, all of which were dedicated to expounding his philosophy of life.

Ies was always a very formal man, a European man, who took life and Ethical Culture, to which he was wholeheartedly devoted, very seriously. And because he did, many of us take it seriously as well.

There is no doubt that Dr. Spetter's understanding of humanism and Ethical Culture intimately emerged from his personal life experience. To give you a taste of his humanism, I would like to quote from the very beginning of his book *Man the Reluctant Brother.* His opening words are rather harrowing. He wrote as follows:

> I need truth because I was an eyewitness to the premeditated murder of children.

> The killers were men and women of a nation much akin to my own. The children were ours.

> I need truth because my generation allowed the ultimately impermissible and because such killing continues. Men everywhere, while protesting their abhorrence, are still willing to permit the impermissible, still willing to kill as "a necessary evil," still willing to appease their conscience with justifications which fasten the tyranny of evil upon their souls.

> I need truth and therefore, behind the veil of language and the logic of argument of this book stands my personal urgency.

> If no one is willing to renounce the murder of children, how will we then be answerable for anything?

> The murder I witnessed was of the children of Europe in World War II. But many more murders have since been added. The killing was against children from France and Holland and Norway and Poland and Russia. They were of all religious backgrounds, though the children of defenseless minorities were the prime targets. Their very defenselessness fanned the

ferocity of the killers. Some children were suffocated by gas; some children were buried alive, some children were torn to pieces by fragmentation or fire bombs; some children were given neither food nor water.

All children were taken to be killed: lame children and blind children, children in   hospitals   and   children in the street coming from school, children in light summer clothes, children who had gone for a swim. Yes, even children were taken who wept because they

I have seen this and speak of it not with sentimentality, but with outrage, and I will not permit it to be locked from your heart.

No doubt, my colleague Dr. Spetter did not have a sunny view of the human condition. As a young man he had witnessed and was a survivor of the darkest underside of human behavior. But he was by no means a defeatist or fatalist. His commitment to humanism was forged out of that sense of the evil propensities of which human beings are capable. And he often said of Ethical Culture, and of us, that our mission is to rescue the human spirit from all those forces that seek to degrade it. "Whatever we do," I recall him saying years ago, "we must not hold human life cheaply." It is a lesson that has stayed with me ever since.

Just as he begins his book with horror, so he ends it with a note of hope. He wrote:

I hold deeply that each life is a gift which the centuries bestow upon the continuity of existence.

A *Passio Humana*, a "passion for Man," is what will negate totalitarianism and oppression, it will open the jail doors of history, provided our mutuality and love outpace our tools. All of us are constantly close to death and yet we are also in touch with the perpetuation of life through what we create and build.

The sense of future derived from this position has resulted for me in an infusion of insight, which, even at moments during my captivity, when death seemed certain and sealed, did not desert me.

Spetter, philosophically, was a kind of existentialist, believing that we can and we must forge our own lives and futures out of our experience, and out of the best that lies within us. His writings and speeches are frequently sprinkled with references to the great humanist Albert Camus, who wrote movingly of the courage and greatness of human beings; human beings who, when confronted by adversity, have the ability for sacrifice and courage as life calls us to be courageous. He also quoted often from Martin Buber, who wrote poetically about the irreducibility of the humanity that lies within each of us.

It was such ideas that framed Matthew Spetter's understanding of humanism. His humanism reached deeply and ranged widely across human experience. He saw the life of men and women lived out between good and evil, life and death, triumph and tragedy, courage and frailty, hope and despair, what the world is and what it might be. And throughout, his mission was to inspire us to summon our agency and courage to fashion a world in which, again, the lives and humanity of women, men, and children would be esteemed and not held cheaply. His humanism was a richer and deeper humanism. And from my own humble perspective, I think that my venerable colleague got it right.

I rest upon Spetter's humanism as a prelude to try to explain my understanding of humanism. And to do so I want to focus on the cherished value of reason, and the place of reason in a humanistic philosophy of life.

There is little doubt in my mind, that Dr. Spetter was a rationalist, and so am I. What I mean by this is that I highly value reason and try to conduct my life by its guiding light. In the most intimate sense, I measure my beliefs by the test of reason. I tend to be what you might call an intellectual rigorist. In other words, I like to think of myself as adopting a belief as my own only when it conforms to evidence and to the canons of reason. I want my beliefs to be proportionate to the facts, so to speak, and if a proposition contradicts the facts, the preponderance of evidence or rational consistency, then my inclination is to reject it. I affirm that there is no dignity in asserting what reason tells us is not true. When presented with a proposition that does not sound right to me, my first inclination is to say "prove it," skeptic that I am. When I say that my beliefs need to pass these tests in order for me to accept them, I am not saying that I must personally and directly be witness to the facts and to the evidence that emerges from them. Most of us appropriately accept the beliefs of other people, credentialed and experienced scientists, or other experts, for example, whose authority we trust. And this is the way it must be. Our beliefs must often rest upon secondhand authority, authority that we believe also passes the tests of evidence and reason.

I want not only my beliefs but my choices in life to be guided by reason. Without reason, we flop around lost, guided only by our hunches, our intuitions, and our impulses. We need reason as the basis of living a good, productive, and dignified life. And we need reason for the sake of sustaining an orderly and civilized society.

Mentioning science, I note that science is the most powerful and productive application of reason that humankind has ever created. Science is the most reliable tool ever forged to grasp a handle on how reality is put together. And the application of science continues to phenomenally expand our understanding of the natural world and to transform the condition of society in ways that would have been totally unimaginable to people just a few centuries ago. I am not a scientist, but I greatly esteem science and the power of the scientific method. If we had to point to a single enterprise that represents the success of the human species, it would be, I submit, the career of science and the application of science in creating the modern world. I think it is only a fool who dismisses the deliverances of scientific knowledge. And, unfortunately, there are many such fools.

And finally, I believe that reason can be elegant. I suspect that mathematicians, philosophers, and scientists know this well. When previously disassociated and confused ideas rationally pull together, not only do they compellingly grip the mind, they also stimulate our aesthetic sensibilities. In short, ideas and ideas ordered by the template of reason can be beautiful.

It is my commitment to reason and the test of evidence that long ago caused me to give up a belief in a Divine Custodian, a supernatural Being who lords over us, cares for us, and judges us. I simply see no evidence, moral or empirical, for such a Being.

It is the cherishing of reason and the salient place that it has in my life and character that leads me to identify myself as a rationalist. But I must say that, having so declared myself, I do not equate humanism, as I understand it, with rationalism. To put it more pointedly, reason alone does not a humanist make. Or, to state it more dryly, reason is a necessary but not sufficient condition to serve as the exclusive basis for humanism.

To be candid, what leads me to deal with this topic is the recent emergence of a multitude of organizations that are known as "rationalist," "secular," or "atheist" groups. Some are very new and some have been around a long while but are experiencing a period of revitalization. All but the last cluster would identify themselves as humanist organizations And since they identify themselves as humanist, and so do we, it is easy for those inside Ethical Culture and outside of it to assume that these groups and Ethical Culture are one and the same, and that they are virtually interchangeable with regard to their underlying and animating philosophies. Among the groups I have in mind are the American Humanist Association, which has been around since the 1930s; the Council for Secular Humanism, which publishes *Free Inquiry* magazine; the Secular Coalition; the Coalition of Reason; and others. And since many of these groups for the moment seem to be flourishing and are in the public eye, there is a natural tendency to move toward them.

Let me state squarely that I don't share this tendency. But I must be clear about where I do stand. I wish these organizations well. They do things I believe in and support. And I also firmly believe in coalitions, and I think that Ethical Culture, especially since it is a small organization, should seek to join coalitions with which we have important overlapping interests.

Coalitions, by definition, are organizations that are set up for a single purpose, or a small set of purposes, and are made up of organizations that may have very different philosophies and goals but find common cause in this one project or purpose. When I represented the Ethical Culture movement on the board of the National Coalition Against the Death Penalty, a coalition of many organizations, I was happy to sit at the same table with a representative of the Roman Catholic Church, an organization that shared my distain for capital punishment, but with which I shared little else. After all, he represented an organization of sixty million, I, three thousand, and we each had equally one vote on the coalition's board.

Likewise, when the secular and rationalist groups are fighting to protect the rights of secularists, or are defending the separation of church and state, or are trying the beat back the churches in their takeover of the public square, or legitimate the place of secularists and atheists in the fabric of American society, I am happy to join in coalition with them to fight for these concerns. These are things I care about. In fact, militantly so.

But my willingness to join with them to support common projects does not to my mind suggest an identification with such organizations, because in significant ways I differ from them and have a very different view as to what humanism means. I simply do not resonate with their music. Their dance is not a dance I do.

I may be an outlier in the Ethical Culture movement, and even among my professional colleagues, in that I have never joined nor have I ever been a member of any organization that calls itself "humanist" other than Ethical Culture. This is my sole organizational identification, and Ethical Culture is where my exclusive loyalty lies and always has. I may occasionally attend the meetings of other groups, and even write for their magazines, and, as mentioned, am eager to work with them to common political goals, but as an outsider and not as an insider. I have some important things in common with them, but not enough wherein I feel that I belong with them as a fellow member.

And to proclaim a heresy, and for the sake of honest disclosure, I sometimes feel more comfortable and more at home among liberal clergy of the traditional religions, who root their ethics in ancient, venerable, and rich traditions, than I do among the members of rationalist and secular groups, whose agendas I often find limited and whose understanding of humanism I often find one dimensional, dry, and, in a certain sense, brittle. It is this that I need to explain at greater length, because it is at the heart of my message.

First, I need to say that this address may seem to some to be an exemplification of what Sigmund Freud brilliantly referred to as the "narcissism of small differences"; that I am making something big out of something small. But I don't think so. I have been a professional in Ethical Culture, if I include my training, for what is now forty-four years. It is not a job, but a life-absorbing vocational commitment that has long become part and parcel of who I am. It is with me and in me all the time. My humanism is something I live and breathe, and in that sense is near and dear to me and very deeply felt. It helps define where my center of gravity of lies. It is something that I think about and reinforce constantly. And out of this lived commitment, I come to the conclusion and the conviction that humanism encompasses far more than reason or rationalism can contain.

Here is what I mean. However essential reason is to my identity as a humanist, I recognize that reason in the final analysis is a tool. However glorious, reason remains a tool, an instrumentality, a means that enables us to achieve goals and interests that themselves transcend reason and that reason has little to do with. In other words, the nature of human beings is such that the ultimate ends we seek are not themselves rational. For whatever reasons, some people cannot be happy unless they risk their lives scaling mountains, or work endless hours to become prima ballerinas. Some find meaning in turning their bodies into living sculptures through hanging out at the gym and the extraordinary effort of lifting weights six hours a day, six days a week. Others find meaning by teaching others new skills, or by beating out the next guy on the stock market, by being entertainers or winning scrabble competitions, or dedicating themselves to communicating to others ethical values and social ideals. Many others yearn to be parents and nurture children, and their lives would be diminished if they were childless. One of the most interesting things about human beings is the almost infinite variety of their values, goals, dreams, and aspirations. And these things we yearn for most do not emerge from reason; they come from the deepest recesses of our being, our hearts, if you will, and very often they emerge from us unbidden. We simply find meaning and pursue our happiness for causes that are diverse and often arbitrary, just as we might prefer chocolate to pistachio, and reason may help us achieve our aspirations and our wants. But reason is not their source. As the philosopher Schopenhauer once said, "I can do what I want, but I cannot want what I want." Our wants and desires arise in us from our inner depths, just as our impulses do.

We are creatures of reason, to be sure. And reason is essential to life, and it ennobles us. But our humanity extends far more broadly than our reason does. We are also creatures of love and desire, compassion and aspiration, of devotion, of hate and fear, of foibles and foolishness, of joy and sorrow, of courage and self-doubt, and irrationality, too, and much, much more. There is much to life that reason cannot penetrate nor explain. There is irony and paradox, tragedy and contradiction, and even aspects of human experience that are mysterious and defy rational understanding. Out of these depths both known and unknown to us comes our creativity, the human impulse to create art and music and poetry and to fulfill our infinite longings, in the service of which we seek fulfillment and our need to put the stamp of meaning on our lives. This is all part of the human experience, and a wider humanism embraces it, but reason, not so.

Another way to state this is that reason is cold. Reason does not provide warmth or belonging and does satisfy the need for love, friendship, family, charity, sympathy, devotion, sanctity, or forgiveness. But my point is that my understanding of humanism does.

The Roman playwright Terence, wrote, "I am a human being. Therefore nothing human is alien from me." The infinite varieties of human expression should be a source of curiosity and interest for us. The secularist and rationalist groups tend to be antireligious, condemning the religions on the grounds that so many of the beliefs and doctrines of the traditional faiths are patently irrational. Indeed the very idea of faith as a justification for holding beliefs that are counterrational is itself irrational. There is, of course, much that is valid in this critique, and I agree with its validity as far as it goes. And much evil is perpetrated in the name of religion, to be sure. Parenthetically, for me one imposing question is what role the new pope, whose ascension is reported with such saccharine goodness and light, really played in Argentina's "dirty war," in which vast swaths of the Catholic Church had complicity with fascism, murder, torture, and repression. I am not naïve to the evil done in the name of religion or when religion is conjoined with political force.

But there is another side. If religion is a human creation, and I believe that it is, then it is a human expression, just as art and music are human expressions, and, like art and music, is very widespread and has given birth to traditions that are both ancient and very complex and, in their own ways, highly sophisticated. Religion can also be a quest for ultimate meaning, and therefore its significance shouldn't be alien to us. If this is the case, then it seems that religion should at least be an object of curiosity and fascination as a human expression, rather than wholesale rejection. And we can see aspects of religion within the humanist frame and not exclusively as humanism's enemy.

A wider humanism can even understand the irrational as a human expression. The Greek tragedians certainly understood the suffering of tragic figures who were victimized by their own fatal flaws, which were as much part of their humanity as was their capacity for reason. And out of their irrational actions, generated by those tragic flaws, the ancient playwrights created great art that speaks to our common humanity over a gulf of more than two thousand years.

I am by no means saying that we should embrace beliefs, religious or otherwise, that our reason tells us are not so. We can reject them and refute them. Only that we appreciate those beliefs as human expressions that in their exploration broaden and enrich our own sense of the human experience and what it means to be human.

My message should be clear. Need humanism be reasonable? Yes, absolutely, but it need be much more. I think that a humanism that identifies humanism merely with the rational is flat, one dimensional, and, from my point of view, badly impoverished. It may be the reason why so many of these rational and secular groups are overly intellectualistic, have no communal life, and barely appreciate the humanity of association that embraces families and children. They are also politically quietistic for the most part. In their overemphasis on winnowing the human experience to its rational core and their aversion to anything that doesn't meet the test of reason, they seem to me not at all different from the religious devotees who are overly fastidious with the purity of doctrine, that is, those whom they readily condemn.

My humanism and specifically Ethical Culture, which is not focused primarily on reason, but on the humanity that dwells within each of us, potentially allows for a wider appreciation of human expression in its multidimensionality and its myriad expressions. Moreover, our commitment to "deed above creed" keeps our sights away from picayune arguments about belief, rational and otherwise, and more directed on alleviating human suffering in concrete ways. Ethical Culture thereby keeps us focused on interpersonal engagement and action in ways in which these other associations, in my view, don't.

In closing, I seek a humanism that is sensitive to human experience in its multiple manifestations; that is moved not only by reason, but by matters of the heart that reason does not reach. I want a humanism that honors reason, but is also moved by compassion and love. I want a humanism that rejoices in the triumphs of human beings, but also embraces the human being, knowing his frailties and imperfections. I want a humanism that can respect the achievements of great men and women, but is no less moved by the precious and ineffable humanity we encounter when we look upon the face of a child.

March 2013

About the Author

For more than forty-five years, Dr. Joseph Chuman has served as the professional leader of the Ethical Culture Society of Bergen County, New Jersey. He also serves part-time as a leader of the New York Society for Ethical Culture.

He holds a PhD and two master's degrees in religion from Columbia University, where he now works as a professor of human rights for their graduate program. He has also taught human rights at Hunter College, the United Nations University for Peace in Costa Rica, and Fairleigh Dickinson University.

Throughout his extensive career as a progressive social activist, he has commonly lectured on topics including politics, philosophy, social ethics, and religion. He has also written a wide range of articles for newspapers, journals of opinion, academic texts, and encyclopedias.

Not just an academic, Chuman is passionate about living out his beliefs by helping others, and has spent years guiding his Ethical Culture congregants through their toughest life transitions.

Made in the USA
Lexington, KY
26 March 2014